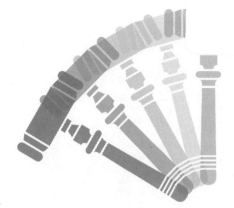

Casenote™ Legal Briefs

EVIDENCE

Keyed to
Waltz and Park's
Evidence: Cases and Materials,
Tenth Edition

ASPEN
PUBLISHERS

111 Eighth Avenue, New York, NY 10011
www.aspenpublishers.com

This publication is designed to provide accurate and authoritative information in regard to the subject matter covered. It is sold with the understanding that the publisher is not engaged in rendering legal, accounting, or other professional services. If legal advice or other expert assistance is required, the services of a competent professional person should be sought.

— From a *Declaration of Principles* adopted jointly by
a Committee of the American Bar Association and a
Committee of Publishers and Associates

FORMAT FOR THE CASENOTE LEGAL BRIEF

PARTY ID: Quick identification of the relationship between the parties.

NATURE OF CASE: This section identifies the form of action (e.g., breach of contract, negligence, battery), the type of proceeding (e.g., demurrer, appeal from trial court's jury instructions) or the relief sought (e.g., damages, injunction, criminal sanctions).

FACT SUMMARY: This is included to refresh the student's memory and can be used as a quick reminder of the facts.

CONCISE RULE OF LAW: Summarizes the general principle of law that the case illustrates. It may be used for instant recall of the court's holding and for classroom discussion or home review.

FACTS: This section contains all relevant facts of the case, including the contentions of the parties and the lower court holdings. It is written in a logical order to give the student a clear understanding of the case. The plaintiff and defendant are identified by their proper names throughout and are always labeled with a (P) or (D).

ISSUE: The issue is a concise question that brings out the essence of the opinion as it relates to the section of the casebook in which the case appears. Both substantive and procedural issues are included if relevant to the decision.

HOLDING AND DECISION: This section offers a clear and in-depth discussion of the rule of the case and the court's rationale. It is written in easy-to-understand language and answers the issue(s) presented by applying the law to the facts of the case. When relevant, it includes a thorough discussion of the exceptions to the case as listed by the court, any major cites to other cases on point, and the names of the judges who wrote the decisions.

CONCURRENCE / DISSENT: All concurrences and dissents are briefed whenever they are included by the casebook editor.

EDITOR'S ANALYSIS: This last paragraph gives the student a broad understanding of where the case "fits in" with other cases in the section of the book and with the entire course. It is a hornbook-style discussion indicating whether the case is a majority or minority opinion and comparing the principal case with other cases in the casebook. It may also provide analysis from restatements, uniform codes, and law review articles. The editor's analysis will prove to be invaluable to classroom discussion.

QUICKNOTES: Conveniently defines legal terms found in the case and summarizes the nature of any statutes, codes, or rules referred to in the text.

PALSGRAF v. LONG ISLAND R.R. CO.
Injured bystander (P) v. Railroad company (D)
N.Y. Ct. App., 248 N.Y. 339, 162 N.E. 99 (1928).

NATURE OF CASE: Appeal from judgment affirming verdict for plaintiff seeking damages for personal injury.

FACT SUMMARY: Helen Palsgraf (P) was injured on R.R.'s (D) train platform when R.R.'s (D) guard helped a passenger aboard a moving train, causing his package to fall on the tracks. The package contained fireworks which exploded, creating a shock that tipped a scale onto Palsgraf (P).

CONCISE RULE OF LAW: The risk reasonably to be perceived defines the duty to be obeyed.

FACTS: Helen Palsgraf (P) purchased a ticket to Rockaway Beach from R.R. (D) and was waiting on the train platform. As she waited, two men ran to catch a train that was pulling out from the platform. The first man jumped aboard, but the second man, who appeared as if he might fall, was helped aboard by the guard on the train who had kept the door open so they could jump aboard. A guard on the platform also helped by pushing him onto the train. The man was carrying a package wrapped in newspaper. In the process, the man dropped his package, which fell on the tracks. The package contained fireworks and exploded. The shock of the explosion was apparently of great enough strength to tip over some scales at the other end of the platform, which fell on Palsgraf (P) and injured her. A jury awarded her damages, and R.R. (D) appealed.

ISSUE: Does the risk reasonably to be perceived define the duty to be obeyed?

HOLDING AND DECISION: (Cardozo, C.J.) Yes. The risk reasonably to be perceived defines the duty to be obeyed. If there is no foreseeable hazard to the injured party as the result of a seemingly innocent act, the act does not become a tort because it happened to be a wrong as to another. If the wrong was not willful, the plaintiff must show that the act as to her had such great and apparent possibilities of danger as to entitle her to protection. Negligence in the abstract is not enough upon which to base liability. Negligence is a relative concept, evolving out of the common law doctrine of trespass on the case. To establish liability, the defendant must owe a legal duty of reasonable care to the injured party. A cause of action in tort will lie where harm, though unintended, could have been averted or avoided by observance of such a duty. The scope of the duty is limited by the range of danger that a reasonable person could foresee. In this case, there was nothing to suggest from the appearance of the parcel or otherwise that the parcel contained fireworks. The guard could not reasonably have had any warning of a threat to Palsgraf (P), and R.R. (D) therefore cannot be held liable. Judgment is reversed in favor of R.R. (D).

DISSENT: (Andrews, J.) The concept that there is no negligence unless R.R. (D) owes a legal duty to take care as to Palsgraf (P) herself is too narrow. Everyone owes to the world at large the duty of refraining from those acts that may unreasonably threaten the safety of others. If the guard's action was negligent as to those nearby, it was also negligent as to those outside what might be termed the "danger zone." For Palsgraf (P) to recover, R.R.'s (D) negligence must have been the proximate cause of her injury, a question of fact for the jury.

EDITOR'S ANALYSIS: The majority defined the limit of the defendant's liability in terms of the danger that a reasonable person in defendant's situation would have perceived. The dissent argued that the limitation should not be placed on liability, but rather on damages. Judge Andrews suggested that only injuries that would not have happened but for R.R.'s (D) negligence should be compensable. Both the majority and dissent recognized the policy-driven need to limit liability for negligent acts, seeking, in the words of Judge Andrews, to define a framework "that will be practical and in keeping with the general understanding of mankind." The Restatement (Second) of Torts has accepted Judge Cardozo's view.

QUICKNOTES

FORESEEABILITY – The reasonable anticipation that damage is a likely result from certain acts or omissions.

NEGLIGENCE - Failure to exercise that degree of care which a person of ordinary prudence would exercise under similar circumstances.

PROXIMATE CAUSE – Something which in natural and continuous sequence, unbroken by any new intervening cause, produces an event, and without which the injury would not have occurred.

NOTE TO STUDENTS

Aspen Publishers is proud to offer *Casenote Legal Briefs*—continuing thirty years of publishing America's best-selling legal briefs.

Casenote Legal Briefs are designed to help you save time when briefing assigned cases. Organized under convenient headings, they show you how to abstract the basic facts and holdings from the text of the actual opinions handed down by the courts. Used as part of a rigorous study regime, they can help you spend more time analyzing and critiquing points of law than on copying out bits and pieces of judicial opinions into your notebook or outline.

Casenote Legal Briefs should never be used as a substitute for assigned casebook readings. They work best when read as a follow-up to reviewing the underlying opinions themselves. Students who try to avoid reading and digesting the judicial opinions in their casebooks or on-line sources will end up shortchanging themselves in the long run. The ability to absorb, critique, and restate the dynamic and complex elements of case law decisions is crucial to your success in law school and beyond. It cannot be developed vicariously.

Casenote Legal Briefs represent but one of the many offerings in Aspen's Study Aid Timeline, which includes:

- Casenotes *Legal Briefs*
- Emanuel *Outlines*
- *Examples & Explanations* Series
- *Introduction to Law* Series
- Emanuel *Law in a Flash* Flashcards
- Emanuel *CrunchTime* Series

Each of these series is designed to provide you with easy-to-understand explanations of complex points of law. Each volume offers guidance on the principles of legal analysis and, consulted regularly, will hone your ability to spot relevant issues. We have titles that will help you prepare for class, prepare for your exams, and enhance your general comprehension of the law along the way.

To find out more about Aspen Study Aid publications, visit us on-line at www.aspenpublishers.com or e-mail us at legaledu@aspenpubl.com. We'll be happy to assist you.

Free access to Briefs on-line!

Download the cases you want in your notes or outlines using the full cut-and-paste feature accompanying our on-line briefs. Please fill out this form for full access to this useful feature. No photocopies of this form will be accepted.

① **Name:** _____ **Phone:** (____) _____

Address: _____ **Apt.:** _____

City: _____ **State:** _____ **ZIP Code:** _____

Law School: _____ **Year (circle one):** 1st 2nd 3rd

② **Cut out the UPC found on the lower left-hand corner of the back cover of this book. Staple the UPC inside this box. Only the original UPC from the book cover will be accepted. (No photocopies or store stickers are allowed.)**

Attach UPC inside this box.

③ **E-mail:**_____ **(Print LEGIBLY or you may not get access!)**

④ **Title (course subject) of this book** _____

⑤ **Used with which casebook (provide author's name):** _____

⑥ **Mail the completed form to:**   Aspen Publishers, Inc.
Legal Education Division
Casenote On-line Access
675 Massachusetts Ave., 11th floor
Cambridge, MA 02139

I understand that on-line access is granted solely to the purchaser of this book for the academic year in which it was purchased. Any other usage is not authorized and will result in immediate termination of access. Sharing of codes is strictly prohibited.

_____

Signature

Upon receipt of this completed form, you will be e-mailed codes so that you may access the Briefs for this Casenote Legal Brief. On-line Briefs may not be available for all titles. For a full list of available titles please check www.aspenpublishers.com/casenotes.

HOW TO BRIEF A CASE

A. DECIDE ON A FORMAT AND STICK TO IT

Structure is essential to a good brief. It enables you to arrange systematically the related parts that are scattered throughout most cases, thus making manageable and understandable what might otherwise seem to be an endless and unfathomable sea of information. There are, of course, an unlimited number of formats that can be utilized. However, it is best to find one that suits your needs and stick to it. Consistency breeds both efficiency and the security that when called upon you will know where to look in your brief for the information you are asked to give.

Any format, as long as it presents the essential elements of a case in an organized fashion, can be used. Experience, however, has led *Casenotes* to develop and utilize the following format because of its logical flow and universal applicability.

NATURE OF CASE: This is a brief statement of the legal character and procedural status of the case (e.g., "Appeal of a burglary conviction").

There are many different alternatives open to a litigant dissatisfied with a court ruling. The key to determining which one has been used is to discover *who is asking this court for what.*

This first entry in the brief should be kept as *short as possible.* The student should use the court's terminology if the student understands it. But since jurisdictions vary as to the titles of pleadings, the best entry is the one that apprises the student of who wants what in this proceeding, not the one that sounds most like the court's language.

CONCISE RULE OF LAW: A statement of the general principle of law that the case illustrates (e.g., "An acceptance that varies any term of the offer is considered a rejection and counteroffer").

Determining the rule of law of a case is a procedure similar to determining the issue of the case. Avoid being fooled by red herrings; there may be a few rules of law mentioned in the case excerpt, but usually only one is *the* rule with which the casebook editor is concerned. The techniques used to locate the issue, described below, may also be utilized to find the rule of law. Generally, your best guide is simply the chapter heading. It is a clue to the point the casebook editor seeks to make and should be kept in mind when reading every case in the respective section.

FACTS: A synopsis of only the essential facts of the case, i.e., those bearing upon or leading up to the issue.

The facts entry should be a short statement of the events and transactions that led one party to initiate legal proceedings against another in the first place. While some cases conveniently state the salient facts at the beginning of the decision, in other instances they will have to be culled from hiding places throughout the text, even from concurring and dissenting opinions. Some of the "facts" will often be in dispute and should be so noted. Conflicting evidence may be briefly pointed up. "Hard" facts must be included. Both must be *relevant* in order to be listed in the facts entry. It is impossible to tell what is relevant until the entire case is read, as the ultimate determination of the rights and liabilities of the parties may turn on something buried deep in the opinion.

The facts entry should never be longer than one to three *short* sentences.

It is often helpful to identify the role played by a party in a given context. For example, in a construction contract case the identification of a party as the "contractor" or "builder" alleviates the need to tell that that party was the one who was supposed to have built the house.

It is always helpful, and a good general practice, to identify the "plaintiff" and the "defendant." This may seem elementary and uncomplicated, but, especially in view of the creative editing practiced by some casebook editors, it is sometimes a difficult or even impossible task. Bear in mind that the *party presently* seeking something from this court may not be the plaintiff, and that sometimes only the cross-claim of a defendant is treated in the excerpt. Confusing or misaligning the parties can ruin your analysis and understanding of the case.

ISSUE: A statement of the general legal question answered by or illustrated in the case. For clarity, the issue is best put in the form of a question capable of a "yes" or "no" answer. In reality, the issue is simply the Concise Rule of Law put in the form of a question (e.g., "May an offer be accepted by performance?").

The major problem presented in discerning what is *the* issue in the case is that an opinion usually purports to raise and answer several questions. However, except for rare cases, only one such question is really the issue in the case. Collateral issues not necessary to the resolution of the matter in controversy are handled by the court by language known as *"obiter dictum"* or merely *"dictum."* While dicta may be included later in the brief, it has no place under the issue heading.

To find the issue, the student again asks *who wants what* and then goes on to ask *why did that party succeed or fail in getting it.* Once this is determined, the "why" should be turned into a question.

The complexity of the issues in the cases will vary, but in all cases a single-sentence question should sum up the issue. *In a few cases,* there will be two, or even more rarely, three issues of equal importance to the resolution of the case. Each should be expressed in a single-sentence question.

Since many issues are resolved by a court in coming to a final disposition of a case, the casebook editor will reproduce the portion of the opinion containing the issue or issues most relevant to the area of law under scrutiny. A noted law professor gave this advice: "Close the book; look at the title on the cover." Chances are, if it is Property, the student need not concern himself with whether, for example, the federal government's treatment of the plaintiff's land really raises a federal question sufficient to support jurisdiction on this ground in federal court.

The same rule applies to chapter headings designating sub-areas within the subjects. They tip the student off as to what the text is designed to teach. The cases are arranged in a casebook to show a progression or development of the law, so that the preceding cases may also help.

It is also most important to remember to *read the notes and questions* at the end of a case to determine what the editors wanted the student to have gleaned from it.

HOLDING AND DECISION: This section should succinctly explain the rationale of the court in arriving at its decision. In capsulizing the "reasoning" of the court, it should always include an application of the general rule or rules of law to the specific facts of the case. Hidden justifications come to light in this entry; the reasons for the state of the law, the public policies, the biases and prejudices, those considerations that influence the justices' thinking and, ultimately, the outcome of the case. At the end, there should be a short indication of the disposition or procedural resolution of the case (e.g., "Decision of the trial court for Mr. Smith (P) reversed").

The foregoing format is designed to help you "digest" the reams of case material with which you will be faced in your law school career. Once mastered by practice, it will place at your fingertips the information the authors of your casebooks have sought to impart to you in case-by-case illustration and analysis.

B. BE AS ECONOMICAL AS POSSIBLE IN BRIEFING CASES

Once armed with a format that encourages succinctness, it is as important to be economical with regard to the time spent on the actual reading of the case as it is to be economical in the writing of the brief itself. This does not mean "skimming" a case. Rather, it means reading the case with an "eye" trained to recognize into which "section" of your brief a particular passage or line fits and having a system for quickly and precisely marking the case so that the passages fitting any one particular part of the brief can be easily identified and brought together in a concise and accurate manner when the brief is actually written.

It is of no use to simply repeat everything in the opinion of the court; the student should only record enough information to trigger his or her recollection of what the court said. Nevertheless, an accurate statement of the "law of the case," i.e., the legal principle applied to the facts, is absolutely essential to class preparation and to learning the law under the case method.

To that end, it is important to develop a "shorthand" that you can use to make margin notations. These notations will tell you at a glance in which section of the brief you will be placing that particular passage or portion of the opinion.

Some students prefer to underline all the salient portions of the opinion (with a pencil or colored underliner marker), making marginal notations as they go along. Others prefer the color-coded method of underlining, utilizing different colors of markers to underline the salient portions of the case, each separate color being used to represent a different section of the brief. For example, blue underlining could be used for passages relating to the concise rule of law, yellow for those relating to the issue, and green for those relating to the holding and decision, etc. While it has its advocates, the color-coded method can be confusing and time-consuming (all that time spent on changing colored markers). Furthermore, it can interfere with the continuity and concentration many students deem essential to the reading of a case for maximum comprehension. In the end, however, it is a matter of personal preference and style. Just remember, whatever method you use, underlining must be used sparingly or its value is lost.

For those who take the marginal notation route, an efficient and easy method is to go along underlining the key portions of the case and placing in the margin alongside them the following "markers" to indicate where a particular passage or line "belongs" in the brief you will write:

N   (NATURE OF CASE)

CR   (CONCISE RULE OF LAW)

I   (ISSUE)

HC   (HOLDING AND DECISION, relates to the CONCISE RULE OF LAW behind the decision)

HR   (HOLDING AND DECISION, gives the RATIONALE or reasoning behind the decision)

HA   (HOLDING AND DECISION, APPLIES the general principle(s) of law to the facts of the case to arrive at the decision)

Remember that a particular passage may well contain information necessary to more than one part of your brief, in which case you simply note that in the margin. If you are using the color-coded underlining method instead of margin notation, simply make asterisks or checks in the margin next to the passage in question in the colors that indicate the additional sections of the brief where it might be utilized.

The economy of utilizing "shorthand" in marking cases for briefing can be maintained in the actual brief writing process itself by utilizing "law student shorthand" within the brief. There are many commonly used words and phrases for which abbreviations can be substituted in your briefs (and in your class notes also). You can develop abbreviations that are personal to you and which will save you a lot of time. A reference list of briefing abbreviations will be found elsewhere in this book.

C. USE BOTH THE BRIEFING PROCESS AND THE BRIEF AS A LEARNING TOOL

Now that you have a format and the tools for briefing cases efficiently, the most important thing is to make the time spent in briefing profitable to you and to make the most advantageous use of the briefs you create. Of course, the briefs are invaluable for classroom reference when you are called upon to explain or analyze a particular case. However, they are also useful in reviewing for exams. A quick glance at the fact summary should bring the case to mind, and a rereading of the concise rule of law should enable you to go over the underlying legal concept in your mind, how it was applied in that particular case, and how it might apply in other factual settings.

As to the value to be derived from engaging in the briefing process itself, there is an immediate benefit that arises from being forced to sift through the essential facts and reasoning from the court's opinion and to succinctly express them in your own words in your brief. The process ensures that you understand the case and the point that it illustrates, and that means you will be ready to absorb further analysis and information brought forth in class. It also ensures you will have something to say when called upon in class. The briefing process helps develop a mental agility for getting to the *gist* of a case and for identifying, expounding on, and applying the legal concepts and issues found there. Of most immediate concern, that is the mental process on which you must rely in taking law school examinations. Of more lasting concern, it is also the mental process upon which a lawyer relies in serving his clients and in making his living.

ABBREVIATIONS FOR BRIEFING

acceptance	acp		offer	O
affirmed	aff		offeree	OE
answer	ans		offeror	OR
assumption of risk	a/r		ordinance	ord
attorney	atty		pain and suffering	p/s
beyond a reasonable doubt	b/r/d		parol evidence	p/e
bona fide purchaser	BFP		plaintiff	P
breach of contract	br/k		prima facie	p/f
cause of action	c/a		probable cause	p/c
common law	c/l		proximate cause	px/c
Constitution	Con		real property	r/p
constitutional	con		reasonable doubt	r/d
contract	K		reasonable man	r/m
contributory negligence	c/n		rebuttable presumption	rb/p
cross	x		remanded	rem
cross-complaint	x/c		res ipsa loquitur	RIL
cross-examination	x/ex		respondeat superior	r/s
cruel and unusual punishment	c/u/p		Restatement	RS
defendant	D		reversed	rev
dismissed	dis		Rule Against Perpetuities	RAP
double jeopardy	d/j		search and seizure	s/s
due process	d/p		search warrant	s/w
equal protection	e/p		self-defense	s/d
equity	eq		specific performance	s/p
evidence	ev		statute of limitations	S/L
exclude	exc		statute of frauds	S/F
exclusionary rule	exc/r		statute	S
felony	f/n		summary judgment	s/j
freedom of speech	f/s		tenancy in common	t/c
good faith	g/f		tenancy at will	t/w
habeas corpus	h/c		tenant	t
hearsay	hr		third party	TP
husband	H		third party beneficiary	TPB
in loco parentis	ILP		transferred intent	TI
injunction	inj		unconscionable	uncon
inter vivos	I/v		unconstitutional	unconst
joint tenancy	j/t		undue influence	u/e
judgment	judgt		Uniform Commercial Code	UCC
jurisdiction	jur		unilateral	uni
last clear chance	LCC		vendee	VE
long-arm statute	LAS		vendor	VR
majority view	maj		versus	v
meeting of minds	MOM		void for vagueness	VFV
minority view	min		weight of the evidence	w/e
Miranda warnings	Mir/w		weight of authority	w/a
Miranda rule	Mir/r		wife	W
negligence	neg		with	w/
notice	ntc		within	w/i
nuisance	nus		without prejudice	w/o/p
obligation	ob		without	w/o
obscene	obs		wrongful death	wr/d

TABLE OF CASES

A

Abel, United States v. 114
Adams v. The New York Central Railroad
    Co. 51
Adkins v. Brett 44
Ando v. Woodberry 97
Atkinson v. Hall 155

B

Baker v. State 50
Ballou v. Henri Studios, Inc. 4
Barrett, United States v. 41
Beasley, United States v. 83
Beech Aircraft Corporation v. Rainey 60
Big Mack Trucking Co., Inc. v.
    Dickerson 32
Bourjaily v. United States 37, 68
Brackeen, United States v. 109
Brown, United States v. 22, 164

C

Carlson, State v. 29
Carrillo, United States v. 82
Cassidy, State v. 89
Chambers v. Mississippi 72
Chapple, State v. 179
Clark v. State 119
Cleghorn v. New York Center & H. River
    Ry. Co. 80
Coles v. Harsch 112
Collins, People v. 77
Collins, State ex rel. v. Superior Court 143
Copelin, United States v. 102
Cunningham, United States v. 84

D

Daubert v. Merrell Dow Pharmaceuticals,
    Inc. 169
Davidson v. Prince 96
Dent, United States v. 65
DiDomenico, United States v. 34
Dockins, United States v. 138
Doerr, United States v. 36
Drake, United States v. 104
Duncan, United States v. 54
Dyer v. MacDougall 153

E

Ellis v. State 180
English, State v. 10
Enskat, People v. 137

F

Farber, Matter of 126
First State Bank of Denton v. Maryland
    Casualty Co. 139
Fun-Damental Too, Ltd. v. Gemmy Industries
    Corp. 16

G

Gardeley, People v. 167
G.M. McKelvey Co. v. General Casualty Co. of
    America 40
Goldberg, United States v. 35
Grady, United States v. 62
Grand Jury, In re 125
Green v. Georgia 73

H

Halloran v. Virginia Chemicals Inc. 88
Hahnemann University Hospital v. Dudnick 56
Hernandez, United States v. 17
Herzig v. Swift & Co. 135
Higgins v. Los Angeles Gas & Electric Co. 150
Hill v. Skinner 142
Hogan, United States v. 100
Holden, Commonwealth v. 159
Hoosier, United States v. 28
Horn, United States v. 176
Huddleston v. United States 86

I

Idaho v. Wright 69
Inadi, United States v. 67
Ingram v. McCuiston 163

J

Jaffee v. Redmond 122
Jaramillo-Suarez, United States v. 20
Johnson v. Elk Lake School District 92
Johnson v. Lutz 52
Johnson v. Misericordia Community Hospital 14
Jones, State v. 26

K

Kammer v. Young 79
Knapp, Commonwealth v. 18
Knapp v. State 2
Kristiansen, United States v. 168
Kuhmo Tire Company, Ltd. v. Carmichael 170

L

Lawrence, State v. 149

Legille v. Dann 154
Lewis v. Baker 58
Lilly v. Virginia 71
Lindstrom, United States v. 111
Lira v. Albert Einstein Medical Center 25
Luce v. United States 110

M

Mahlandt v. Wild Canid Survival & Research
    Center, Inc. 30
McCray v. Illinois 131
Menendez v. Superior Court 123
Meyers v. United States 136
Michelson v. United States 81
Mountain, People v. 78
Murdock, Estate of 11
Mutual Life Ins. Co. of New York v. Hillmon 45

N

Nixon, United States v. 129

O

Oates, United States v. 61
Odom, State v. 161
Ohio v. Roberts 66
Old Chief v. United States 3
Olden v. Kentucky 90
Oswalt, State v. 101
Owens, United States v., 484 U.S. 554 49
Owens, United States v., 21 M.J. 117 103

P

Palmer v. Hoffman 57
Perrin v. Anderson 87
Pheaster, United States v. 47
Piccinonna, United States v. 174
Platero, United States v. 91
Porter, State v. 173
Prink v. Rockefeller Center, Inc. 121

R

Reed v. McCord 27
Reynolds, United States v. 128
Rhodes, United States v. 21
Ries Biologicals, Inc. v. Bank of Santa Fe 15
Rock v. Arkansas 144
Roder, People v. 156
Roviaro v. United States 130

S

Saada, United States v. 105
Sabel v. Mead Johnson & Co. 33

Saelee, United States v. 171
Salerno, United States v. 39
Sanders, United States v. 107
San Francisco, City & County of, v. Superior
    Court 118
Scheffer, United States v. 175
Scop, United States v. 162
Shepard v. United States 46
Silver v. New York Central Railroad 19
Simon v. Kennebunkport 94
Sirico v. Cotto 134
Smith v. Rapid Transit, Inc. 152
Soles v. State 23
Stroud v. Cook 63
Subramaniam v. Public Prosecutor 12

T

Tanner v. United States 145
Tome v. United States 113
Trammel v. United States 124
Tran Trong Cuong, United States v. 166
Travelers Fire Ins. Co. v. Wright 38
Truck Insurance Exchange v. Michling 24
Tucker v. State 85
Tuer v. McDonald 95
Turbyfill v. International Harvester Co. 64

U

Upjohn Co. v. United States 117

V

Varcoe v. Lee 148
Vigneau, United States v. 53
Vinyard v. Vinyard Funeral Home, Inc. 13
Virgin Islands, Government of v. Knight 160

W

Webster Groves, City of v. Quick 23
White v. Illinois 70
Williams v. Alexander 55
Williamson, United States v. 42
Wong, United States v. 108
Woodruff, United States v. 116

Y

Yates v. Bair Transport, Inc. 59

Z

Zenni, United States v. 18
Zippo Manufacturing Co. v. Rogers Imports,
    Inc. 48
Zolin, United States v. 120

CHAPTER TWO*
AN INTRODUCTION TO RELEVANCE

QUICK REFERENCE RULES OF LAW

1. **Relevance.** The determination of the relevancy of a particular item of evidence rests on whether proof of that evidence would reasonably tend to help resolve the primary issue on trial. (Knapp v. State)

2. **Exclusion of Relevant Evidence.** Relevant evidence may be excluded when its risk of unfair prejudice substantially outweighs its probative value, in view of the availability of alternative evidence on the same point. (Old Chief v. United States)

3. **Prejudicial Impact of Probative Values.** Under Fed. R. Evid. 403, when a court endeavors to balance the probative value of evidence against its prejudicial effect it must give the evidence that amount of probative value it would have if the evidence is believed, not the extent to which the court finds it believable. (Ballou v. Henri Studios, Inc.)

*There are no cases in Chapter 1.

KNAPP v. STATE

Convicted murderer (D) v. State (P)

Ind. Sup. Ct., 168 Ind. 153, 79 N.E. 1076 (1907).

NATURE OF CASE: Appeal from conviction for murder.

FACT SUMMARY: Knapp's (D) defense to a charge of murder was self defense. He testified that he had been told that the victim had killed another man. The prosecution was allowed to prove the victim had not caused the other death.

CONCISE RULE OF LAW: The determination of the relevancy of a particular item of evidence rests on whether proof of that evidence would reasonably tend to help resolve the primary issue on trial.

FACTS: Knapp (D) was charged with the murder of the marshal of Hagerstown. He claimed the killing was in self defense. At trial, he testified that some people around Hagerstown, whom he could not identify, had told him that the marshal had killed an old man he had arrested by beating him to death. Over Knapp's (D) objection, the prosecution was permitted to show that the old man referred to had died of natural causes and had not been beaten. Knapp (D) appealed his conviction on the grounds the evidence of the actual nature of the old man's death was immaterial. He asserted that the only issue was whether he had heard the story, not whether it was true.

ISSUE: Will the determination of the relevancy of a particular item of evidence depend on whether proof of that evidence would reasonably tend to help resolve a primary issue on trial?

HOLDING AND DECISION: (Gillett, J.) Yes. Knapp (D) was correct in asserting that the issue was whether or not he had heard the story about the death of the old man at the hands of the victim. But evidence may be relevant that does not bear directly on the issue on trial. It is enough that the evidence, once proved, may shed some light on a primary issue without necessarily conclusively resolving it. Truth-telling is a basic human instinct. When Knapp (D) was unable (or unwilling) to reveal the source of his information about the victim, the prosecution was entitled to show the improbability of the story. By showing that the victim had not, in fact, caused the old man's death, the prosecution pointed up the improbability of Knapp's (D) testimony. If people tend to tell the truth, and Knapp's (D) version of the old man's death was false, it is improbable that anyone told it to him. No error having been shown, the conviction is affirmed.

EDITOR'S ANALYSIS: The question of admissibility of evidence proving a collateral fact is, for the most part, within the discretion of the trial judge to resolve. One of the major considerations in his decision is whether the amount of time that may be consumed is justified in view of the connection to the primary issue. The more direct the connection, the more leeway that will be allowed and vice versa.

NOTES:

OLD CHIEF v. UNITED STATES

Convicted felon (D) v. Federal government (P)

519 U.S. 172 (1997).

NATURE OF CASE: Appeal from conviction for possession of firearm.

FACT SUMMARY: Old Chief (D) offered to stipulate to a prior felony conviction to avoid admitting the full record of his prior offense when he was charged with violation of a statute prohibiting the possession of firearms.

CONCISE RULE OF LAW: Relevant evidence may be excluded when its risk of unfair prejudice substantially outweighs its probative value, in view of the availability of alternative evidence on the same point.

FACTS: Old Chief (D) was charged with violation of a statute that prohibited the possession of a firearms by anyone convicted of a crime punishable by imprisonment exceeding one year. Old Chief (D) had a previous felony conviction of assault that fell within the purview of the statute. At trial, Old Chief (D) moved to exclude the name and nature of his prior conviction in exchange for a stipulation that he had been convicted of a crime punishable by imprisonment exceeding one year. The trial judge refused Old Chief's (D) stipulation, and the jury convicted him on all counts. Old Chief (D) appealed.

ISSUE: May relevant evidence be excluded when its risk of unfair prejudice substantially outweighs its probative value, in view of the availability of alternative evidence on the same point?

HOLDING AND DECISION: (Souter, J.) Yes. Relevant evidence may be excluded when its risk of unfair prejudice substantially outweighs its probative value which is judged in context the availability of alternative evidence on the same point. Although the prosecution is entitled to prove its case by the evidence of its own choice, this rule has no application where the evidence is not essential in providing a continuous story of its case against the defendant. The proper test is to balance the degrees of probative value and unfair prejudice for the evidence in question and for alternative, relevant evidence. The alternative evidence may be admitted if carries the same or greater probative value but a lower risk of unfair prejudice than the evidence in question. Reversed and remanded.

EDITOR'S ANALYSIS: The term "unfair prejudice" speaks to the capacity of some concededly relevant evidence to lure the fact finder into declaring guilt on a ground different from proof specific to the offense charged. In other words, a defendant's earlier bad act may be generalized into bad character, thereby raising the odds that he did the act he is charged with. Even worse, some juries might feel justified in practicing "preventive conviction," even if they believe the defendant is momentarily innocent.

BALLOU v. HENRI STUDIOS, INC.
Estate decedent (P) v. Employer of driver (D)
656 F.2d 1147 (5th Cir. 1981).

NATURE OF CASE: Exclusion of evidence as prejudicial.

FACT SUMMARY: Henri (D) challenged the trial court's exclusion of evidence showing Ballou (P) was intoxicated when struck by a vehicle, contending its relevance outweighed its prejudicial impact.

CONCISE RULE OF LAW: Under Federal Rule of Evidence 403, when a court endeavors to balance the probative value of evidence against its prejudicial effect it must give the evidence that amount of probative value it would have if the evidence is believed, not the extent to which the court finds it believable.

FACTS: Ballou (P) was killed when he was struck by a vehicle driven by an employee of Henri Studios (Henri) (D). Ballou's (P) representatives sued Henri (D) for the negligence of its employee. Prior to trial, Ballou's (P) representatives filed a motion in limine seeking an order to exclude the results of a blood test indicating Ballou (P) was intoxicated at the time of the collision, on the basis the report's prejudicial impact outweighed its probative value. The district court held a pretrial hearing on the motion, at which Ballou's (P) representatives introduced evidence to refute the results. They placed a nurse on the stand who testified she had examined Ballou (P) very closely a few hours before the collision and she was positive he was not then intoxicated. In response, Henri (D) described the chain of events leading from the removal of the blood from the body to the test results. The district court held that the nurse's testimony sufficiently showed the tests lacked credibility, and held that under Fed. R. Evid. 403, its prejudicial impact outweighed its probative value and granted the motion. Henri (D) appealed.

ISSUE: Under Fed. R. Evid. 403, must a court ascribe that amount of probative value which the evidence would have if it is believed and not merely the value the court would give it based on the courts evaluation of its probity?

HOLDING AND DECISION: (Williams, J.) Yes. Under Fed. R. Evid. 403, when a court endeavors to balance the probative value of a piece of evidence against its prejudicial impact it must give the evidence that amount of probative value it would have if the evidence is believed, not the value the court ascribes to it based on the extent to which it finds it believable. The court must leave to the jury the question of believability. In this case, Ballou's (P) intoxication would strongly tend to show contributory negligence. This issue goes directly to the allocation of fault and thus is highly relevant. Further, the test results, although clearly prejudicial, are not unfairly so. They were scientifically obtained and relate to the primary issue in the case. Therefore, it cannot be said that the results are more prejudicial than probative, and the motion should have been denied. Reversed and remanded.

EDITOR'S ANALYSIS: Evidence must meet two fundamental tests of relevancy. It must be both logically relevant in that it has some tendency in reason to prove or disprove a fact in controversy. Also, it must be legally relevant. This means that its prejudicial impact cannot substantially outweigh its probative value. It is important to remember that merely because evidence is prejudicial, it will not lack legal relevancy unless this prejudicial property substantially outweighs its logical relevancy. This is so, because all evidence worthy of an advocate's attempt to admit it will necessarily be prejudicial to some extent. It is only where it is so prejudicial that the jury may ascribe too much weight to it for emotional reasons that it will be said to lack legal relevancy.

NOTES:

4

CHAPTER THREE
THE HEARSAY RULE

QUICK REFERENCE RULES OF LAW

1. **Admissions of Guilt.** The voluntary murder confession of a third-party, coupled with circumstances pointing to its truth, is not competent evidence in behalf of the defendant charged with the murder. (State v. English)

2. **Statements Not Offered for the Truth of the Matter Asserted.** The hearsay rule does not preclude all out-of-court statements offered to show its truth; rather, it precludes reliance on the credibility of an out-of-court declarant to guarantee the right of meaningful cross-examination. (Estate of Murdock)

3. **Out-of-court Statements on Hearer.** Evidence of the out-of-court statements of a person not present at trial is hearsay only when the statements are offered for their truth, not as evidence of the fact they were made. (Subramaniam v. Public Prosecutor)

4. **Statements as Circumstantial Evidence of Knowledge.** Where, regardless of the truth or falsity of a statement, the fact that it has been made is relevant, the hearsay rule does not apply and the statement may be admitted into evidence. (Vinyard v. Vinyard Funeral Home, Inc.)

5. **Statements Not Proferred for the Truth of the Matter Asserted.** Evidence must be presented for its truth in order to be excluded as hearsay. (Johnson v. Misericordia Community Hospital)

6. **Statements Admitted as Proof They Were Made.** Oral statements expressly offered for a non-hearsay purpose, that is, to prove that the statements were made, are admissible evidence. (Ries Biologicals, Inc. v. Bank of Santa Fe)

7. **Declarant's State-of-mind Exception.** Statements, otherwise excluded as hearsay, may be received into evidence to show the declarant's then-existing state of mind. (Fun-Damental Tool, Ltd. v. Gemmy Industries Corp.)

8. **Statements Admitted for the Truth of the Matter Asserted.** Evidence relied upon not as proof of a witness' state of mind at the inception of an investigation, but as evidence of a defendant's guilt, is inadmissible hearsay under Federal Rule of Evidence 802. (United States v. Hernandez)

9. **Assertion as Hearsay.** Non-assertive verbal conduct is not covered by the hearsay rule and is therefore admissible. (United States v. Zenni)

10. **Assertive Conduct.** A person who has committed a heinous crime, but has gone undiscovered, and who thereafter commits suicide, has, by that act, confessed the commission of that crime. (Commonwealth v. Knapp)

11. **Hearsay Exemptions.** Evidence of no complaints is too remote to show a lack of defect unless there is evidence of similar circumstances of the persons not complaining and evidence that they had an opportunity to complain. (Silver v. New York Central Railroad)

12. **Hearsay.** The rule against hearsay does not bar admission of ledgers as circumstantial evidence that show the character and use of a place where the ledgers were found. (United States v. Jaramillo-Suarez)

13. [Rule of law not stated in casebook excerpt.] (United States v. Rhodes)

14. **Definition of Hearsay.** If the conclusions as to which one testifies are based on the statements of out-of-court declarants, they constitute inadmissible hearsay. (United States v. Brown)

15. **Out-of-court Statement as Hearsay.** The hearsay rule is inapplicable to what the witness, on the stand and subject to cross-examination, observed, either through his own senses or through the use of scientific instruments. (City of Webster Groves v. Quick)

16. **Dying Declaration Exception to the Hearsay Rule.** It is not error for a trial judge who has himself determined that a dying declaration was made with an impending sense of death to refuse to instruct the jury that they must not consider the declaration if they find that the declaration was made without an impending sense of death. (Soles v. State)

17. **Res Gestae Exception to the Hearsay Rule.** For declarations to be admissible in evidence as part of the res gestae, there must be evidence of an act itself admissible in the case independently of the declaration that accompanies it. (Truck Insurance Exchange v. Michling)

18. **Statements of Medical Opinion.** A physician's extrajudicial medical opinion is inadmissible at trial as hearsay evidence. (Lira v. Albert Einstein Medical Center)

19. **Present Sense Impressions.** The present sense impression exception to the hearsay rule requires that an extrajudicial statement evidence contemporaneousness and that the declarant made it from his personal knowledge. (State v. Jones)

20. **Admission Exemption from Hearsay Rule.** Admissions against interest by a party of any fact material to the issue qualifies as an exception to the hearsay rule and is admissible as evidence. (Reed v. McCord)

21. **Adoptive Admissions.** Where one of the parties to the action has manifested his adoption of or belief in the truth of a statement that would otherwise constitute hearsay, it is admissible under an exception to the hearsay rule for admissions by a party opponent. (United States v. Hoosier)

22. **Intent to Adopt, Agree or Approve.** The intent to adopt, agree with, or approve of the contents of another's statement, a precondition to the admissibility of evidence offered under O.E.C. § 801(4)(b)(B), is a preliminary question of fact for the trial judge under O.E.C. § 104(1). (State v. Carlson)

23. **Federal Rule of Evidence 801(d)(2)(D).** Federal Rule of Evidence 801(d)(2)(D) makes statements made by agents within the scope of their employment admissible and there is no implied requirement that the declarant have personal knowledge of the facts underlying his statement. (Mahlandt v. Wild Canid Survival & Research Center, Inc.)

24. **Vicarious Admissions.** An agent's hearsay statements should be received against the principal as vicarious admissions only when the trial judge finds, as a preliminary fact, that the statements were authorized. (Big Mack Trucking Co., Inc. v. Dickerson)

25. **Statements of Third-party Non-agents.** Out-of-court statements made by an individual who is not a party's agent are not admissible under Federal Rule of Evidence 801(d)(2) as an admission against the party. (Sabel v. Mead Johnson & Co.)

26. **Co-conspirator Statements.** Statements made during and in furtherance of a conspiracy to commit a crime or a civil wrong are not made inadmissible by the hearsay rule. (United States v. DiDominico)

27. **Traditional Co-conspirator Exception.** A late-joining conspirator takes the conspiracy as he finds it. (United States v. Goldberg)

28. **Co-conspirator Exception.** Where a co-conspirator of a party makes a statement against the party which, reasonably concluded, furthers the conspiracy, then this statement may be admitted at the party's subsequent trial in respect to the conspiracy. (United States v. Doerr)

29. **Constitutionality of Co-conspirator Exception.** Federal Rule of Evidence 801(d)(2)(E), excluding out-of-court statements in furtherance of conspiracy from being considered hearsay, does not violate the Confrontation Clause. (Bourjaily v. United States)

30. **Prior Testimony Exception to the Hearsay Rule.** Complete identity of the parties is not required where prior recorded testimony given in a criminal trial is not sought to be admitted in a civil trial. (Travelers Fire Insurance Co. v. Wright)

31. **Prior Testimony Exception to the Hearsay Rule.** Federal Rule of Evidence 804(b)(1) permits the admission of former testimony of an unavailable witness if the party against whom the testimony is now offered had an opportunity and similar motive to develop the testimony by direct, cross- or redirect examination. (United States v. Salerno)

32. **Declarations against Interest.** A declaration against interest by one not a party or in privity with a party to an action is admissible where the declarant (1) is either dead or unavailable; (2) had peculiar means of knowing the facts stated; (3) made a declaration that was against his pecuniary or proprietary interest; and (4) had no probable motive to falsify the facts stated. (G.M. McKelvey v. General Casualty of America)

33. **Declarations against Interest.** Under the Federal Rules of Evidence, a statement tending to expose the declarant to criminal liability and offered to exculpate the accused is not admissible under the exception to the hearsay rule for declarations against interest, unless corroborating circumstances clearly indicate the trustworthiness of the statement. (United States v. Barrett)

34. **Out-of-court, Non-self-inculpatory Statements.** Federal Rule of Evidence 804(b)(3) does not allow admission of non-self-inculpatory statements, even if they are made within a broader narrative that is generally self-inculpatory. (Williamson v. United States)

35. **State of Mind Exception to the Hearsay Rule.** Statements expressing the declarant's state of mind at the time of the utterances are admissible as exceptions to the hearsay rule, notwithstanding that some portions of the statements do not describe state of mind and tend to damage the defendant. (Adkins v. Brett)

36. **Declaration of Intent as Hearsay Exception.** Whenever a party's intention is, of itself, a distinct and material fact in a chain of circumstances, it may be proved by contemporaneous oral or written declarations of the party. (Mutual Life Insurance Co. of New York v. Hillmon)

37. **Statements Based on Memory.** Declarations of present memory, looking backwards to a prior occurrence, are inadmissible to prove, or tend to prove, the existence of the occurrence. (Shepard v. United States)

38. **Admissibility of Statements of Interest to Do Something with Another Person.** The *Hillmon* doctrine permits introduction of hearsay declarations as evidence that the declarant carried out his intention to perform the act they indicate it was his intention to perform, even if its accomplishment requires action by others. (United States v. Pheaster)

39. **Admissibility of Surveys.** If adequate statistical and procedural safeguards are taken, a survey is admissible evidence under the "existing present state of mind, belief, or opinion" exception to the hearsay rule. (Zippo Manufacturing Co. v. Rogers Imports, Inc.)

40. **Previous Identification Testimony.** A witness in a criminal trial may testify about an earlier identification even if he can no longer testify as to the basis for that identification. (United States v. Owens)

41. **Refreshing Recollection.** Anything can be used to refresh a witness's recollection of an event, even a memorandum made by another, and it need not meet the standards applicable to a record of past recollection. (Baker v. State)

42. **Limitation on Past Recollection Recorded Exception.** When a witness's own recollection is not refreshed by a written memoranda that he made, that writing is not admissible as evidence. (Adams v. The New York Central Railroad Co.)

43. **Business Records Exception to the Hearsay Rule.** While a statute may allow the admission into evidence of business records that are kept in the regular course of business, even without firsthand knowledge of the record by the recorder, entries that include hearsay statements of third parties not engaged in the business related to the record may not be admitted. (Johnson v. Lutz)

44. **Limitation on Business Record Exception.** The business records exception to the hearsay rule does not embrace statements contained within a business record that are made by one who is an outsider to the business where the statements are offered for their truth. (United States v. Vigneau)

45. **Multiple Hearsay.** Business records otherwise admissible under an exception to the hearsay rule are not precluded from admission merely because they are based on other business records or the nonhearsay statements of agents on matters within the scope of their agency. (United States v. Duncan)

46. **Business Records Exception to the Hearsay Rule.** The only information which is admissible in a hospital report under the business records exception is that which is recorded in the regular course of business and for the purpose of assisting the hospital in carrying on that business. (Williams v. Alexander)

47. **Computerized Business Records.** A computerized business record is considered trustworthy unless the opposing party comes forward with some evidence to question its reliability. (Hahnemann University Hospital v. Dudnick)

48. **Regular Course of Business Requirement to the Business Records Exception.** A record is considered to be "in the regular course of business" if made systematically or as a matter of routine to reflect events or transactions of the business. (Palmer v. Hoffman)

49. **Business Records Exception to the Hearsay Rule.** A writing or record, whether in the form of an entry in a book or otherwise, made as a memorandum or record of any act, occurrence, or event and pursuant to regular business procedure, is admissible. (Lewis v. Baker)

50. **Statements for Medical Diagnosis Exception to the Hearsay Rule.** A doctor's report prepared in anticipation of litigation is admissible under the business records exception if the court finds that the reports have an inherent probability of trustworthiness. (Yates v. Bair Transsport, Inc.)

51. **Public Records and Reports Exception to the Hearsay Rule.** The public records and reports exception to the hearsay rule permits introduction of opinions and conclusions contained in public records and reports. (Beech Aircraft Corp. v. Rainey)

52. **Official Records Exception to the Hearsay Rule.** Evaluative and law enforcement reports which fail to qualify under the "public records" exception to the hearsay rule cannot be admitted as "business." (United States v. Oates)

53. Official Records Exception to the Hearsay Rule. While Fed. R. Evid. 803(8)(B) does exclude records and reports setting forth "matters observed by police officers and other law enforcement personnel" from its "public records" exception to the hearsay rule, this exclusionary language covers only police officers' reports of their contemporaneous observations of crime. (United States v. Grady)

54. Admissibility of Prior Conviction. A prior state misdemeanor conviction is admissible in a subsequent federal court action to establish civil liability for the conduct that resulted in the conviction. (Stroud v. Cook)

55. Residual Exceptions to the Hearsay Rule. Under Federal Rule of Evidence 804(b)(5), a statement not specifically covered by a hearsay exception may be admitted if (1) it is made under equivalent guarantees of trustworthiness; (2) it is offered to prove a material fact; (3) it is more probative than other reasonably obtained evidence; and (4) the general purposes of the hearsay exceptions and the interests of justice will be served by its admission into evidence. (Turbyfill v. International Harvester Co.)

56. Hearsay Exception. Hearsay evidence of an unavailable witness that does not fall within a specific hearsay exception may be admitted if there are particularized guarantees of trustworthiness shown to satisfy Federal Rule of Evidence 804(b)(5) and the Confrontation Clause. (United States v. Dent)

57. Hearsay and the Right of Confrontation. The right to confrontation is not violated by the presentation of the transcript testimony where there was an adequate opportunity to cross-examine the witness at the official proceeding at which the testimony was given. (Ohio v. Roberts)

58. Hearsay and the Right of Confrontation. The Confrontation Clause does not require that a nontestifying co-conspirator be unavailable to testify as a condition for admission of the co-conspirator's out-of-court statements into evidence. (United States v. Inadi)

59. Reliability of Co-conspirator Statements. The Confrontation Clause does not require a court to make an independent inquiry into the reliability of out-of-court statements made by an alleged co-conspirator that otherwise satisfy the requirements of Federal Rule of Evidence 801(d)(2)(E). (Bourjaily v. United States)

60. "Residual" Hearsay Exception. An out-of-court statement of an unavailable declarant which does not fall within a "firmly rooted" hearsay exception is not admissible under the "residual" hearsay exception as particularly trustworthy merely because other evidence corroborates the statement. (Idaho v. Wright)

61. Excited Utterances. The Sixth Amendment Confrontation Clause does not prohibit the admission of testimony under the "spontaneous declaration" and "medical examination" exceptions to the hearsay rule. (White v. Illinois)

62. Admissibility of Non-testifying Co-conspirator's Confession. A confession by a non-testifying accomplice to a crime that shifts or spreads blame is presumptively unreliable, and therefore violates the criminal defendant's rights under the Confrontation Clause. (Lilly v. Virginia)

63. Impeachment by Party of Own Witnesses. Where constitutional rights directly affecting the ascertainment of guilt are implicated the hearsay rule may not be applied mechanically so to defeat the ends of justice. (Chambers v. Mississippi)

64. Due Process and Hearsay. The hearsay rule will not apply where exclusion of the evidence would deny a criminal defendant due process of law. (Green v. Georgia)

STATE v. ENGLISH
State (P) v. Convicted murderer (D)
N.C. Sup. Ct., 201 N.C. 295, 159 S.E. 318 (1931).

NATURE OF CASE: Appeal from conviction for second-degree murder.

FACT SUMMARY: In the State's (P) criminal action against English (D) for second-degree murder, the trial court excluded evidence, over English's (D) exceptions, of a third-party's extrajudicial confession to the murder, whereby English (D) was subsequently convicted.

CONCISE RULE OF LAW: The voluntary murder confession of a third-party, coupled with circumstances pointing to its truth, is not competent evidence in behalf of the defendant charged with the murder.

FACTS: After Dave Locke's confession to the murder of English's (D) wife, which circumstances appeared to authenticate, English (D) was arrested and charged with his wife's murder. During trial, English (D) offered evidence of Locke's confession, which was, in turn, excluded by the court. Subsequently, the court, despite English's (D) exceptions to the exclusion of the evidence, convicted him of second-degree murder, which was affirmed on appeal. English (D) appealed.

ISSUE: Is the voluntary murder confession of a third party, coupled with circumstances pointing to its truth, competent evidence in behalf of the defendant charged with the murder?

HOLDING AND DECISION: (Brogden, J.) No. The voluntary murder confession of a third party, coupled with circumstances pointing to its truth, is not competent evidence in behalf of the defendant charged with the murder. This rule is in agreement with the weight of authority which excludes such testimony. Specifically, the court in *State v. May*, 15 N.C. 328, excluded evidence of the previously described nature on the legal principle of hearsay. Moreover, although there is a well-argued view which would contrarily permit such testimony on the basis of common sense, if proffered testimony is technically and legalistically hearsay, then the technical interpretation must prevail and such evidence must be excluded. In the instant case, the trial judge was correct in excluding evidence of Locke's murder confession, which was in the interest of English (D), the accused. Affirmed.

EDITOR'S ANALYSIS: Judge Brogden points out in the opinion that the patriarchal case from which the above rule proceeds, *State v. May*, 15 N.C. 328, may have had as one of its purposes the eradication of proffered testimony regarding extrajudicial confessions illegitimately procured by slave masters from slaves as a means of placing the blame for wrongs committed by the former onto the latter. Given that the confessor in the above case was African-American, and given the time period (1931, North Carolina), the fact that the North Carolina Supreme Court chose to hold to traditional legal principles may have been out of the same procuration concerns that faced the *May* court.

NOTES:

ESTATE OF MURDOCK
Children of deceased (P) v. Children of deceased (D)
32 Muc. 352 (1983).

NATURE OF CASE: Appeal from the exclusion of evidence as hearsay.

FACT SUMMARY: The trial court excluded testimonial evidence, relating a statement made to the witness by Arthur Murdock showing Murdock to have died after his wife, on the basis that the statement was hearsay.

CONCISE RULE OF LAW: The hearsay rule does not preclude all out-of-court statements offered to show its truth; rather, it precludes reliance on the credibility of an out-of-court declarant to guarantee the right of meaningful cross-examination.

FACTS: Sarah and Arthur Murdock each executed separate wills. Sarah left her entire estate to Arthur should she predecease him. Should she survive him, her estate was to go to her children by a prior marriage. Arthur's will was identical, leaving Sarah his estate if she survived him, and leaving his children by a prior marriage the estate should he survive her. Subsequently, their private airplane crashed, killing them both. Litigation arose concerning which one died first. Arthur's children attempted to introduce testimony of a deputy sheriff to the effect that upon arriving at the scene, he clearly saw Sarah was dead, and that Arthur whispered, "I'm still alive." The trial court excluded the statement as hearsay solely because it was an out-of-court statement offered for its truth. Arthur's children appealed.

ISSUE: Does the hearsay rule prohibit the admission of all out-of-court statements offered for their truth?

HOLDING AND DECISION: (Kaplan, J.) No. The hearsay rule does not preclude all out-of-court statements offered to show their truth. Rather, it precludes reliance on the credibility of an out-of-court declarant in order to guarantee the right of meaningful cross-examination. In this case, the statement—merely by the fact it was made—shows Arthur survived his wife. Dead people do not make statements. As a result, it is improper to apply hearsay analysis to this statement as there is no doubt as to its credibility. The only question of credibility involves whether the statement was indeed made, and on that point the deputy sheriff was available for cross-examination. Therefore, the statement should have been admitted. Reversed.

CONCURRENCE: (Park, J.) What Murdock said is irrelevant; the fact that he could say anything showed that he was still alive. The majority's opinion stands for the proposition that an utterance is not hearsay when its value at trial does not depend to any degree on the credibility of an out-of-court declarant. However, that does not mean that when the use of a statement *does* require some dependence on credibility of the declarant, the statement is automatically hearsay; a statement may not be hearsay even though its value varies with the credibility of an out-of-court declarant.

EDITOR'S ANALYSIS: In determining what weight, if any, to give to a particular piece of testimony, a trier of fact evaluates the credibility of the declarant. This evaluation requires consideration of the plausibility of the truth of the statement along with the demeanor of the declarant when the statement is made. Further, declarants must be subject to meaningful cross-examination by the opposing party. When a statement is made out of court the trier is deprived of the ability to evaluate the declarant's demeanor and the opponent is deprived of his right to cross-examine. As a result, statements made out of court are considered inherently unreliable and are excluded under the hearsay rule.

NOTES:

SUBRAMANIAM v. PUBLIC PROSECUTOR
Convicted firearm possessor (D) v. Prosecution (D)
Jud. Comm. of Privy Counsel, 100 Solic.Jour. 566 (1956).

NATURE OF CASE: Appeal, by special leave, from dismissal of appeal for conviction for illegal firearm possession.

FACT SUMMARY: Subramaniam (D) was arrested for possession of prohibited firearm ammunition. He sought to testify as to threats made against him by terrorists who, he claimed, forced him to carry the ammunition. The testimony was excluded as hearsay.

CONCISE RULE OF LAW: Evidence of the out-of-court statements of a person not present at trial is hearsay only when the statements are offered for their truth, not as evidence of the fact they were made.

FACTS: Under emergency regulations in effect in Kuala Lumpur, possession of prohibited firearms or ammunition was a capital offense. Subramaniam (D) was charged with violation of the regulation when he was found in possession of twenty rounds of ammunition. At the time of his arrest, Subramaniam (D) claimed that he had been captured and wounded by terrorists who had forced him to carry the ammunition. At his trial, Subramaniam (D) sought to support his claim of duress by testifying about the threats made against him by the terrorists. This testimony was excluded as hearsay since the terrorists could not be called for cross-examination. Subramaniam (D) brought this appeal, by special leave, after his original appeal had been dismissed.

ISSUE: Is evidence of the out-of-court statements of a person not present in court hearsay if the statements are not offered for truth but rather as evidence of the fact they were made?

HOLDING AND DECISION: (Mr. L.M.D. De Silva) No. Subramaniam's (D) defense of duress was severely hampered by his inability to testify as to the threats made against him by the terrorists. Evidence of the out-of-court statements of another are hearsay only if the statements are offered for their truth. Such out-of-court statements are not hearsay if they are offered merely to establish they were made without regard for their truth. Whether or not the terrorists' threats were true is not at issue. For the defense of duress, all that needed to be established was whether Subramaniam (D) believed those threats. Since those statements were not to be offered for their truth, their exclusion as hearsay was improper and the appeal should be allowed.

EDITOR'S ANALYSIS: Whether a statement is offered for its truth is sometimes an elusive concept. Typical examples of such statements that are not offered for their truth include statements offered to show another's reaction thereto; statements altered to show the declarant's state of mind by inference; statements offered to show that the listener had knowledge of certain information; and, as in the principal case, statements offered as a basis for a person's reasonable belief.

VINYARD v. VINYARD FUNERAL HOME, INC.
Slip-and-fall victim (P) v. Premises owner (D)
St. Louis Ct. App., 435 S.W.2d 392 (1968).

NATURE OF CASE: Appeal from award of damages for personal injuries.

FACT SUMMARY: In Vinyard's (P) suit against Vinyard Funeral Home, Inc. (D) for personal injuries received when Vinyard (P) fell in the parking lot of the Funeral Home (D), the Funeral Home (D) contended that evidence that people complained to the Funeral Home (D) that the surface of the parking lot was slippery when wet was improperly admitted because it was hearsay.

CONCISE RULE OF LAW: Where, regardless of the truth or falsity of a statement, the fact that it has been made is relevant, the hearsay rule does not apply and the statement may be admitted into evidence.

FACTS: Vinyard (P), the daughter-in-law of the Vinyard Funeral Home, Inc. (D) president, fell and was injured in the parking lot of the Funeral Home (D) when she slipped on the pavement of the lot on a rainy night. At trial, evidence was admitted that people had complained to the Funeral Home (D) that the sealed surface of the lot was slippery when wet. The Funeral Home (D) objected to the admission of this evidence as hearsay. Vinyard (P) received a judgment in her favor, and the Funeral Home (D) appealed.

ISSUE: Where, regardless of the truth or falsity of a statement, the fact that it has been made is relevant, does the hearsay rule not apply and may the statement be admitted into evidence?

HOLDING AND DECISION: (Clemens, J.) Yes. Where, regardless of the truth or falsity of a statement, the fact that it has been made is relevant, the hearsay rule does not apply, and the statement may be admitted into evidence. Here, questions and answers about the slickness of the parking lot when wet were improper as hearsay if offered only to prove the fact that the sealed area was slick. But aside from the fact of slickness, there was the issue of the Funeral Home's (D) knowledge of slickness. Evidence of complaints of slickness made to the Funeral Home (D) was relevant to the material issue of the Funeral Home's (D) knowledge. Vinyard (P), to make her case, was obliged to show that the Funeral Home's (D) officers knew about the slickness. The trial court properly admitted evidence that this knowledge had come to the offices through complaints of patrons that the parking lot's sealed area was slick when wet. Affirmed.

EDITOR'S ANALYSIS: Hearsay must be a statement or other communicative conduct offered to prove the truth of the matter asserted. This presupposes a lack of personal knowledge of the truth of the matter asserted on the witness' part. To qualify as hearsay, the declaration must have been made out of court; that is, at least not made at the hearing at which it is offered in evidence.

NOTES:

JOHNSON v. MISERICORDIA COMMUNITY HOSPITAL
Patient (P) v. Hospital (D)
Wis. Ct. App., 97 Wis.2d. 521, 294 N.W.2d. 501 (1980).

NATURE OF CASE: Appeal from a damage award for negligence.

FACT SUMMARY: Misericordia (D) contended the trial court erred in admitting evidence of other hospitals' records regarding the fitness of a doctor subsequently hired by Misericordia (D), contending such were hearsay.

CONCISE RULE OF LAW: Evidence must be presented for its truth in order to be excluded as hearsay.

FACTS: Johnson (P) sued Misericordia (D) contending the hospital was negligent in hiring Dr. Salinksy and allowing him to perform operations. At trial, evidence was presented showing that had Misericordia (D) checked Salinksy's credentials, it would have found records at other hospitals which would have placed it on notice of Salinksy's incompetence. Misericordia (D) appealed an award of damages for Johnson (P) contending such records were inadmissible as hearsay. Johnson (P) contended the records were admitted to show this information existed, not to prove Salinksy's incompetence.

ISSUE: Must evidence be introduced for the truth of its assertions in order for it to be subject to a hearsay objection?

HOLDING AND DECISION: [Judge not stated in casebook excerpt.] Yes. In order for evidence to be subject to a hearsay objection, it must be offered to prove the truth of the assertions made. If Johnson (P) had presented the records to show the truth of its assertions, that is, that Salinksy was incompetent, than it could be classified as hearsay. Because it was introduced merely to show such information existed, it cannot be considered hearsay and was properly admitted. Affirmed.

EDITOR'S ANALYSIS: The rationale behind the exclusion of hearsay evidence is that such is inherently untrustworthy. The trier of fact is deprived of an opportunity to observe the declarant when the statement is made. It is this missed opportunity which allows for the exclusion of evidence even where the witness testifying was the declarant.

NOTES:

RIES BIOLOGICALS, INC. v. BANK OF SANTA FE
Distributor of medical supplies (P) v. Bank (D)
780 F.2d 888 (10th Cir. 1986).

NATURE OF CASE: Appeal from award of damages for breach of oral promise.

FACT SUMMARY: In Ries Biologicals, Inc's (P) suit against the Bank of Santa Fe (D) for breach of oral promise, the Bank (D) contended that the trial court erroneously admitted evidence of statements made by the senior vice-president of the Bank (D), guaranteeing payment of approved shipments made by Ries (P), because those statements were hearsay.

CONCISE RULE OF LAW: Oral statements expressly offered for a non-hearsay purpose, that is, to prove that the statements were made, are admissible evidence.

FACTS: Ries Biologicals, Inc. (P) was a distributor of medical supplies. Ries (P) began selling supplies to Dialysis Management Systems, Inc. (DMS), but DMS started to have financial problems and accumulated a debt to Ries (P) of $42,000. Ries (P) stopped shipping supplies to DMS because of the debt, but resumed shipment on credit based on Ries's (P) reliance on the Bank of Santa Fe's (D) oral agreement to guarantee payment for orders which were approved in advance. Ries (P), however, was not paid in full and sued the Bank (D). The trial court found for Ries (P), and the Bank (D) appealed, contending that the court erroneously admitted evidence of statements made by the senior vice-president of the Bank (D), guaranteeing payment of approved shipments made by Ries (P), because those statements were hearsay.

ISSUE: Are oral statements expressly offered for a non-hearsay purpose, that is, to prove that the statements were made, admissible evidence?

HOLDING AND DECISION: (Crow, J.) Yes. Oral statements expressly offered for a non-hearsay purpose, that is, to prove that the statements were made, are admissible evidence. The oral statements of Philip Levitt, the Bank's (D) senior vice-president, were expressly offered for a non-hearsay purpose. The relevance of Levitt's statements is not their truth or falsity, rather it is the fact the statements were made. The relevance of the statements depends, therefore, not on the credibility of the out-of-court declarant, Levitt, but on that of the testifying witness. Thus, there was no manifest error in the admission of Levitt's oral statements. Affirmed.

EDITOR'S ANALYSIS: Where the probative value of evidence is dependent on the perception, memory, or integrity of an out-of-court source who cannot be subjected to cross-examination, the evidence is hearsay. However, an out-of-court assertion is only hearsay if it is offered to prove the truth of the matter asserted. If the statement is not used as an assertion of substantive fact, but is relevant simply because it was made, the inability to cross-examine the person who made the out-of-court statements is not crucial.

NOTES:

FUN-DAMENTAL TOO, LTD. v. GEMMY INDUSTRIES CORP.

Manufacturer (P) v. Alleged Infringer (D)

111 F.3d 993 (2d Cir. 1997).

NATURE OF CASE: Appeal from judgment for plaintiff in trade dress infringement case.

FACT SUMMARY: Gemmy (D) alleged that the testimony of Fun-Damental's national sales manager was inadmissible hearsay and could not support a finding of actual confusion.

CONCISE RULE OF LAW: Statements, otherwise excluded as hearsay, may be received into evidence to show the declarant's then-existing state of mind.

FACTS: Fun-Damental (P), a novelty toy manufacturer, claimed that Gemmy (D) copied a coin bank it manufactured to produce and sell an almost identical version at a lower price. Fun-Damental (P) successfully sued Gemmy (D) for trade dress infringement under the Lanham Act. Gemmy (D) alleged that the testimony by Fun-Damental's (P) sale manager, suggesting that some retail customers complained because they thought Fun-Damental (P) was selling its product at a lower price to other retailers, should not have been admitted because it was hearsay. Gemmy (D) appealed, arguing that the evidence, even if admissible, did not support a finding of actual confusion.

ISSUE: May statements, otherwise excluded as hearsay, be received into evidence to show the declarant's then-existing state of mind?

HOLDING AND DECISION: (Cardamone, J.) Yes. Statements, otherwise excluded as hearsay, may be received into evidence to show the declarant's then-existing state of mind. The testimony in question was not offered to prove that Fun-Damental (P) was actually selling at a lower price, but was probative of the declarant's confusion. Affirmed.

EDITOR'S ANALYSIS: Hearsay is an out of court statement admitted for the truth of the matter asserted. Some statements, otherwise excluded as hearsay, may still be admitted if they fall under one of the exceptions to the hearsay rule. Fed. R. Evid. 803(3) allows statements to be received to show the declarant's then-existing state of mind.

QUICKNOTES

HEARSAY - An out-of-court statement made by a person other than the witness testifying at trial that is offered in order to prove the truth of the matter asserted.

PROBATIVE - Tending to establish proof.

STATE OF MIND - A declarant's mental state, testimony regarding state of mind is ordinarily not considered hearsay because it is indicative of motivation and therefore has circumstantial guarantees of trustworthiness.

NOTES:

UNITED STATES v. HERNANDEZ
Federal government (P) v. Drug dealer (D)
750 F.2d 1256 (5th Cir. 1985).

NATURE OF CASE: Appeal from conviction for possession and distribution of cocaine.

FACT SUMMARY: In the government's (P) prosecution of Hernandez (D) for possession and distribution of cocaine, Hernandez (D) contended that the prosecution attorney elicited inadmissible testimony from a government witness, and that, therefore, Hernandez's (D) conviction should be reversed.

CONCISE RULE OF LAW: Evidence relied upon not as proof of a witness' state of mind at the inception of an investigation, but as evidence of a defendants guilt, is inadmissible hearsay under Federal Rule of Evidence 802.

FACTS: An informant, Gholson, and a Drug Enforcement Administration (DEA) special agent, Saulnier, arranged with Hernandez (D) a meeting where Hernandez (D) allegedly offered to sell Gholson and Saulnier a kilo of cocaine. When Gholson accepted the cocaine from Hernandez (D) and the two were proceeding to the place where payment to Hernandez (D) would take place, Hernandez (D) was arrested. Hernandez (D) testified he had been set-up by Gholson and objected to the admission into evidence of Saulnier's statement that U.S. Customs had identified Hernandez (D) as a drug smuggler. The statement was admitted into evidence, Hernandez (D) was convicted of possession and distribution of cocaine, and he appealed, contending that the prosecutor had elicited evidence from a government (P) witness which was inadmissible because it was not relevant to show Saulnier's state of mind and was therefore hearsay.

ISSUE: Is evidence relied upon not as proof of a witness' state of mind at the inception of the investigation, but as evidence of a defendant's guilt, inadmissible hearsay under Fed. R. Evid. 802?

HOLDING AND DECISION: (Rubin, J.) Yes. Evidence relied upon not as proof of a witness' state of mind at the inception of the investigation, but as evidence of a defendant's guilt, is inadmissible hearsay under Fed. R. Evid. 802. The government's (P) argument that this testimony was not hearsay and was relevant to show Saulnier's state of mind lacks merit. Saulnier's state of mind was not at issue. The testimony was, therefore, hearsay. The government's (P) protestation that the evidence was not elicited to prove Hernandez (D) was a drug smuggler, but merely to explain the motivation behind DEAs investigation is unconvincing from both a common-sense perspective and from the government's (P) subsequent use of that testimony. This type of evidence is inadmissible. Reversed.

EDITOR'S ANALYSIS: The hearsay rule forbids evidence of out-of-court assertions to prove the facts asserted in them. If the purpose of offered testimony is to use an out-of-court statement to evidence the truth of facts therein stated, the hearsay objection cannot be removed by eliciting the meaning of the statement in an indirect form. That is, evidence about the meaning of "information received" by the witness, or testimony of the results of investigations made by other persons, offered as proof of the facts asserted out of court, are properly classed as hearsay.

NOTES:

UNITED STATES v. ZENNI
Federal government (P) v. Alleged bookmaker (D)
492 F. Supp. 464 (E.D. Ky. 1980).

NATURE OF CASE: Prosecution for illegal bookmaking.

FACT SUMMARY: Humphrey (D) contended that testimony of government agents concerning phone conversations they had with callers to Humphrey's (D) premises after his arrest, wherein the callers stated directions for placing bets, was inadmissible hearsay.

CONCISE RULE OF LAW: Non-assertive verbal conduct is not covered by the hearsay rule and is therefore admissible.

FACTS: While executing a search warrant on Humphrey's (D) premises, government agents answered the phone several times pursuant to the warrant's authority to search for illegal book-making activities. The unknown callers stated directions for placing bets on various sporting events. Humphrey (D) was arrested, and at trial the government (P) proposed to introduce the conversations to show that the callers believed that the premises were being used in betting operations, and that the existence of such belief tends to prove they were so used. Humphrey (D) objected, contending the conversations were offered for their truth and were inadmissible hearsay.

ISSUE: Is non-assertive verbal conduct covered by the hear-say rule?

HOLDING AND DECISION: (Bertelsman, J.) No. Non-assertive verbal conduct is not considered to be an effort on the part of the actor to communicate any fact inferable from the conduct. Therefore, the hearsay rule does not apply. Fed. R. Evid. 801 defines hearsay as an out-of-court statement offered to prove its truth. A statement is then defined as an assertion intended to be an assertion. In this case, the callers did not by their calls intend to assert that Humphrey's (D) premises were being used for bookmaking. That fact is inferred from the callers unassertive conduct and therefore was not hearsay. Therefore, the conversations are not rendered inadmissible as hearsay.

EDITOR'S ANALYSIS: A statement for purposes of the hearsay rule may be written or oral, or it may be manifested by conduct. A policeman who raises his hand with his palm forward is intending to communicate or assert a message to another to stop. This is clearly a statement also. Hand motions indicating acquiescence are also statements and if offered to prove the actor agreed to a particular thing are hearsay, yet they fall within the exception. The difference between these statements and the non-assertive conduct illustrated in this case is the intent to communicate the inferred fact.

COMMONWEALTH v. KNAPP
Federal government (P) v. Aider and Abettor (D)
Mass. Sup. Jud. Ct., VII American State Trials 395 (1830).

NATURE OF CASE: Criminal prosecution for murder.

FACT SUMMARY: Knapp (D) was tried for murder on the basis he had aided and abetted the person who actually committed the killing. That person had committed suicide before Knapp's (D) trial, and the prosecution asserted that such an act was proof of his guilt.

CONCISE RULE OF LAW: A person who has committed a heinous crime but has gone undiscovered, and who thereafter commits suicide, has, by that act, confessed the commission of that crime.

FACTS: Knapp (D) was accused of aiding and abetting the murder of Joseph White. The prosecution maintained that the actual killing had been accomplished by a man named Crowninshield. Subsequent to the killing, but prior to the trial, Crowninshield had committed suicide. In order to prove Knapp's (D) guilt, the prosecution had to establish that Crowninshield had committed the killing. The prosecutor, Daniel Webster, sought to infer Crowninshield's guilt from his suicide.

ISSUE: May the suicide of a person suspected of a crime be properly inferred as a confession to the commission of the crime suspected?

HOLDING AND DECISION: (Prosecutor's Argument) Yes. No crime goes undetected or unpunished. Even in the rare instance when the perpetrator successfully conceals his guilt from other men, he must still face the wrath of God. Further, the knowledge of his own guilt preys heavily on the perpetrator's heart and soul. Such guilt begins to build an irresistible pressure for confession. When the perpetrator can no longer stand the pressure, yet he cannot bring himself to speak the confession, one alternative remains. Suicide is the only refuge from confession, yet the suicide itself speaks confession as loudly as the words themselves.

EDITOR'S ANALYSIS: Assertive conduct which may communicate an idea (so called Morgan hearsay) may be viewed on two levels. First, the relevance of such conduct to the issue on trial must be established. (In the principal case, for instance, Crowninshield's suicide could also be attributable to his shame for being falsely accused or because he was in financial trouble). If relevance can be established, then the conduct can be excluded as Morgan hearsay. However, the exceptions to Morgan hearsay are more numerous than for traditional (or Wigmore) hearsay. Therefore, similar items of evidence will usually be admissible under either system.

SILVER v. NEW YORK CENTRAL RAILROAD
Passenger (P) v. Railroad (D)
Mass. Sup. Jud. Ct., 329 Mass. 14, 105 N.E.2d 923 (1952).

NATURE OF CASE: Action for damages for personal injuries resulting from low temperature.

FACT SUMMARY: In order to prove that the temperature on New York Central's (D) train was not too low, New York Central (D) sought to introduce evidence that no one else complained to the porter of the lack of heat.

CONCISE RULE OF LAW: Evidence of no complaints is too remote to show a lack of defect unless there is evidence of similar circumstances of the persons not complaining and evidence that they had an opportunity to complain.

FACTS: Silver (P) alleged that an ailment she had was worsened because the temperature on New York Central's (D) railroad car was too low. In order to prove that the temperature was not too low, New York Central (D) sought to have the porter testify that none of the other passengers complained of the cold. The court would not allow this evidence.

ISSUE: Does the hearsay rule prevent evidence of the lack of complaints to show the lack of a defect?

HOLDING AND DECISION: (Wilkins, J.) No. The hearsay rule does not prevent such testimony. However, such evidence should be considered to be too remote, and inadmissible, unless the non-complaining parties were in a similar position as the plaintiff, and they had an adequate opportunity to complain. In this case, the passengers on the train were all in a similar position with Silver (P), and it is not likely that they would refrain from complaining if the temperature dropped below what was proper. The porter was also the proper person to testify to such matters because he would be the person who would probably hear the complaints. Therefore, as there was an opportunity for the passengers to complain, the evidence of the lack of complaints was wrongfully excluded from evidence. Exceptions sustained.

EDITOR'S ANALYSIS: The situation in this case, and the food situation the court talked about are, the classic areas in which a silence is the basis of an affirmative inference. While some courts have treated such cases as hearsay, most courts ignore any hearsay problem and base exclusion solely on relevancy. This is the way this court handled the problem. This explains the large number of courts which allow the lack of complaints to be admitted to show the lack of a defective condition. The trend is in the direction of admitting such evidence as non-hearsay. This trend finds support in recent statutes and rules.

NOTES:

UNITED STATES v. JARAMILLO-SUAREZ
Federal government (P) v. Drug dealer (D)
950 F.2d 1378 (9th Cir. 1991).

NATURE OF CASE: Review of a criminal conviction for cocaine and conspiracy offenses.

FACT SUMMARY: Suarez (D) contended that a "pay/owe" sheet recording drug transactions was inadmissible hearsay and the district court erred by allowing it into evidence.

CONCISE RULE OF LAW: The rule against hearsay does not bar admission of ledgers as circumstantial evidence that show the character and use of a place where the ledgers were found.

FACTS: Suarez (D) was accused of cocaine and conspiracy offenses. The United State (P) offered evidence that a "pay/owe" sheet was found in an apartment frequented and rented by Suarez (D). The United States (P) presented expert testimony that the "pay/owe" sheet essentially recorded drug transactions. The United States (P) also presented other evidence found in the apartment, such as vehicle registration slips belonging to Suarez (D). The district court admitted the "pay/owe" sheet into evidence over Suarez's (D) objection that it constituted inadmissible hearsay. The court of appeals granted review.

ISSUE: Does the rule against hearsay bar admission of ledgers as circumstantial evidence that show the character and use of a place where the ledgers were found?

HOLDING AND DECISION: (Canby, J.) No. The rule against hearsay does not bar admission of ledgers as circumstantial evidence that show the character and use of a place where the ledgers were found. The rule against hearsay prohibits the admission of drug ledgers or "pay/owe" sheets to prove the truth of the matter asserted in the documents, unless a proper foundation has been laid. In this case, no foundation had to be laid because the "pay/owe" sheet was not offered to prove the truth of the matter asserted on the document. Instead, it was offered only to show that the document was evidence of drug-related activity, that the document was linked to the apartment where it was found, and that Suarez (D) was connected to the apartment. Furthermore, the trial court properly instructed the jury that the "pay/owe" sheet was being admitted for the limited purposes of showing character and use of the place it was found and not for the truth of the matter asserted in the document. Affirmed.

EDITOR'S ANALYSIS: Under Fed. R. Evid. 801(c), a statement is hearsay if there is match between what the proponent seeks to prove and what the declarant intends to communicate. Whether the match exists is for the trial judge alone to decide. In this case, if the "pay/owe" sheet had been offered to prove the truth of the matter asserted, then a proper foundation would have had to be laid as to the authenticity of the document. As Suarez (D) argued unsuccessfully in the case, the United States (P) would have had to show that Suarez (D) either authored or was in some way connected to the document.

NOTES:

UNITED STATES v. RHODES
Federal government (P) v. Master sergeant (D)
Trial by General Court Martial, Ft. McNair, D.C. 1958.

NATURE OF CASE: Military court martial.

FACT SUMMARY: Rhodes (D) was tried for espionage. At his court martial, the prosecution was permitted to introduce a memorandum between two Russian agents which implicated Rhodes as a spy.

CONCISE RULE OF LAW: [Rule of law not stated in casebook excerpt.]

FACTS: Rhodes (D) was a Master Sergeant in the United States Army. He was accused of conspiring with Russian agents to violate the espionage laws of the United States. At his court martial, a memorandum between two known Russian agents was admitted into evidence against Rhodes (D). The memorandum contained some general biographical informaton about Rhodes (D) and described briefly how he had been recruited as a spy. Also contained in the memo was a description of his military duties and a statement that he had agreed to continue supplying information to the Russians. The memorandum had been seized from the hiding place of a Russian agent by the Federal Bureau of Investigation (FBI). Rhodes's (D) counsel objected to admission of the memo, asserting it was hearsay.

ISSUE: None reported, however the memorandum was admitted.

HOLDING AND DECISION: [Holding and decision not stated in casebook excerpt.]

EDITOR'S ANALYSIS: This memorandum is in fact not just hearsay, but hearsay on hearsay. The author was not relaying information personally known to him but was merely passing on what he had been told by his Moscow sources. Therefore, the memo itself was hearsay as was the information contained therein. While the memo may have had a high degree of relevance, its reliability is questionable at best. It is this type of unreliable information that the hearsay rule was designed to exclude.

NOTES:

UNITED STATES v. BROWN

Federal government (P) v. Income tax preparer (D)

548 F.2d 1194 (5th Cir. 1977).

NATURE OF CASE: Appeal from a conviction for counseling and procuring false tax returns.

FACT SUMMARY: Brown argued that an Internal Revenue Service (IRS) agent offered hearsay testimony at his trial when she testified that between 90% and 95% of about 160 returns he had prepared contained overstated itemized deductions.

CONCISE RULE OF LAW: If the conclusions as to which one testifies are based on the statements of out-of-court declarants, they constitute inadmissible hearsay.

FACTS: As a part-time income tax preparer, Brown (D) was convicted by a jury of counseling, procuring, and advising the preparation and presentation of fraudulent and false U.S. income tax returns for others. On appeal, he contended that the trial court had improperly admitted the testimony of an IRS agent who testified that between 90% and 95% of about 160 returns Brown (D) had prepared contained overstated itemized deductions. Brown (D) argued that this testimony was hearsay inasmuch as the tax returns would not show overstated deductions on their face but that a conclusion that there were overstatements had to be based on out-of-court statements by the taxpayers the agent had audited.

ISSUE: Does it constitute inadmissible hearsay when one attempts to testify to conclusions he has made based on the statements of out-of-court declarants?

HOLDING AND DECISION: (Brown, C.J.) Yes. When a witness attempts to testify to conclusions he has made on the basis of the statements of out-of-court declarants, such constitutes hearsay, which is generally inadmissible. Here, the information this IRS agent obtained from the out-of-court statements made by the 160 taxpayers whose returns she audited was absolutely vital to her ultimate in-court conclusion. There was no chance to test such statements by cross-examination and the jury had no way to examine the trustworthiness of the agent's testimony because it could not examine the taxpayers' statements upon which such testimony was directly and substantially founded. A clearer case of hearsay testimony would be difficult to imagine. Reversed and remanded for a new trial.

DISSENT: (Gee, J.) The IRS agent merely testified as to her own personal knowledge about the results of tax audits she conducted, and that is not within the definition of hearsay.

EDITOR'S ANALYSIS: The rule against hearsay was a late development of the common law, not really crystallizing until the late 17th century. Although such a qualification did not last long, there was a short period in which hearsay, although not independently admissible, was permitted into evidence as confirmation of other evidence.

NOTES:

CITY OF WEBSTER GROVES v. QUICK
City (P) v. Speeding motorist (D)
St. Louis Ct. App., 323 S.W.2d 386 (1959).

NATURE OF CASE: Appeal from or conviction for violation of a speed ordinance.

FACT SUMMARY: Quick (D) was convicted of speeding by the testimony of the arresting police officer who testified as to the readings of the electric timer used to clock defendant's speed. Quick (D) contended that the introduction of the electronic timer reading constituted hearsay.

CONCISE RULE OF LAW: The hearsay rule is inapplicable to what the witness, on the stand and subject to cross-examination, observed, either through his own senses or through the use of scientific instruments.

FACTS: Quick (D) was convicted of speeding, based on the use of an electric timer which determined his speed to be 40 [in a 30] mph zone. The electric timing device had been tested for accuracy on the morning in question. The arresting officer testified as to the readings of the electric timer, and Quick (D) contended that the court erred in permitting this testimony because it constituted hearsay.

ISSUE: Is the hearsay rule applicable to what the witness, on the stand and subject to cross-examination, observed through the use of scientific instruments?

HOLDING AND DECISION: (Anderson, J.) No. Hearsay is an extrajudicial utterance, including both oral statements and writings. The hearsay rule is not applicable to what the witness, on the stand and subject to cross-examination, observed, either through his own senses or through the use of scientific instruments. The officer here testified to the reading of the mechanism in question and not to what someone else had told him. The witness was under oath and thoroughly cross-examined, thus satisfying the principal requirements of the hearsay rule. The evidence in question here was not dependent on the perception, memory, or sincerity of an absent declarant. Thus, the lower court did not err in allowing the evidence, and its decision is affirmed.

EDITOR'S ANALYSIS: The rationale for rejecting hearsay evidence is that if such evidence were admissible the adversary party would be deprived of his right to cross-examine the out-of-court declarant. In addition, other reasons given for denying hearsay evidence include lack of oath, lack of confrontation, danger of mistake in transmitting the extrajudicial words, and lack of trustworthiness of such evidence. Note that none of these rationales for invoking the hearsay rule are present in the case at bar.

SOLES v. STATE
Convicted murderer (D) v. State (P)
Fla. Sup. Ct., 97 Fla. 61, 119 So. 791 (1929).

NATURE OF CASE: Appeal from conviction for manslaughter.

FACT SUMMARY: The trial judge admitted the dying declaration of the victim, but did not instruct the jury to determine whether the statement was made with an impending sense of death.

CONCISE RULE OF LAW: It is not error for a trial judge who has himself determined that a dying declaration was made with an impending sense of death to refuse to instruct the jury that they must not consider the declaration if they find that the declaration was made without an impending sense of death.

FACTS: Soles (D) was charged with the murder of Long. At trial, the prosecution offered testimony by Long's father and sister that after Long was shot, but before he lapsed into unconsciousness, he stated, "Oh, Daddy! Carl Soles shot me with a 22 rifle. I have got to die." The trial court admitted this as a dying declaration, and therefore falling within an exception to the hearsay rule, but refused to instruct the jury that they must not consider the statement if they concluded that the declaration was made without an impending sense of death. Soles (D) was convicted of manslaughter and appealed based on the refusal to give the requested jury instruction.

ISSUE: Is it for the trial judge alone to determine whether a dying declaration sought to be admitted as evidence was made with an impending sense of death?

HOLDING AND DECISION: (Brown, J.) Yes. It would be erroneous for the trial court, having first admitted the dying declaration, to instruct the jury to disregard it if they conclude that the legal requirement as to consciousness of death does not in their opinion exist. The jury may determine the weight of the evidence, and after the evidence is admitted, its credibility; while they are at liberty to ignore the circumstances which the judge relied upon for proof, they should not be encouraged to do so. Affirmed.

EDITOR'S ANALYSIS: Virtually all courts have insisted that the declarant have given up all hope of recovery, and strongly believed in the imminence of his own death. Since the declarant is, of course, unavailable to testify, the preliminary finding of the necessary precedent conditions must be made by the court.

TRUCK INSURANCE EXCHANGE v. MICHLING
Company exchange (D) v. Wife of decedent (P)
Tex. Sup. Ct., 364 S.W.2d 172 (1963).

NATURE OF CASE: Appeal from award of death benefits provided by the Texas Worker's Compensation Act.

FACT SUMMARY: In Mrs. Michling's (P) suit against Truck Insurance Exchange (D) to recover death benefits provided by the Texas Worker's Compensation Act because of the death of her husband, Texas Insurance Exchange (D) contended that testimony given by Mrs. Michling (P) was not a res gestae utterance and was, therefore, inadmissible hearsay.

CONCISE RULE OF LAW: For declarations to be admissible in evidence as part of the res gestae, there must be evidence of an act itself admissible in the case independently of the declaration that accompanies it.

FACTS: Mr. Michling, the deceased, sustained an accidental, but fatal, injury allegedly in the scope of his employment. The only evidence offered to prove that the deceased had received the injury in the scope of his employment was testimony given by Mrs. Michling (P). Mrs. Michling (P) said that her husband told her that he had hit his head on the bulldozer he was driving and that his head hurt so much that he had to come home. Mrs. Michling (P) sued Truck Insurance Exchange (D) to recover death benefits provided by the Texas Worker's Compensation Act, and the trial court ruled in her favor. The Exchange (D) appealed, contending that the testimony given by Mrs. Michling (P) about her husband's death was not a res gestae utterance and, therefore, inadmissible hearsay.

ISSUE: For declarations to be admissible in evidence as part of the res gestae, must there be evidence of an act itself admissible in the case independently of the declaration that accompanies it?

HOLDING AND DECISION: (Culver, J.) Yes. For declarations to be admissible in evidence as part of the res gestae, there must be evidence of an act itself admissible in the case independently of the declaration that accompanies it. A hearsay statement, as res gestae, is admitted as an exception to the hearsay rule because it is made under circumstances which raise a reasonable presumption that it is the spontaneous utterance of thought created by the occurrence itself, and, thus, becomes part of the occurrence. Here, the only evidence of the occurrence is the hearsay statement. There is not any independent proof that the deceased suffered any injury at approximately the time and place alleged. Therefore, Mrs. Michling's (P) testimony about statements made by the deceased cannot be considered as res gestae and is inadmissible hearsay. Reversed.

EDITOR'S ANALYSIS: Two main policies are discernable in recognizing res gestae, or spontaneous statements, as admissible evidence. One is a desire to allow each witness to tell his story in a natural way by telling all that happened at the time of the narrated incident. The other is the recognition of spontaneity as the source of special trustworthiness. The quality of spontaneity characterizes almost all types of statements labeled as res gestae.

LIRA v. ALBERT EINSTEIN MEDICAL CENTER
Patient (P) v. Hospital (D)
Pa. Super. Ct., 384 Pa. Super. Ct. 503, 559 A.2d 550 (1989).

NATURE OF CASE: Appeal from grant of motion for new trial.

FACT SUMMARY: In Lira's (P) medical malpractice action against Albert Einstein (D), the trial court awarded Albert Einstein's (D) motion for a new trial after admitting evidence of a physician's extrajudicial opinion regarding Lira's (P) treatment which led to a judgment in her favor.

CONCISE RULE OF LAW: A physician's extrajudicial medical opinion is inadmissible at trial as hearsay evidence.

FACTS: After Dr. Silberman's extrajudicial statement unfavorable to Albert Einstein (D) regarding Ms. Lira's (P) condition was admitted into evidence in her medical malpractice suit against Albert Einstein (D), the jury returned a verdict in Ms. Lira's (P) favor. In recounting the events leading up to this statement, Ms. Lira (P) testified, in effect, that Dr. Silberman, upon commencing his examination of her, subsequent to her medical treatment by Albert Einstein (D), asked her "Who's the butcher who did this?" After the verdict, Albert Einstein (D) moved for a new trial, which was granted by the trial court, Lira (P) appealed.

ISSUE: Is a physician's extrajudicial medical opinion inadmissible at trial as hearsay evidence?

HOLDING AND DECISION: (Wieand, J.) Yes. A physician's extrajudicial medical opinion is inadmissible at trial as hearsay evidence. This rule was derived from carefully examining the common law. In doing this, the common law has failed to recognize a physicians opinion as falling within a recognized exception to the exclusionary rule for hearsay evidence (for example, excited utterance of present sense impression). Aside from this, although hearsay evidence may be received upon proof of exceptional circumstances, cross-examination may be an alternative where it is the only means for testing the reliability of an opinion regarding disputed facts. In the instant case, since Dr. Silberman's extrajudicial statement was clearly an opinion, and since no extenuating circumstances necessitate the admittance of his opinion as opposed to merely cross-examining him regarding the validity of his opinion, then the court was correct in awarding Albert Einstein's (D) motion for a new trial.

EDITOR'S ANALYSIS: The above rule is in line with pretrial discovery principles, whereby if one party interviews an expert witness, then the adverse party must be informed of this interview in order to, among other things, safeguard against surprise at trial. This concern is reflected in the above case since such a witness has a tremendous swaying effect on the jury. Presumably, this swaying effect will be neutralized by requiring that a physician be present at trial to face cross-examination regarding his alleged opinion.

NOTES:

STATE v. JONES
State (P) v. State trooper (D)
Md. Ct. App., 311 Md. 23, 532 A.2d 169 (1987).

NATURE OF CASE: Appeal from exclusion of extrajudicial statements.

FACT SUMMARY: In the State's (P) criminal action against Jones (D) for sexual assault, the court of special appeals, reversing the trial court's ruling, excluded extrajudicial statements regarding the circumstances surrounding the alleged assault, which led to Jones' (D) exoneration.

CONCISE RULE OF LAW: The present sense impression exception to the hearsay rule requires that an extrajudicial statement evidence contemporaneousness and that the declarant made it from his personal knowledge.

FACTS: During the State's (P) criminal action against Jones (D) for sexual assault, the trial court admitted extrajudicial statements regarding the circumstance surrounding the alleged assault into court. These circumstances, in important part, included the alleged sexual assault by Jones (D), a state trooper, of a motorist and Jones' (D) subsequent fleeing of the scene, with the boyfriend of the motorist in hot pursuit. During this pursuit, another trooper, Byrd, allegedly heard consecutive radio transmissions regarding the spectacle which respectively said, "Look at Smokey Bear southbound with no lights on at a high rate of speed," and, "Look at that little car trying to catch up with him." After admitting these statements, the trial court convicted Jones (D), in important part, of a third-degree sexual offense. On appeal, however, the court of special appeals rejected the admissibility of the evidence and reversed. The State (P) appealed.

ISSUE: Does the present sense exception to the hearsay rule require that an extrajudicial statement evidence contemporaneousness and that the declarant made it from his personal knowledge?

HOLDING AND DECISION: (McAuliffe, J.) Yes. The present sense impression exception to the hearsay rule requires that an extrajudicial statement evidence contemporaneousness and that the declarant made it from his personal knowledge. This rule presumes that an extrajudicial statement made spontaneously (i.e., before reasonable time elapses between observation and utterance) is truthful. Likewise, it presumes that such a statement made from a declarant's personal knowledge is also truthful. Moreover, since the aim of the hearsay rule, for present purposes, is to exclude statements made presumably by incredible declarants, then requiring that an extrajudicial statement meet these two criteria appears to logically support this aim. However, meeting these two conditions does not necessarily ensure the admissability of evidence. On the contrary, further corroborating evidence may be needed, depending on the circumstances. In the instant case, since Byrd's description of the statements and his recollection of the circumstances surrounding them appear to reasonably support a conclusion that they were made contemporaneously and through the declarant's personal knowledge, and since the circumstances do not necessitate further corroborating evidence, then the trial court was at liberty to admit evidence of the statements. Reversed and remanded.

EDITOR'S ANALYSIS: Since the present sense impression exception to the hearsay rule applies differently to each extrajudicial statement, based upon the circumstances, this leaves a court with wide discretion in respect to admitting or excluding such statements. Obviously, then, other factors come into play, i.e., the type of action involved and, among other things, the sheer believability of the adverse parties. In the above case, the plaintiff's version of the events was probably more believable to the Maryland Court of Appeals, which might explain its propensity to admit the extrajudicial statements despite the court of special appeals' ruling

NOTES:

REED v. McCORD

Estate of decedent (P) v. Employer of derrick operator (D)

N.Y. Ct. App., 160 N.Y. 330, 54 N.E. 737 (1899).

NATURE OF CASE: Action to recover damages on a theory of negligence.

FACT SUMMARY: Reed's (P) intestate sought to have damaging admissions made by McCord (D) at coroner's inquest admitted as evidence in later trial for damages.

CONCISE RULE OF LAW: Admissions against interest by a party of any fact material to the issue qualifies as an exception to the hearsay rule and is admissible as evidence.

FACTS: Reed (P) was killed when part of a derrick operated by McCord's (D) employee fell and hit him. At the coroner's inquest, McCord (D) admitted that his employee had failed to follow proper safety procedures. In an action by Reed's (P) intestate against McCord for damages resulting from the employee's negligence, the earlier admission was introduced as evidence. McCord (D) appealed a judgment against him contending the inquest testimony should not have been admitted.

ISSUE: Are party admissions on any material issue admissible as evidence?

HOLDING AND DECISION: (Martin, J.) Yes. Although hearsay, admissions qualify as an exception to the rule. Even though McCord (D) was not a witness to the accident, an admission does not have to be based on first-hand knowledge in order to be admissible. Admissions against interest qualify as an exception to the hearsay rule because it is highly improbable that a party will not admit or state anything against himself or against his own interest unless it is true.

EDITOR'S ANALYSIS: Most courts do not require that an admission be based on first-hand knowledge before it can be admitted as reliable evidence. The theory behind this is that a man will not speak against his own interest until he has made a comprehensive investigation.

NOTES:

UNITED STATES v. HOOSIER
Federal government (P) v. Convicted armed robber (D)
542 F.2d 687 (6th Cir. 1976).

NATURE OF CASE: Appeal from a conviction for armed robbery.

FACT SUMMARY: A witness at Hoosier's (D) armed robbery trial was permitted to testify to certain statements Hoosier's (D) girlfriend had made in Hoosier's (D) presence and to which he had offered no denial.

CONCISE RULE OF LAW: Where one of the parties to the action has manifested his adoption of or belief in the truth of a statement that would otherwise constitute hearsay, it is admissible under an exception to the hearsay rule for admissions by a party opponent.

FACTS: Hoosier (D) was convicted of armed robbery in a trial where the court allowed a witness to testify as to certain statements by Hoosier's (D) girlfriend. Hoosier (D) argued they constituted inadmissible hearsay. The witness testified that he saw Hoosier (D) and his girlfriend three weeks after the robbery and that Hoosier (D) had money and was wearing diamond rings. He further testified that the girlfriend had commented on Hoosier's (D) affluence, telling the witness, "That ain't nothing, you should have seen the money we had in the hotel room," thereafter speaking of "sacks of money." In the face of these statements, Hoosier (D) made no denial or other comment.

ISSUE: Can a statement which would otherwise be hearsay be admitted against a party to the action who manifested his adoption of or belief in the truth of the statement?

HOLDING AND DECISION: (Per curiam) Yes. There is an exception to the hearsay rule for admission by a party opponent, and it allows introduction into evidence of a statement which would otherwise constitute hearsay where one of the parties to the action had manifested his adoption of or belief in the truth of that statement. Adoption or acquiescence in the statement of another can be manifested in any appropriate manner -including failure to protest an untrue statement made in one's presence when such a protest would normally be forthcoming under the circumstances were the statement untrue. In such case, the decision calls for an evaluation in terms of probable human behavior. In this case, there is little likelihood that Hoosier's (D) silence in the face of his girlfriend's statements was due to "advice of counsel" or assertion of his fifth amendment right to remain silent. Under the total circumstances, probable human behavior would have been for him to deny her statements were they not true. Thus, admission of the statements was proper. Affirmed.

EDITOR'S ANALYSIS: Use of much of this type of evidence in criminal cases has been circumscribed by the constitutional restraints of Miranda and its progeny. When accusations are made, a defendant's failure to respond will usually be the result of his having been informed that his utterances might be used against him and it is his right to remain silent. Thus, use of this type of silence to admit such accusations would be unconstitutional.

NOTES:

STATE v. CARLSON
State (P) v. Drug possessor (D)
Or. Sup. Ct., 311 Or. 201, 808 P.2d 1002 (1991).

NATURE OF CASE: Appeal from conviction for unlawful possession of a controlled substance.

FACT SUMMARY: In the State's (P) criminal action against Carlson (D) for unlawful possession of a controlled substance, the trial court admitted evidence regarding an extrajudicial statement and Carlson's (D) reaction thereto that led to his conviction.

CONCISE RULE OF LAW: The intent to adopt, agree with, or approve of the contents of another's statement, a precondition to the admissibility of evidence offered under O.E.C. § 801(4)(b)(B), is a preliminary question of fact for the trial judge under O.E.C. § 104(1).

FACTS: After allegedly indulging himself in drugs, Carlson (D) was confronted by police who questioned him regarding needle marks on his arms. In response, Carlson (D) acknowledged, in essence, that he has "a few tracks" and then said that the marks were injuries that he had received from working on a car. Consequently, his girlfriend, Lisa, who was present during the exchange and close enough to hear what was being said, broke in by yelling, "You liar, you got them from shooting up in the bedroom with all your stupid friends." At this point, Carlson (D) "hung his head and shook" it "back and forth." Subsequently, during the State's (P) criminal action against Carlson (D) for, in important part, unlawful possession of a controlled substance, the trial judge admitted, over Carlson's (D) objection, testimony about Lisa's accusation and Carlson's (D) reaction to it. After this admittance, Carlson (D) was convicted of the State's (P) charge, which was affirmed on appeal. Carlson (D) appealed.

ISSUE: Is the intent to adopt, agree with, or approve of the contents of another's statement, a precondition to the admissibility of evidence offered under O.E.C. § 801(4)(b)(B), a preliminary question of fact for the trial judge under O.E.C. § 104(1)?

HOLDING AND DECISION: (Unis, J.) Yes. The intent to adopt, agree with, or approve of the contents of another's statement, a precondition to the admissibility of evidence offered under O.E.C. § 801(4)(b)(B) is a preliminary question of fact for the trial judge under O.E.C. § 104(1). This rule is derived from examining the Legislative Commentary to O.E.C. § 104(1) and from examining the purpose of the hearsay rule. With respect to the former, the Commentary assigns to the trial judge the responsibility for making preliminary determinations regarding, inter alia, the "admissibility of evidence." Accordingly, since proof of an interest to adopt, agree, or approve concerns the admissibility of evidence, then this interest falls within the scope of O.E.C.

§ 104(1). With respect to the latter, the purpose of the hearsay rule is to guard against the risks of misperception, miscollection, misstatement, and insincerity, which are associated with statements of persons made out of court. However, this purpose will not be rightly served by leaving the question of intent to adopt, agree, or approve to the jury since the jury, in passing on the admission by conduct, will have to bear not only evidence about the conduct and the surrounding circumstances, but also the out-of-court statement, as necessary predicates for understanding what the party allegedly adopted. Whereupon, an insubstantially corroborated statement may be heard by the jury. However, even if this statement is deemed inadmissible (i.e., the intent to adopt, agree, or approve is not established), the fact that the jury heard the statement in the first place possibly may taint it. In the instant case, since several reasonable inferences can be drawn from Carlson's (D) ambiguous, nonverbal reaction, no one of which predominates over the others, then the court erred in finding by a preponderance of the evidence that Carlson (D) intended to adopt, agree with, or approve of his wife's accusatory statement. Accordingly, the evidence of his wife's hearsay statement and Carlson's (D) reaction thereto was not admissible under O.E.C. § 801(4)(b)(B). Reversed and remanded.

EDITOR'S ANALYSIS: Although the Oregon Supreme Court reached the above result, it could have allowed the question as to the defendant's intent to adopt, agree, or approve to go to the jury since the jury probably could have handled this question as judiciously as the judge presumably did. However, other factors, such as concerns for policing a burgeoning drug problem, might explain the result, presumably since allowing the judge to handle such questions reduces the risk of defendants facing drug-related charges being exonerated.

NOTES:

MAHLANDT v. WILD CANID SURVIVAL & RESEARCH CENTER, INC.

Injured child (P) v. Wildlife center (D)

588 F.2d 626 (8th Cir. 1978).

NATURE OF CASE: Appeal from denial of damages for negligence.

FACT SUMMARY: The trial court hearing Daniel Mahlandt's (P) civil action against the Center (D) refused to let into evidence certain conclusory statements against interest made by an employee of the Center (D).

CONCISE RULE OF LAW: Federal Rule of Evidence 801(d)(2)(D) makes statements made by agents within the scope of their employment admissible and there is no implied requirement that the declarant have personal knowledge of the facts underlying his statement.

FACTS: Nobody actually saw what happened, but young Daniel Mahlandt (P), who was just under four-years-old at the time, wound up in the enclosure where Mr. Poos (D), the Director of the Center (D), kept Sophie—a wolf belonging to the Center (D) but which he took around to schools and institutions where he showed films and gave programs regarding the nature of wolves. Sophie had been raised at the children's zoo and had there acted in a good-natured and stable manner while in contact with thousands of children. Sophie apparently bit Mahlandt (P) causing him serious injuries. There was some evidence indicating that the child might have crawled under the fence and thereby received his injuries. An offer was made to disprove this theory by introducing evidence that Poos (D) had left a note on the door of the Center's (D) president saying the wolf had bitten a child and that he had made a similar statement later that day when he met the president and was asked what happened. There was also an offer to introduce minutes of a meeting of the Center's (D) board that reflected a great deal of discussion about the legal aspects of the incident of Sophie biting the child. None of this was let into evidence, the judge reasoning that in each case those making the statements had no personal knowledge of the facts and the statements were thus hearsay. A judgment for the Center (D) followed.

ISSUE: Is it necessary to show that the agent had personal knowledge of the facts underlying his statement for a statement made by an agent within the scope of his employment to be admissible under Federal Rule of Evidence 801(d)(2)(D)?

HOLDING AND DECISION: (Van Sickle, J.) No. Fed. R. Evid. 801(d)(2)(D) makes admissible statements made by agents within the scope of their employment. Rule 403 provides for the exclusion of relevant evidence if its probative value is substantially outweighed by the danger of unfair prejudice, etc.

Rule 805 recites, in effect, that a statement containing hearsay within hearsay is admissible if each part of the statement falls within an exception to the hearsay rule. While each provides additional bases for excluding otherwise acceptable evidence, neither rule mandates the introduction into Rule 801(d)(2)(D) of an implied requirement that the declarant have personal knowledge of the facts underlying his statement. Thus, the two statements made by Poos (D) (one in the note he wrote and one he made verbally) were admissible against the Center (D). As to the minutes of the Center's (D) board meeting, there was no servant or agency relationship which justified admitting the evidence of these minutes as against Poos (D) (who was a non-attending, non-participating employee). The only remaining question is whether the trial court's rulings excluding these three items of evidence are at all justified under Rule 403. It is true that none of the statements involved were based on the personal knowledge of the declarant. However, it was recognized by the Advisory Committee on Proposed Rules that this does not necessarily mean they must be rejected as too unreliable to be admitted into evidence. In its discussion of 801(d)(2) exceptions to the hearsay rule, the Committee said: "The freedom which admissions have enjoyed from technical demands of searching for an assurance of trustworthiness in some against-interest circumstances, and from the restrictive influences of the opinion rule and the rule requiring first-hand knowledge, when taken with the apparently prevalent satisfaction with the results, calls for generous treatment of this avenue to admissibility." 28 U.S.C.A., Volume of Federal Rules of Evidence, Rule 801, p. 527, at p. 530. So, here, remembering that relevant evidence is usually prejudicial to the cause of the side against which it is presented, and that the prejudice which concerns us is unreasonable prejudice—and applying the spirit of Rule 801(d)(2)(D)—Rule 403 does not warrant the exclusion of the evidence of Poos' (D) statements as against himself or the Center (D). But the limited admissibility of the corporate minutes, coupled with the repetitive nature of the evidence and the low probative value of the minute record, all justify supporting the judgment of the trial court, under Rule 403, not to admit them into evidence. Reversed and remanded for a new trial.

EDITOR'S ANALYSIS: One of the questions courts have struggled with in this area is whether or not in order to qualify as an admission the statement must have been made by the agent to an outsider (i.e., one other than his principal or another agent).

Continued on next page.

This often comes up when the opposing party in a suit against the principal wants to introduce into evidence a report written or given orally by an agent to the principal or another agent. Just as many courts have refused to let such evidence in as have let it in against the principal as an admission. The Federal Rules of Evidence have been interpreted as recognizing what Wigmore observed: that "communication to an outsider has not generally been thought to be an essential characteristic of an admission." Wigmore on Evidence, § 1557.

NOTES:

BIG MACK TRUCKING CO., INC. v. DICKERSON

Trucking company (D) v. Estate of decedent (P)

Tex. Sup. Ct., 497 S.W.2d 283 (1973).

NATURE OF CASE: Appeal from award of damages for wrongful death.

FACT SUMMARY: In the Dickersons' (P) suit against Big Mack Trucking Co., Inc. (D) for the wrongful death of Mr. Dickerson, Big Mack (D) contended that there was no evidence to support judgment against it because all evidence of the negligence of Big Mack's (D) employee, Leday, was hearsay as to Big Mack (D).

CONCISE RULE OF LAW: An agent's hearsay statements should be received against the principal as vicarious admissions only when the trial judge finds, as a preliminary fact, that the statements were authorized.

FACTS: Dickerson, the deceased, and Leday were employees of Big Mack Trucking Co, Inc. (D). Each was driving a truck-tractor pulling a flatbed trailer loaded with sheet steel across Texas. Both trucks stopped in Waco. Leday parked his truck 15 feet behind Dickerson's and left the vehicle unattended. Dickerson was killed when Leday's truck rolled forward, crushing Dickerson between the two trucks. The Dickersons (P) sued Big Mack (D) for wrongful death and recovered damages in the lawsuit. Big Mack (D) appealed, contending that there was no evidence to support the judgment against it because all the evidence of Leday's negligence and proximate cause was hearsay as to Big Mack (D).

ISSUE: Should an agent's hearsay statements be received against the principal as vicarious admissions only when the trial judge finds, as a preliminary fact, that the statements were authorized?

HOLDING AND DECISION: (Johnson, J.) Yes. An agent's hearsay statements should be received against the principal as vicarious admissions only when the trial judge finds, as a preliminary fact, that the statements were authorized. Here, the Dickersons' (P) theory of liability was predicated upon the fact that Leday's brakes were defective at the time he parked his truck. However, Leday did not testify, and no attempt was made to explain or justify the failure to call Leday, his absence, or his failure to give testimony. The only evidence tending to prove the circumstances of the accident or the elements necessary for the Dickersons' (P) recovery came from two witnesses who could only testify what Leday had previously related to them. The Dickersons (P) assert that in an action against a servant and a master, here, Leday and Big Mack (D), the master having been joined under respondeat superior, it is not necessary that the evidence proving the servant's negligence and proximate cause be competent evidence against the master in order to support a judgment against the master. This view is unacceptable.

Evidence of an servant's negligence must be admissible against the master in order to sustain a judgment against the master and only statements authorized by the master and made by the servant may be received against the master as vicarious admissions exceptions to the hearsay rule. Here, Big Mack (D) did not authorize Leday to make any statements about how the accident occurred, and Leday's statements must, therefore, be classified as inadmissible hearsay. Reversed and remanded.

EDITOR'S ANALYSIS: When a party to a suit has expressly authorized another person to speak on his behalf, it is an obvious extension of the admission rule to admit against the party the statements of such person. The agent is well informed about acts in the course of business. Also, if the admissibility of admissions is viewed as arising from the adversary system, responsibility for statements of one's employee is a consistent aspect of that system.

NOTES:

SABEL v. MEAD JOHNSON & CO.

Pharmaceutical drug user (P) v. Pharmaceutical company (D)
737 F.Supp. 135 (D. Mass. 1990).

NATURE OF CASE: Action by user of an antidepressant medication against the drug's manufacturer claiming the drug caused an adverse reaction (priapism).

FACT SUMMARY: Sabel (P) sought to introduce into evidence a tape of a meeting attended by outside medical experts convened by Mead Johnson & Co. (Mead Johnson) (D), the manufacturer of a drug taken by Sabel (P) that Sabel (P) claimed caused priapism.

CONCISE RULE OF LAW: Out-of-court statements made by an individual who is not a party's agent are not admissible under Federal Rule of Evidence 801(d)(2) as an admission against the party.

FACTS: Sabel (P) used Desyrel, an antidepressant manufactured by Mead Johnson & Co. (Mead Johnson) (D). He brought suit claiming that Desyrel caused him to develop priapism. At trial, Sabel (P) sought to introduce a tape of a meeting convened by Mead Johnson (D) and attended by outside medical experts to explore several aspects of the unexpected, but increasingly apparent, association of Desyrel with priapism. Two Mead Johnson (D) employees also attended. An outside expert who had previously conducted research sponsored by Mead Johnson (D) chaired the meeting. Topics discussed at the meeting included the mechanisms by which the drug could cause priapism, avenues of research into the association between the drug and priapism, and what warnings to physicians should accompany Desyrel. Mead Johnson (D) did not control the manner or means of discussion and analysis used at the meeting, nor were the experts empowered to speak or act on behalf of Mead Johnson (D). The opinions expressed at the meeting were diverse and the experts' differences of opinion were not resolved at its conclusion. Sabel (P) asserted the tape and its transcript were admissible as an admission of Mead Johnson (D) under Fed. R. Evid. 801(d)(2), as an exception to the hearsay rule.

ISSUE: Are out-of-court statements made by an individual who is not a party's agent admissible under Fed. R. Evid. 801(d)(2) as an admission against the party?

HOLDING AND DECISION: (Wolf, J.) No. Out-of-court statements made by an individual who is not a party's agent are not admissible under Fed. R. Evid. 801(d)(2) as an admission against the party. Fed. R. Evid. (801)(d)(2) provides that an out-of-court statement is not hearsay if "[t]he statement is offered against a party and is (C) a statement by a person authorized by the party to make a statement concerning the subject, or (D) a statement by the party's agent or servant concerning a matter within the scope of the agency or employment . . . ." Admissibility is thus governed by the scope of the principal-agent relationship as determined by principles of agency. Here, a principal-agent relationship was not created between Mead Johnson (D) and the experts. A critical element of that relationship is the right of the principal to control the agent's conduct with respect to matters within the scope of the agency. Here, Mead Johnson (D) did not control the meeting, although it financed it. In addition to Mead Johnson's (D) apparent lack of control, there was no evidence that the experts were speaking on its behalf. Mead Johnson (D) did not express an intent to be bound by the experts' recommendations. Instead, the meeting was a type of brainstorming session that did not establish Mead Johnson's (D) official position. Here, Sabel (P) failed to show that the experts possessed any power to act or speak on Mead Johnson's (D) behalf. Therefore, the statements made by the outside experts were inadmissible hearsay.

EDITOR'S ANALYSIS: The court ruled, however, that the statements made by the full-time Mead Johnson (D) employees were admissible. By definition, the employees satisfied the agency requirement of Fed. R. Evid. 801(d)(2) because they were acting within the scope of their employment at the time they made the taped statements, which related to a matter within the scope of their employment.

NOTES:

UNITED STATES v. DiDOMENICO
Federal government (P) v. Accused (D)
78 F.3d. 294 (7th Cir. 1996).

NATURE OF CASE: Appeal from a conviction for criminal conspiracy.

FACT SUMMARY: DiDomenico (D) was convicted after some out of court statements were admitted under the exception for statements of co-conspirators.

CONCISE RULE OF LAW: Statements made during and in furtherance of a conspiracy to commit a crime or a civil wrong are not made inadmissible by the hearsay rule.

FACTS: DiDomenico (D) was convicted in a criminal conspiracy. The testimony of a co-conspirator was admitted under an exception to the hearsay rule. The exception is based on the fact that conspirators are considered each others' agents and therefore principals. A principal is bound by the agent's words and deeds, provided they are within the scope of the agency relationship, so that an admission by one is considered an admission by all. DiDomenico (D) appealed, alleging that the statements were made in a conspiracy to conceal an earlier, completed conspiracy and that statements made in furtherance of the second conspiracy could not be admissible in evidence to demonstrate participation in the acts of the first.

ISSUE: Are statements made during and in furtherance of a conspiracy to commit a crime or a civil wrong made inadmissible by the hearsay rule?

HOLDING AND DECISION: (Posner, J.) No. Statements made during and in furtherance of a conspiracy to commit a crime or a civil wrong are not made inadmissible by the hearsay rule. Statements designed to prevent a conspiracy from collapsing are not to be equated to statements designed to cover up a finished conspiracy. In the first case, unlike the second, there is only one conspiracy; the statements are made in a effort to shore it up and keep it going; they are therefore inadmissible against the conspirators. Affirmed.

EDITOR'S ANALYSIS: The court in this case distinguished the situation in the instant case from cases involving two conspiracies, usually involving a later conspiracy to cover-up an earlier conspiracy. Where there are two conspiracies, statements made in the course of one conspiracy cannot be introduced to prove the facts of the other conspiracy. But the court noted that this was not such a case, since the statements at issue were merely made to shore up the conspiracy, not to conceal it.

QUICKNOTES

AGENCY - A relationship where one person acts with the consent and on the behalf of, and holds all the powers and authority prescribed by, another person.

AGENT - An individual who has the authority to act on behalf of another.

CONSPIRACY - Concerted action by two or more persons to accomplish some unlawful purpose.

HEARSAY - An out-of-court statement made by a person other than the witness testifying at trial that is offered in order to prove the truth of the matter asserted.

PRINCIPAL - A person or entity who authorizes another (the agent) to act on its behalf and subject to its authority to the extent that the principal may be held liable for the actions of the agent.

NOTES:

UNITED STATES v. GOLDBERG
Federal government (P) v. Accused (D)
105 F.3d. 770 (1st Cir. 1997).

NATURE OF CASE: Appeal from a conviction for federal fraud and tax offenses.

FACT SUMMARY: Goldberg (D) contended that out of court statements made by co-conspirators before he joined the conspiracy should not have been introduced into evidence against him.

CONCISE RULE OF LAW: A late-joining conspirator takes the conspiracy as he finds it.

FACTS: Goldberg (D) was convicted of fraud when out of court statements made by co-conspirators were admitted against him. Goldberg (D) appealed, alleging that the statements were not admissible against him because they were made before he joined the conspiracy.

ISSUE: Does a late-joining conspirator take the conspiracy as he finds it?

HOLDING AND DECISION: (Boudin, J.) Yes. A late-joining conspirator takes the conspiracy as he finds it. A conspiracy is like a train; when a party steps aboard, he is part of the crew and assumes conspirator's responsibility for the existing freight. This is the traditional approach to the co-conspiracy exception to the hearsay rule, presumptively adopted by the Federal Rules of Evidence. It is followed in most circuits, including this one. Affirmed.

EDITOR'S ANALYSIS: The court in this case declined to follow the holding of an earlier case, *United States v. Petrozziello*, 548 F.2d 20 (1st Cir. 1977). In that case, the court held that if it is more likely than not that the declarant and the defendant were members of a conspiracy when the hearsay statement was made, and the statement was in furtherance of the conspiracy, the hearsay is admissible. That narrow version of the hearsay exception was not followed by later cases in that circuit, however.

QUICKNOTES

AGENCY - A relationship where one person acts with the consent and on the behalf of, and holds all the powers and authority prescribed by, another person.

CONSPIRACY - Concerted action by two or more persons to accomplish some unlawful purpose.

HEARSAY - An out-of-court statement made by a person other than the witness testifying at trial that is offered in order to prove the truth of the matter asserted.

UNITED STATES v. DOERR
Federal government (P) v. Prostitution co-conspirator (D)
886 F.2d 944 (7th Cir. 1989).

NATURE OF CASE: Appeal from admittance of extrajudicial statements.

FACT SUMMARY: In the government's (P) criminal action against Doerr (D) for an unlawful prostitution conspiracy, the federal district court admitted the extrajudicial statements of co-conspirators with Doerr (D) into court over Doerr's (D) objections.

CONCISE RULE OF LAW: Where a co-conspirator of a party makes a statement against the party which, reasonably concluded, furthers the conspiracy, then this statement may be admitted at the party's subsequent trial in respect to the conspiracy.

FACTS: During the government's (P) criminal action against Doerr (D), representing Pixley (D) and himself, for, in important part, an unlawful prostitution conspiracy, Meyer and John Patrick Doerr, Doerr's (D) half-brother and fellow conspirator with Meyer and the defendants, offered challenged statements during their testimony regarding conversations they had with the defendants in respect to the latter's unlawful enterprise conducted in the rear, or terrace area, of two clubs and a massage parlor. In the first challenged statement, Meyer testified that Pixley (D) mentioned, during their conversation, that "when he was hired back there that Josephine had a curtain put up in the terrace of the patio area, how ridiculous it was, it was asking for problems with the police." In the second challenged statement, John Patrick testified that during a conversation with Doerr (D), the latter said, "I can't believe—I don't believe—I can't believe you don't know what's going on, or you didn't know what's going on." These statements were admitted into court over Doerr's (D) objections. Doerr (D) appealed.

ISSUE: Where a co-conspirator of a party makes a statement against the party which, reasonably concluded, furthers the conspiracy, may this statement be admitted at the party's subsequent trial in respect to the conspiracy?

HOLDING AND DECISION: (Ripple, J.) Yes. Where a conspirator of a party makes a statement which, reasonably concluded, furthers the conspiracy, then this statement may be admitted at the party's subsequent trial in respect to the conspiracy. This rule merely restates Fed. R. Evid. 801(d)(2)(E), which provides that a statement is not hearsay if it is "offered against a party and is . . . a statement by a co-conspirator of a party [made] during the course and in furtherance of the conspiracy." Moreover, the "in furtherance" requirement is satisfied so long "as some reasonable basis exists for concluding that the statement furthered the conspiracy." See *Garlington v.*

O'Leary, 879 F.2d 277, 283 (7th Cir. 1989). In the instant case, since Mr. Pixley's (D) discussion of the red curtain with Meyer cannot reasonably be characterized as part of an attempt to induce Meyer to join or assist the conspiracy, and since Doerr's (D) statement to his brother in no way furthered the ends of the conspiracy, the trial court erred in admitting the challenged statements. Reversed.

EDITOR'S ANALYSIS: Like the present sense impression exception to the hearsay rule, the co-conspirator exception leaves a court with wide discretion to determine the admissibility of an extrajudicial statement, since a reasonable standard comes into play. Again, various, unexplained circumstances may determine whether a court admits or excludes a particular statement. In the above case, the fact that the case was brought in federal court may explain why the statements were, in the final determination, excluded, presumably since the gravity of a federal court carries more weight, whereupon further corroborating evidence may be needed to induce statement admittance.

NOTES:

BOURJAILY v. UNITED STATES
Convicted drug dealer (D) v. Federal government (P)
483 U.S. 171 (1987).

NATURE OF CASE: Appeal of conviction of conspiracy to distribute narcotics.

FACT SUMMARY: Bourjaily (D) argued that Federal Rule of Evidence 801(d)(2)(E), excluding out-of-court statements in furtherance of conspiracy from being considered hearsay, violated the Confrontation Clause.

CONCISE RULE OF LAW: Federal Rule of Evidence 801(d)(2)(E), excluding out-of-court statements in furtherance of conspiracy from being considered hearsay, does not violate the Confrontation Clause.

FACTS: Bourjaily (D) was accused of conspiracy to distribute narcotics. The court admitted an out-of-court statement by the alleged co-conspirator. This was permitted under Fed. R. Evid. 801(d)(2)(E), which categorizes such statements as nonhearsay. Bourjaily (D) was convicted. On appeal, he argued that admission of the statement violated the Confrontation Clause. The court of appeals affirmed. The Supreme Court granted certiorari.

ISSUE: Does Fed. R. Evid. 801(d)(2)(E), excluding out-of-court statements in furtherance of conspiracy from being considered hearsay, violate the Confrontation Clause?

HOLDING AND DECISION: (Rehnquist, C.J.) No. Fed. R. Evid. 801(d)(2)(E), excluding out-of-court statements in furtherance of conspiracy from being considered hearsay, does not violate the Confrontation Clause. Because the Confrontation Clause and the hearsay rule essentially address the same concerns, that which is admissible under the hearsay rule requires no independent inquiry into reliability in order to be sufficient for Confrontation Clause purposes. The co-conspirator exception is deeply rooted in the jurisprudence of evidence, and to reject it as unconstitutional would effect a great change in evidence law for no good purpose. Affirmed.

EDITOR'S ANALYSIS: The Court had, prior to this case, partially passed on the issue here. In *U.S. v. Inadi*, 475 U.S. 387 (1966), it had been argued that unavailability of the declarant was required for admission under 801(d)(2)(E) to satisfy the Confrontation Clause. The Court rejected that argument there and affirmed that holding here.

NOTES:

TRAVELERS FIRE INS. CO. v. WRIGHT

Insurance company (D) v. Insured (P)

Okla. Sup. Ct., 322 P.2d 417, 70 A.L.R. 2d 1170 (1958).

NATURE OF CASE: Action to recover under terms of two fire insurance policies.

FACT SUMMARY: When witnesses called by Travelers Insurance (D) refused to testify in civil trial, Travelers (D) sought to admit the witnesses' prior recorded testimony in a trial for arson.

CONCISE RULE OF LAW: Complete identity of the parties is not required where prior recorded testimony given in a criminal trial is not sought to be admitted in a civil trial.

FACTS: J.B. Wright (P) and J.C. Wright (P) sued to recover under the terms of fire insurance policies. Travelers Fire Insurance Co. (D) defended on the ground that J.B. Wright (P) had deliberately caused the fire with intent to defraud. To prove this, the insurer called two witnesses, Eppler and Brown. However, they refused to testify, claiming the privilege against self-incrimination. The insurer (D) then sought to have admitted a transcript of Eppler's and Brown's testimonies which were given in J.B. Wright's (P) earlier trial for arson.

ISSUE: Where prior recorded testimony given in a criminal trial is now sought to be admitted in a civil trial, is complete identity of the parties required?

HOLDING AND DECISION: (Jackson, J.) No. All that is required for testimony from a criminal case to be introduced in a subsequent civil trial is that (1) it is impossible to obtain the testimony of the witness who testified in the criminal case; (2) that there was an opportunity to cross-examine the witness by the party against whom the testimony is sought to be used in the civil case, or by one whose motive and interest in cross-examination was the same; and (3) that there is an identity of issues. Complete identity of parties is not required. While J.C. Wright (P) did not have an opportunity to cross-examine in the criminal case, J.B. Wright (P), who was present then, had the same motive and interest in cross-examining Eppler and Brown. The issue—deliberate causing of the fire—was the same in both cases. Although Eppler and Brown are now unavailable to testify, there is sufficient protection accorded the Wrights (P) to permit the prior recorded testimony to be admitted in the civil case as an exception to the hearsay rule.

EDITOR'S ANALYSIS: Many courts still follow the traditional view requiring complete identity between the parties. However, even these courts would not require 100% identity where a party in the second trial is a successor in interest to one of the parties in the first trial. Some would not apply it where there were additional parties in the first case who were not present in the second.

NOTES:

UNITED STATES v. SALERNO
Federal government (P) v. Organized crime member (D)
505 U.S. 317 (1992).

NATURE OF CASE: Review of a reversal of a criminal conviction for numerous federal offenses.

FACT SUMMARY: Salerno (D) contended that the district court erred by not admitting grand jury testimony under Federal Rule of Evidence 804(b)(1) as former testimony of an unavailable witness.

CONCISE RULE OF LAW: Federal Rule of Evidence 804(b)(1) permits the admission of former testimony of an unavailable witness if the party against whom the testimony is now offered had an opportunity and similar motive to develop the testimony by direct, cross- or redirect examination.

FACTS: Salerno (D), along with six other defendants, was indicted on a variety of federal offenses involving organized crime and attempts to defraud the New York construction industry. The main focus of the case was on a concrete company called Cedar Park, which was owned by DeMatteis and Bruno. During the grand jury investigation, DeMatteis and Bruno were given immunity to testify. They repeatedly denied any participation with the "Club" of six companies under investigation. During trial, the United States (P) attempted to show that Cedar Park did participate in the "Club." In order to rebut the United States' (P) evidence, Salerno (D) subpoenaed DeMatteis and Bruno to repeat the exculpatory testimony they had given to the grand jury. However, DeMatteis and Bruno invoked the Fifth Amendment privilege against self-incrimination and refused to testify. Salerno (D) then attempted to introduce the transcripts of their grand jury testimony, but the district court refused to admit them. The court of appeals reversed. The Supreme Court granted certiorari.

ISSUE: Does Fed. R. Evid. 804(b)(1) permit the admission of former testimony of an unavailable witness if the party against whom the testimony is now offered had an opportunity and similar motive to develop the testimony by direct, cross- or redirect examination?

HOLDING AND DECISION: (Thomas, J.) Yes. Fed. R. Evid. 804(b)(1) permits the admission of former testimony of an unavailable witness if the party against whom the testimony is now offered had an opportunity and similar motive to develop the testimony by direct, cross- or redirect examination. However, in order to admit former testimony under Rule 804 (b)(1), the proponent must satisfy each element of the Rule, including a showing of a "similar motive." Typically, during a grand jury investigation, the prosecution must maintain secrecy and is therefore motivated to not expose contradictory evidence. Furthermore, the prosecution may not be aware of important

issues in the case until trial and thus may not fully develop grand jury testimony. In this case, the United States (P) may or may not have had a similar motive to develop testimony at the grand jury proceedings as it would at trial. Reversed and remanded for determination of this issue.

EDITOR'S ANALYSIS: Former testimony that meets the requirements under Fed. R. Evid. 804(b)(1) is admissible even though it is hearsay because the former testimony is considered reliable. The former testimony is made under oath and subject to direct and/or cross-examination. Another consideration for admitting the former testimony is that the witness is unavailable and there is no other practical means of attaining the evidence.

NOTES:

G.M. McKELVEY CO. v. GENERAL CASUALTY CO. OF AMERICA

Insured company (P) v. Insurer (D)

Ohio Sup. Ct., 166 Ohio St. 401, 142 N.E.2d 854 (1957).

NATURE OF CASE: Suit to recover proceeds on an insurance policy.

FACT SUMMARY: Employees of McKelvey (P) misappropriated money and later signed written confessions admitting their defalcations. In an action by McKelvey (P) against General (D) to recover insurance proceeds covering such loss, McKelvey (P) sought to prove, by the confessions, the fact and amount of loss.

CONCISE RULE OF LAW: A declaration against interest by one not a party or in privity with a party to an action is admissible where the declarant: (1) is either dead or unavailable; (2) had peculiar means of knowing the facts stated; (3) made a declaration that was against his pecuniary or proprietary interest; and (4) had no probable motive to falsify the facts stated.

FACTS: Employees of McKelvey misappropriated money belonging to McKelvey (P). Although they could not now be located within the jurisdiction, they had signed written confessions admitting to the defalcations and the amount taken. McKelvey (P) was insured against such losses by General (D), and in an action to recover under the insurance policy, McKelvey (P) sought to prove the misappropriation and the amount taken by means of the written confessions.

ISSUE: Is a declaration against interest by one not a party or in privity with a party to an action admissible where the declarant: (1) is either dead or unavailable; (2) had peculiar means of knowing the facts stated; (3) made a declaration that was against his pecuniary or proprietary interest; and (4) had no probable motive to falsify the facts stated?

HOLDING AND DECISION: (Matthias, J.) Yes. A declaration against interest by one not a party or in privity with a party to an action is admissible where the declarant: (1) is either dead or unavailable; (2) had peculiar means of knowing the facts stated; (3) made a declaration that was against his pecuniary or proprietary interest; and (4) had no probable motive to falsify the facts stated. The employees here were the only ones who could know the amounts taken, their statements were against their pecuniary interests since it subjected them to liability, and they were unavailable as witnesses. No claim was made that they falsified their statements; therefore, the statements are admissible to prove the fact and amount of loss.

EDITOR'S ANALYSIS: This case follows the majority of cases which permit the declaration against interest where such declaration would affect the declarant's pecuniary interest, and where it is shown that the declarant knew the facts stated without motive to falsify. Also, many cases hold that absence from jurisdiction is sufficient to make the witness unavailable. It is, however, uncertain whether the court would have reached the same result had the confessions not been signed but only admitted under oral testimony.

NOTES:

UNITED STATES v. BARRETT
Federal government (P) v. Convicted thief (D)
539 F.2d 244 (1st Cir. 1976).

NATURE OF CASE: Appeal from conviction for theft.

FACT SUMMARY: Barrett (D) contended that Tilley's out-of-court statement indicating Barrett (D) was not involved in a stamp collection theft should have been admitted because the rest of Tilley's statement tended to be against Tilley's own penal interest by advertising his likely complicity in the crime.

CONCISE RULE OF LAW: Under the Federal Rules of Evidence, a statement tending to expose the declarant to criminal liability and offered to exculpate the accused is not admissible under the exception to the hearsay rule for declarations against interest, unless corroborating circumstances clearly indicate the trustworthiness of the statement.

FACTS: After being convicted of crimes arising from the theft and sale of a collection of postage stamps from a museum, Barrett (D) appealed. He argued that Tilley, who died prior to trial, had made certain statements to one Melvin to the effect that Barrett (D) was not involved in the theft. The rest of the statements indicated Tilley's knowledge of the circumstances of the theft. Barrett (D) argued that Melvin should have been allowed to testify as to these statements under the exception to the hearsay rule for declarations against interest. He claimed that Tilley's statements tended against Tilley's penal interest by advertising his likely complicity in the crime.

ISSUE: Is an out-of-court statement tending to expose the declarant to criminal liability and offered to exculpate the accused admissible only if corroborating circumstances clearly indicate its trustworthiness?

HOLDING AND DECISION: (Campbell, J.) Yes. Under the Federal Rules of Evidence, an exception to the hearsay rule exists as to out-of-court declarations against interest made by one unavailable at trial, and this covers any statement which at the time it was made was so far contrary to the declarant's pecuniary or proprietary interest or so far tended to subject him to civil or criminal liability that a reasonable man in his position would not have made the statement unless he believed it to be true. However, a statement tending to expose the declarant to criminal liability and offered to exculpate the accused is not admissible under this exception unless corroborating circumstances clearly indicate its trustworthiness. In this case, the offered statements allegedly made by Tilley were statements against interest within the Rule. Thus, the district court should have sought to determine if there was sufficient corroboration so as to warrant their admission. Reversed and remanded.

EDITOR'S ANALYSIS: In providing for the admission of declarations against penal interest in addition to those against pecuniary or proprietary interest, the Federal Rules departed from the common-law tradition. This was a matter of heated debate in Congress. The court in the above case noted that "Rule 804(b)(3) reflects Congress' attempt to strike a fair balance between exclusion of trustworthy evidence . . . and indiscriminate admission of less trustworthy evidence which, because of the lack of opportunity for cross-examination and the absence of the declarant, is open to easy fabrication."

NOTES:

41

WILLIAMSON v. UNITED STATES
Convicted drug dealer (D) v. Federal government (P)
512 U.S. 594 (1994).

NATURE OF CASE: Appeal from conviction of possession of cocaine with intent to distribute, conspiracy to possess cocaine with intent to distribute, and traveling interstate to promote the distribution of cocaine.

FACT SUMMARY: Williamson (D) contended that the district court erred in allowing the testimony of a Drug Enforcement Administration (DEA) agent in court who related arguably self-inculpatory statements made out of court to him by Harris, one of Williamson's (D) employees, regarding the possession and transport of the cocaine.

CONCISE RULE OF LAW: Federal Rule of Evidence 804(b)(3) does not allow admission of non-self-inculpatory statements, even if they are made within a broader narrative that is generally self-inculpatory.

FACTS: Harris, an employee of Williamson (D), was stopped by the police while he was driving. The police, after searching the car, found 19 kilograms of cocaine in the car and arrested Harris. After his arrest, Harris was interviewed by telephone by a DEA agent, Walton. Harris told Walton that he had gotten the cocaine from a Cuban, that the cocaine belonged to Williamson (D), and that Harris was delivering it to a particular dumpster for pickup. Shortly thereafter, Walton interviewed Harris personally; Harris then told Walton that he was transporting the cocaine to Atlanta for Williamson (D), that Williamson (D) was traveling ahead of him in another car at the time of the arrest, and that Williamson (D) had apparently seen the police searching Harris' car and had fled. Harris told Walton that he had initially lied about the source of the cocaine because he was afraid of Williamson (D). Harris implicated himself in his statements to Walton but did not want his story to be recorded and refused to sign a written transcript of the statement. Walton later testified that Harris was not promised any reward for cooperating. Williamson (D) was eventually charged and convicted of various drug-related offenses. When Harris was called to testify at Williamson's (D) trial, he refused to do so. The district court then ruled that, under Fed. R. Evid. 804(b)(3), Agent Walton could relate what Harris told him because Harris' statements were against his own interests. Williamson (D) was convicted, and the court of appeals affirmed. On appeal, Williamson (D) argued that both lower courts erred by allowing Walton to testify regarding Harris' out-of-court statements.

ISSUE: Does Fed. R. Evid. 804(b)(3) allow admission of non-self-inculpatory statements, even if they are made within a broader narrative that is generally self-inculpatory?

HOLDING AND DECISION: (O'Connor, J.) No. Fed. R. Evid. 804(b)(3) does not allow admission on non-self-inculpatory statements, even if they are made within a broader narrative that is generally self-inculpatory. The district court may not just assume, for purposes of Rule 804(b)(3), that a statement is self-inculpatory because it is part of a fuller confession, and this is especially true when the statement implicates someone else. The question under the Rule is always whether the statement was sufficiently against the declarant's penal interest that a reasonable person would not have made the statement unless believing it to be true. This question can only be answered in light of all the surrounding circumstances. In this case, some of Harris' confession would clearly have been admissible under the Rule. For instance, when he said he knew there was cocaine in the car, he forfeited his only defense to the charge of cocaine possession—lack of knowledge. But other parts of his confession, especially those in which he implicated Williamson (D), did little to subject Harris to criminal liability. A reasonable person in Harris' position might think that implicating someone else would decrease his own exposure to criminal liability at sentencing. Nothing in the record shows that the district court or court of appeals inquired whether each of the statements in Harris' confession was truly self-inculpatory. Remanded to the court of appeals to conduct this inquiry.

CONCURRENCE: (Ginsburg, J.) Fed. R. Evid. 804(b)(3) excepts from the general hearsay rule only those declarations or remarks within a narrative that are individually self-inculpatory. However, Harris' statements, as recounted by Walton, do not fit, even in part, within the exception described in the Rule for Harris' arguably inculpatory statements are too closely intertwined with his self-serving declarations to be ranked as trustworthy. To the extent that some of these statements tended to incriminate Harris, they provided only marginal or cumulative evidence of his guilt. They project the image of a person's acting not against his penal interest but striving mightily to shift principal responsibility to someone else. Therefore, Harris' hearsay statements should not be admissible under Rule 804(b)(3).

CONCURRENCE: (Kennedy, J.) Rule 804(b)(3) establishes a hearsay exception for statements against penal, proprietary, pecuniary, and legal interest. The text of the Rule does not tell us whether collateral statements are admissible. The Court resolves this issue by adopting the extreme position that no collateral statements are admissible under the Rule. The Court reaches that conclusion by relying on the "principle behind the Rule" that reasonable people do not make statements against their interest

Continued on next page.

unless they are telling the truth, and reasons that this policy "expressed in the statutory text" simply does not extend to collateral statements. To the contrary, three sources indicate that the Rule allows the admission of some collateral statements: first, the Advisory Committee Note to the Rule establishes that some collateral statements are admissible; second, at common law, collateral statements were admissible, and we can presume that Congress intended the principle and terms used in the Federal Rules of Evidence to be applied as they were at common law; third, absent a textual direction to the contrary, we should assume that Congress intended the penal interest exception for inculpatory statements to have some meaningful effect. The exclusion of collateral statements would cause the exclusion of almost all inculpatory statements.

EDITOR'S ANALYSIS: As indicated by the Court in *Williamson*, Rule 804(b)(3) requires that self-inculpatory statements should be examined in terms of the reasonable person and that the declarant believe the statement to be against interest. In order to analyze whether the declarant truly believes his statement was against interest, the identity of the person to whom the statement was made should be considered. Although the situation wherein a declarant makes his statement to the authorities is the prime example of a statement against interest, if such a statement was made to a trusted friend (who was expected to keep the information secret), it has not necessarily been held that this eliminates the disserving nature of the statement.

NOTES:

ADKINS v. BRETT
Husband (P) v. Adulterer (D)
Cal. Sup. Ct., 184 Cal. 252, 193 P. 251 (1920).

NATURE OF CASE: Suit for damages for alienation of affections.

FACT SUMMARY: Adkins (P) sued Brett (D), charging him with the alienation of Adkins' (D) wife. The court admitted statements by which Mrs. Adkins expressed her preference for Brett (D) and admitted that she had seen him socially and received gifts from him. This evidence was admitted on the theory that it was within the state-of-mind exception to the hearsay rule.

CONCISE RULE OF LAW: Statements expressing the declarant's state of mind at the time of the utterances are admissible as exceptions to the hearsay rule, notwithstanding that some portions of the statements do not describe state of mind and tend to damage the defendant.

FACTS: Adkins (P) sued Brett (D), charging him with alienation of Adkins' (P) wife. At trial, evidence was introduced of a statement in which Brett (D) admitted to having sexual relations with Mrs. Adkins. Evidence was also admitted of her conversations with her husband (P) in which she declared that Adkins (P) was distasteful to her and that Brett (D) was able to show her a good time. Brett (D) objected to the admissibility of Mrs. Adkins' statements, citing the hearsay rule, but the evidence was accepted on the theory that, being indicative of the declarant's feelings, it was admissible to show her state of mind. From a judgment for Adkins (P), Brett (D) appealed, alleging error in the admission of the evidence described.

ISSUE: May statements expressing declarant's state of mind at the time of the utterances be admitted as exceptions to the hearsay rule, notwithstanding that some portions of the statements do not describe state of mind and tend to damage the defendant?

HOLDING AND DECISION: (Olney, J.) Yes. Statements expressing the declarant's state of mind at the time of the utterances are admissible as exceptions to the hearsay rule, notwithstanding that some portions of the statements do not describe state of mind and tend to damage the defendant. Brett's (D) objection that the verdict was unsupported by the evidence must fail because, although much of the evidence offered was entirely contradictory, the jury was entitled to believe the evidence presented by Adkins (P). Moreover, Brett's (D) objection that evidence of statements made out of his presence was inadmissible is unsupported by any rule of evidence. And, although the evidence of Mrs. Adkins' statements was clearly hearsay, it was nevertheless admissible as indicative of her feelings and therefore of her state of mind at the time of their utterance. Unfortunately, the statements, in addition to establishing Mrs. Adkins' state of mind, include many observations which are damaging to Bretts (D) position. It is, nevertheless, the well-settled rule that evidence admissible for one purpose is not rendered inadmissible by its failure to meet the standards required by another rule of admissibility. When evidence is admissible for one purpose only, however, the court must insure against prejudice to the party opposing the evidence either by a limiting instruction, deletion of highly prejudicial portions, or any other method reasonably calculated to mitigate the potential damaging effect of the evidence. In this case, no adequate instruction was given to protect Brett (D) from prejudice. Therefore, the evidence of the conversation between Adkins (P) and his wife was improperly admitted, and the judgment in favor of Adkins (P) must be reversed.

EDITOR'S ANALYSIS: A well-recognized exception to the hearsay rule exists for statements which are expressive of the declarant's state of mind. The basis for acceptance of such statements is their typical spontaneity with its attendant probability of sincerity. Although the exception was probably designed to include only those statements which constitute direct assertions of the declarant's state of mind, many courts apply the exception as well to statements which tend to prove his state of mind only circumstantially.

NOTES:

MUTUAL LIFE INSURANCE CO. OF NEW YORK
v. HILLMON
Insurance company (D) v. Estate of decedent (P)
145 U.S. 285 (1892).

NATURE OF CASE: Action to recover proceeds of insurance policy.

FACT SUMMARY: Mutual Life (D) refused to pay off on a life insurance policy on Hillmon's life because of a conflict over the identity of the decedent.

CONCISE RULE OF LAW: Whenever a party's intention is, of itself, a distinct and material fact in a chain of circumstances, it may be proved by contemporaneous oral or written declarations of the party.

FACTS: Hillmon was missing. A body which could have been his was buried at Crooked Creek. Hillmon's wife (P), the beneficiary of his life insurance, filed suit against two insurance companies (D) to recover the policy proceeds. Mutual Life (D) defended on the basis that it could not adequately be established that Hillmon was dead, since the body could not be positively identified. Some evidence was admitted which tended to show that Hillmon had gone to Crooked Creek at the same time the body was discovered. Mutual Life (D) contended that Walters was the actual decedent at Crooked Creek and tried to introduce a letter written to Walters' fiancee that he intended to go to Crooked Creek at the time the body was discovered. It was alleged that this was within the business-record exception to the hearsay rule. The letter was not admitted, and the jury found for Hillmon's wife (P).

ISSUE: Where a party's intention is, of itself, a distinct and material fact in a chain of circumstances, may it be proved by contemporaneous oral or written declarations of the party?

HOLDING AND DECISION: (Gray, J.) Yes. Where a party's intention is, of itself, a distinct and material fact in a chain of circumstances, it may be proved by contemporaneous oral or written declarations of the party. Here, there is a controversy over the identity of the decedent. Mutual Life (D) contends that the decedent was Walters. While the letters were not within the business-records exception as Mutual (D) argued, they are admissible as falling within the state-of-mind exception. The evidence of Walters' intention is admissible to create the inference that since he intended to go there at the time the letter was written, he did go there. It is not proof that he actually went, only that it is more likely than not that he did. Since the issue was in controversy, it might have tended to influence the jury. Where the bodily or mental feelings of an actor are material to be proved, the usual expression of them is competent and admissible as an exception to the hearsay rules. After death, there is no other way of establishing such facts. Since the letters were probative as to

Walters' current state of mind, it was error to exclude them. Judgment is reversed and the cause is remanded.

EDITOR'S ANALYSIS: Regarding this case, McCormick has said, "Despite the failure until recently to recognize the potential value of declarations of state of mind to prove subsequent conduct, it is now clear that out-of-court statements which tend to prove a plan, design, or intention of the declarant are admissible, subject to the usual limitations as to remoteness in time and apparent sincerity common to all declarations of mental state, to prove that the plan, design, or intention of the declarant was carried out by declarant."

NOTES:

SHEPARD v. UNITED STATES
Physician (D) v. Federal government (P)
290 U.S. 96 (1933).

NATURE OF CASE: Appeal from conviction for murder.

FACT SUMMARY: Trial court had permitted the introduction of testimony that Mrs. Shepard, the victim, had stated shortly before her death, "Dr. Shepard has poisoned me."

CONCISE RULE OF LAW: Declarations of present memory, looking backwards to a prior occurrence, are inadmissible to prove, or tend to prove, the existence of the occurrence.

FACTS: Dr. Shepard (D) was charged with the poison-killing of his wife, who was also his patient. At his trial, the court permitted the prosecution to introduce testimony of a nurse who attended Mrs. Shepard shortly before her death. The nurse testified that Mrs. Shepard asked her to fetch a bottle of whisky from the Doctor's (D) room. The nurse said the wife had drunk from this bottle before collapsing, requested a test, insisted that the smell and taste were strange, and added, "Dr. Shepard has poisoned me." On appeal following Dr. Shepard's (D) conviction, the U.S. Supreme Court ruled that the evidence could not be justified under the rule which makes dying declarations admissible.

ISSUE: Are declarations of present memory, looking backwards to a prior occurrence, inadmissible to prove, or tend to prove, the existence of the occurrence?

HOLDING AND DECISION: (Cardozo, J.) No. Declarations of present memory, looking backwards to a prior occurrence, are inadmissible to prove, or tend to prove, the existence of the occurrence. Since the testimony had been offered and received as proof of a dying declaration, the government may not now argue an appeal that the declarations were offered to show a persistency of a will to live. Because of the stated purpose of the testimony, Dr. Shepard (D) was put off his guard. It would now be unfair for the government to shift its ground. The purpose for which normally hearsay evidence is sought to be admitted must be made clear at the time it is introduced. The government did not use the declarations by Mrs. Shepard to prove her present thoughts and feelings, or even her thoughts and feelings in times past. Rather, they were offered as proof of an act committed by someone else as evidence that she was dying of poison by her husband. The jury is incapable of distinguishing in its mind between these declarations as mere indications of a state of mind and as pointing the finger of guilt at Dr. Shepard (D). The ruling in *Mutual Life Ins. Co. v. Hillmon* [145 U.S. 285 (1892)] represents the high-water line beyond which courts may not go; in that case, the testimony looked forward to prove an occurrence. Here, it looks backward to a past act, and, more importantly, to an act by someone not the speaker. Reversed and remanded.

EDITOR'S ANALYSIS: The rule enunciated here has been heavily criticized but has, nonetheless, survived in the case law. One exception has been in probate cases where the testator's declarations made after the disputed occurrence are admitted to prove that he has made or revoked a will. The reason for this is that the testator is unavailable. Extending this rationale, the Model Code of Evidence would admit all hearsay declarations including statements of memory, when the declarant is unavailable to testify.

NOTES:

UNITED STATES v. PHEASTER
Federal government (P) v. Kidnapping conspirator (D)
544 F.2d 353 (9th Cir. 1976).

NATURE OF CASE: Appeal from convictions in a kidnap-ransom case.

FACT SUMMARY: The trial court admitted into evidence the hearsay statements of the still-missing victim of a kidnap-ransom conspiracy about whom he was going to meet when he disappeared.

CONCISE RULE OF LAW: The *Hillmon* doctrine permits introduction of hearsay declarations as evidence that the declarant carried out his intention to perform the act they indicate it was his intention to perform, even if its accomplishment requires action by others.

FACTS: Pheaster (D) was among those charged with a kidnap-ransom conspiracy revolving around the still-missing Larry Adell, the 16-year-old son of a Palm Springs multimillionaire. Over objection by the defendants that the testimony constituted inadmissible hearsay, one of Larry's friends testified that Larry had left his companions at Sambo's Restaurant on the night he disappeared with the comment that he was going to the parking lot to meet Angelo (another defendant) and would be right back. Other friends were permitted to testify to various statements Larry had made that same afternoon and evening indicating he was going to meet Angelo that night to purchase some marijuana. These statements were admitted under the Hillmon doctrine, which allows hearsay statements to be admitted under the state-of-mind exception to show that an individual intended to perform a particular act. From that intention, the trier of fact may draw the inference that the person carried out his intention and performed the act. On appeal, Pheaster (D) objected to the use of the doctrine when the declarants stated intention is to do something which requires the action of one or more others to be accomplished.

ISSUE: Does the *Hillmon* doctrine permit the introduction of hearsay declarations as evidence that the declarant carried out his intention to perform the act they indicate it was his intention to perform, even if its accomplishment requires action by others?

HOLDING AND DECISION: (Renfrew, J.) Yes. The *Hillmon* doctrine permits introduction of hearsay declarations as evidence that the declarant carried out his intention to perform the act they indicate it was his intention to perform, even if its accomplishment requires action by others. Despite the theoretical problems and valid objections to such application, the authority in favor thereof is impressive and requires this court to uphold the trial court's position. Affirmed.

EDITOR'S ANALYSIS: The *Hillmon* doctrine permits introduction of hearsay declarations as evidence that the declarant carried out his intention to perform the act they indicate it was his intention to perform, even if its accomplishment requires action by others.

NOTES:

ZIPPO MFG. CO. v. ROGERS IMPORTS, INC.
Lighter manufacturer (P) v. Competitor (D)
216 F.Supp. 670 (S.D.N.Y. 1963).

NATURE OF CASE: Action seeking to enjoin others from imitating the size and shape of plaintiff's lighter under trademark infringement and unfair competition causes.

FACT SUMMARY: To establish its case that the shape and size of Zippo (P) lighters had acquired a secondary meaning to the public, Zippo (P) conducted a survey to see whether Rogers' (D) lighters would be confused with Zippo's (P).

CONCISE RULE OF LAW: If adequate statistical and procedural safeguards are taken, a survey is admissible evidence under the "existing present state of mind, belief, or opinion" exception to the hearsay rule.

FACTS: Zippo (P) brought an action against Rogers Imports (Rogers) (D) for allegedly copying its lighter. Zippo (P) sought injunctive relief and damages on a trademark and unfair competition theory. As part of its action for unfair competition, Zippo (P) sought to prove that the size, shape, and appearance had acquired an independent secondary meaning. Therefore, the public, when viewing a copy of a Zippo lighter, would think that it was actually a Zippo. To prove its contentions, Zippo (P) had a survey prepared in which those surveyed had to identify the manufacturer of an unmarked Zippo standard lighter, a Zippo slimline lighter, and an unmarked Rogers (D) lighter. The poll showed that 37% of those viewing the Rogers (D) lighter thought it was a Zippo (P). Rogers (D) objected to the admission of the survey on several grounds. It contended that surveys were inadmissible hearsay, that it had been improperly conducted, and that if the unidentified Rogers (D) lighter had been in its display card, very few of those polled would have been mistaken. The survey was admitted and a verdict was rendered for Zippo (P).

ISSUE: If adequate statistical and procedural safeguards are taken, is a survey admissible evidence under the "existing present state of mind, belief, or opinion" exception to the hearsay rule?

HOLDING AND DECISION: (Feinberg, J.) Yes. If adequate statistical and procedural safeguards are taken, a survey is admissible evidence under the "existing present state of mind, belief, or opinion" exception to the hearsay rule. Most courts allow them as either nonhearsay, admissible hearsay, or for no reported reason. Surveys are technically hearsay, since the belief of those polled is being testified to by the pollster. However, where those being polled have no reason to lie and the questions are simple, direct, and not misleading, there is no real reason to doubt the veracity of the replies. They are admissible as exceptions to the hearsay rule under the "existing state of mind, opinion, or belief" exception. With adequate procedural and statistical

protections there is no reason why they should not be admitted. Probative evidence on public opinion in secondary meaning cases cannot be obtained in any other reasonable manner short of calling every member of the smoking public to trial. Rogers's (D) allegation that the percentage of those identifying its lighter as a Zippo (P) would be greatly diminished if Rogers's (D) display card and markings had been used is valid. However, this merely goes to the weight given the survey. Some of those polled would not have noticed the Rogers (D) name. Therefore, even though its conclusions may be of doubtful value, it does not render the survey inadmissible. Judgment affirmed.

EDITOR'S ANALYSIS: To be valid, surveys must relate to the personal belief, opinion, or state of mind of those polled. Therefore, it would be improper to admit a survey which asks questions concerning the acts, conduct, or belief of others. For example, a poll conducted to ascertain whether the public thinks that a state law is discriminatory would be inadmissible as proof that the law was discriminatory.

NOTES:

UNITED STATES v. OWENS
Federal government (P) v. Convicted murderer (D)
484 U.S. 554 (1988).

NATURE OF CASE: Appeal of conviction for attempted murder.

FACT SUMMARY: Owens (D) was convicted of attempted murder after victim Foster, while unable to identify Owens (D) in court, testified that he had earlier identified him.

CONCISE RULE OF LAW: A witness in a criminal trial may testify about an earlier identification even if he can no longer testify as to the basis for that identification.

FACTS: Foster, a prison guard, was severely beaten. While in the hospital, he identified Owens (D) as the attacker. He later lost independent recollection of the attack and could not explain the basis for his hospital identification. Over defense objection, Foster was allowed to testify regarding his hospital identification. Owens (D) was convicted and appealed. The Ninth Circuit reversed, holding that the Confrontation Clause barred such testimony. The Supreme Court granted review.

ISSUE: May a witness in a criminal trial testify about an earlier identification even if he can no longer testify as to the basis for that identification?

HOLDING AND DECISION: (Scalia, J.) Yes. A witness in a criminal trial may testify about an earlier identification even if he can no longer testify as to the basis for that identification. The Confrontation Clause of the Sixth Amendment has been read to require only the opportunity for effective cross-examination, not whatever sort of cross-examination the defense might wish. When a witness cannot recall the basis for an earlier identification, the opposing party already has a potent cross-examination tool, as a forgetful witness has inherent credibility problems. It has long been held that an expert may give an opinion even if he has forgotten the basis therefor, and this situation is no different. Here, Owens (D) had the opportunity to attack Foster on the basis of his forgetfulness, and that was all the Confrontation Clause required. Reversed.

EDITOR'S ANALYSIS: Owens (D) also contended that Foster's testimony violated the Federal Rules of Evidence. Specifically, Owens (D) contended that Fed. R. Evid. 801(d)(1)(C)'s exclusion from hearsay of a prior identification required that the declarant be subject to cross-examination. Foster, stated Owens (D), was not so subject due to his memory loss. The court disagreed for the same reasons noted in the discussion on the Confrontation Clause.

NOTES:

BAKER v. STATE

Robbery and murder convict (D) v. State (P)

Md. Ct. Spec. App., 35 Md.App. 593, 371 A.2d 699 (1977).

NATURE OF CASE: Appeal from a conviction for first-degree murder and robbery.

FACT SUMMARY: Baker's (D) counsel was not permitted to use a police report prepared by another officer to refresh the recollection of Officer Bolton while he was on the stand testifying.

CONCISE RULE OF LAW: Anything can be used to refresh a witness's recollection of an event, even a memorandum made by another, and it need not meet the standards applicable to a record of past recollection.

FACTS: Baker (D) was convicted of robbery and murder in the first degree. On appeal therefrom, she argued that the trial judge had erred in refusing her counsel the opportunity to refresh the present recollection of a police officer who was testifying by showing him a report written by a fellow officer. In cross-examining Officer Bolton, Baker's (D) counsel sought to elicit from him the fact that the crime victim confronted Baker (D) and stated that she was not one of the persons who had attacked and robbed him. Officer Bolton had stated he did not remember whom it was the crime victim had so confronted, and Baker's (D) counsel sought to have him look at a police report prepared by another officer to refresh his memory on that point. The judge did not allow it.

ISSUE: May a memorandum made by another be used to refresh a witness's recollection of an event, if it does not meet the standards applicable to a record of past recollection?

HOLDING AND DECISION: (Moylan, J.) Yes. Anything can be used to refresh a witness's recollection of an event, even a memorandum made by another, and it need not meet the standards applicable to a record of past recollection. There is no limit as to what can be used to refresh a witness's recollection of an event. The stimulus that is thus used to revive a witness's dormant memory is not itself received in evidence. Thus, it is not to be confused with documents admitted into evidence as embodiments of past recollections recorded and is not subject to the same stringent rules of admission. All that is required is that the stimulus ignite the flash of accurate recall, i.e., that it accomplish the revival which is sought. The stimulus used need not even be in writing. Even if it is a writing, it need not have ever been read by the witness before he sees it at trial nor does the witness have to vouch for it or its accuracy. Under these principles, Baker's (D) counsel should have been allowed to refresh Officer Bolton's present recollection with a follow officer's report. Reversed and remanded for a new trial.

EDITOR'S ANALYSIS: Whatever memory aid is used to refresh a witness's recollection, it is always subject to inspection by the opposing party, who has the right to show it to the jury. The party seeking to use the memory aid may not submit it to the jury for their inspection, however, unless it constitutes evidence that is otherwise admissible.

NOTES:

ADAMS v. THE NEW YORK CENTRAL RAILROAD CO.
Quadraplegic (P) v. Railroad (D)
Ct. of Common Pleas, Cleveland, Ohio, 1961. Docket 724,072 (1961).

NATURE OF CASE: Damages for personal injuries.

FACT SUMMARY: The New York Central Railroad Co. (D) wanted to introduce evidence of an accident Adams (P) had been involved in prior to the accident involving New York Central (P).

CONCISE RULE OF LAW: When a witness's own recollection is not refreshed by a written memoranda that he made, that writing is not admissible as evidence.

FACTS: Adams (P), a quadraplegic, claims his injuries were a result of an accident involving the New York Central Railroad Co. (D). In order to show that Adams' (P) injuries were a result of another accident which occurred prior to the accident involving the parties in this action, New York Central (D) attempted to introduce evidence under the "past recollection recorded" exception to the hearsay rule. In laying the foundation, New York Central (D) had Mr. Raith, an inspector for the John Hancock Mutual Life Insurance Co., testify that he had made a written record of an interview that he had with Adams (P). Mr. Raith testified that he had no present recollection of the interview, even after looking at the record he had made, but he knew that the writing accurately set forth the facts discussed in the interview. He further stated that the writing was made shortly after the interview was conducted while it was still fresh in his mind. After laying this foundation, New York Central (D) attempted to introduce the writing itself into evidence. Adams's (P) attorney objected on the grounds that the writing was not a document made in the course of business and therefore was not admissible.

ISSUE: May a writing be admitted under the "past recollection recorded" exception to the hearsay rule if the witness who made the writing has no independent recollection?

HOLDING AND DECISION: (Trial court ruling from transcript) No. When a witness's own recollection is not refreshed by a written memoranda that he made, that writing is not admissible as evidence. The trial court sustained the objection and refused to let the writing in. The jury returned a verdict for Adams (P) in the amount of $300,000. The judge refused to allow the writing to come in because the witness testified that his own recollection was not refreshed after reading his notes. (It isn't clear whether this is the reason the judge sustained the objection by Adams's (P) attorney or if the judge agreed with Adams's (P) attorney that the writing couldn't come in because it was not a document prepared in the routine course of business.) New York Central (D) made a motion for a new trial on the grounds that the rejection of the proffered memorandum was prejudicial error. Before a ruling was made on the motion, this case was settled for a sum less than the $300,000 verdict.

EDITOR'S ANALYSIS: In a minority of states, the writing is not allowed into evidence under the "past recollection recorded" exception. The witness is allowed to read the memorandum to the jury, but that is all that comes into evidence. The majority of states, however, will allow the writing to be put into evidence. In practically all states, one of the requirements that must be met before this exception is applicable is that the witness must have no present recollection of the information contained in the writing.

NOTES:

JOHNSON v. LUTZ
Estate of decedent (P) v. Truck driver (D)
N.Y. Ct. App., 253 N.Y. 124, 170 N.E. 517 (1930).

NATURE OF CASE: Wrongful death action based on a traffic accident.

FACT SUMMARY: Lutz (D) attempted to get an accident report filed by a policeman into evidence. The report contained statements of witnesses to the traffic accident.

CONCISE RULE OF LAW: While a statute may allow the admission into evidence of business records that are kept in the regular course of business, even without firsthand knowledge of the record by the recorder, entries that include hearsay statements of third parties not engaged in the business related to the record may not be admitted.

FACTS: Johnson (P) was killed in a traffic accident with Lutz (D). In order to prove that he was not at fault, Lutz (D) attempted to have an accident report admitted into evidence. The report was made by a police officer on duty, and included statements of witnesses to the accident. A statute in effect provided that records kept in the normal course of business were admissible without the firsthand knowledge of the recorder. However, the court did not allow the report into evidence.

ISSUE: Where a statute allows the admission into evidence of business records that are kept in the regular course of business, even without firsthand knowledge of the record by the recorder, is an entry in that business record that includes hearsay statements of third parties not engaged in the business related to the record admissible?

HOLDING AND DECISION: (Hubbs, J.) No. While a statute may allow the admission into evidence of business records that are kept in the regular course of business, even without firsthand knowledge of the record by the recorder, entries that include hearsay statements of third parties not engaged in the business related to the record may not be admitted. The purpose of the statute was to allow proof of business transactions without the necessity of calling all the parties involved in situations involving normal business conditions. The essence of this statute was to provide credence to records made by persons in the exercise of the business duty. The intent of the legislature was not to extend this rule to statements made by persons outside the business for which the report was made, such as witnesses to an accident. Therefore, the report was properly excluded.

EDITOR'S ANALYSIS: The statute in question in this case was passed to remedy situations such as the one that existed in the previous case. Had this statute been in effect in that case, as it would have been in most jurisdictions today, the shopbook would have been admissible to prove the account receivable. However, as this case indicates, to apply this type of statute to a record, not only must the recorder be under a business duty to record the information, but the persons giving him the information must be under a similar duty. In other words, it's not enough that the policeman was under a business duty to make the report in this case, but the witnesses must have also been under a business duty in reporting to the police. Obviously, they were not under such a duty and, therefore, the report was not admissible. This rule has been severely criticized, but still stands as the majority rule.

NOTES:

UNITED STATES v. VIGNEAU
Federal government (P) v. Convicted money launderer (D)
187 F.3d 70 (1st Cir. 1999).

NATURE OF CASE: Appeal from conviction for money laundering and illegal drug distribution.

FACT SUMMARY: Vigneau (D) claimed that Western Union "To Send Money" forms that contained his name, address, and telephone number were inadmissible hearsay and not admissible under the business records exception.

CONCISE RULE OF LAW: The business records exception to the hearsay rule does not embrace statements contained within a business record that are made by one who is an outsider to the business where the statements are offered for their truth.

FACTS: Vigneau (D) was convicted on 21 counts of money laundering in connection with a drug distribution scheme. At trial, the court allowed the government (P) to introduce, without redaction and for all purposes, Western Union "To Send Money" forms, under the theory that the forms fell under the business records exception to the hearsay rule. These forms are handed by the sender of money to a Western Union agent after the sender completes the left side of the form by writing (1) the sender's name, address and telephone number; (2) the amount of the transfer; and (3) the intended recipient's name and location. The Western Union clerk then fills in the right side of the form with the clerk's signature, date, amount of the transfer and fee, and a computer-generated control number. At the time Vigneau (D) allegedly filled these forms out, independent proof of the sender's identity was not required. The government (P) had either the original forms completed by the sender or computer records of such forms. Vigneau (D) argued that his name, address and telephone number on the "To Send Money" forms were inadmissible hearsay to identify him as the sender.

ISSUE: Does the business records exception to the hearsay rule embrace statements contained within a business record that are made by one who is an outsider to the business where the statements are offered for their truth?

HOLDING AND DECISION: (Boudin, J.) No. The business records exception to the hearsay rule does not embrace statements contained within a business record that are made by one who is an outsider to the business where the statements are offered for their truth. The forms literally comply with the business records exception because each form (or the computerized information representing the form) is a business record. The problem, however, is that the business records exception does not apply where the statements contained in the record were made by a stranger to the business. That is because when the stranger fills out the forms, there are no safeguards of business

regularity or business checks to assure the truth of the statement to the business. Fed. R. Evid. 803(6), which codifies the business records exception, provides in part that a business record is inadmissible if found to lack trustworthiness. That reference to "trustworthiness," however, does not comprise an independent hearsay exception. Sometimes, the statement by the "outsider" may be admissible not for its truth but for some other purpose. The weakness in the government's (P) position here is that the forms were admitted for all purposes. Clearly, the forms were relevant to the government's (P) case because they showed money transfers that supported the description of drug and money laundering activities. Thus, the forms could have been submitted in redacted form, omitting the information identifying Vigneau (D) as the sender. But because the forms were not redacted, they should not have been admitted for their truth. Here, the error is not harmless. Vacated and remanded as to the money laundering charges.

EDITOR'S ANALYSIS: As the court in this case notes, if there had been independent evidence that the writer of the forms was Vigneau (D), the statements in those forms—his name, address, and telephone number—would constitute party-opponent admissions and would technically not be hearsay under Fed. R. Evid. 801(d)(2). Without such independent evidence, however, the prosecution could not use the forms themselves as bootstrap-proof that Vigneau (D) was the one who made the admission.

NOTES:

UNITED STATES v. DUNCAN
Federal government (P) v. Fraudulent insurance claimants (D)
919 F.2d 981 (5th Cir. 1990).

NATURE OF CASE: Appeal from conviction for mail fraud and conspiracy.

FACT SUMMARY: Duncan (D) defrauded his health insurer by staging accidents and faking injuries, but tried to prevent, on grounds of hearsay, the admission of insurance records based on hospital and doctor reports at his trial for mail fraud and conspiracy.

CONCISE RULE OF LAW: Business records otherwise admissible under an exception to the hearsay rule are not precluded from admission merely because they are based on other business records or the nonhearsay statements of agents on matters within the scope of their agency.

FACTS: Over a period of several years, Duncan (D), his wife, and several of their friends and relatives, staged a series of faked automobile crashes, injuries, and hospital stays in a scheme to defraud several health insurance companies. Mr. & Mrs. Duncan (D) alone were hospitalized over twenty times and collected over $300,000 in insurance proceeds. The government caught up with them, however, and indicted them for mail fraud and conspiracy. At trial, the records of the insurance companies Duncan (D) and the others bilked were introduced under the business records exception to the hearsay rule (Fed. R. Evid. 803(6)). After a two-week trial, a jury found the Duncans (D) guilty. The Duncans (D) appealed, in part on the ground that the insurance records had been improperly admitted because they contained other unauthenticated medical records and statements of doctors which were hearsay not falling within the business records exception.

ISSUE: Are business records otherwise admissible under an exception to the hearsay rule precluded from admission nonetheless because they are based on other business records or on the nonhearsay statements of agents on matters within the scope of their agency?

HOLDING AND DECISION: (Duhé, J.) No. Business records otherwise admissible under an exception to the hearsay rule are not precluded from admission merely because they are based on other business records or the nonhearsay statements of agents on matters within the scope of their agency. Here, the insurance companies compiled their records from the business records of hospitals. Because the medical records from which the insurance companies were made were themselves business records, there was no accumulation of inadmissible hearsay. Further, even if the insurance company records contained some medical information not taken from actual hospital records, that information was admissible as nonhearsay under Fed. R. Evid. 801(d)(2)(C)-(D), which excludes from hearsay statements of agents concerning matters within the scope of their agency. Patients routinely authorize the release of medical records for use by insurance companies, and medical providers who lack such express authorization still are entitled to act as the patient's agent in obtaining payment of medical expenses from insurance companies. Thus, the insurance records were admissible against the Duncans (D). Affirmed.

EDITOR'S ANALYSIS: In most modern businesses, business records are a mass of multiple hearsay; e.g., an order goes from the customer to the salesperson to the home office to the accounting department to the shipping department and back to accounting to be recorded in the books. A business record containing such a chain of multiple hearsay is admissible if each statement in the chain is either: not hearsay for the purpose for which it is offered; within some other exemption or exception; or made by a person under a "business duty" to make such statements. "Business duty" means that it is a regular part of the person's job to make or record such statements.

NOTES:

WILLIAMS v. ALEXANDER
Injured cyclist (P) v. Driver (D)
N.Y. Ct. App., 309 N.Y. 283, 129 N.E.2d 417 (1955).

NATURE OF CASE: Action to recover damages in a personal injury case.

FACT SUMMARY: At the trial of a personal injury lawsuit, Alexander (D) wanted to introduce a portion of the hospital record into evidence in which Williams (P) related how the accident occurred. Williams (P) objected to the introduction of this evidence.

CONCISE RULE OF LAW: The only information which is admissible in a hospital report under the business records exception is that which is recorded in the regular course of business and for the purpose of assisting the hospital in carrying on that business.

FACTS: Williams (P) was struck by Alexander's (D) car as he rode his bike through an intersection, and he brought this action to recover damages for the injuries which he sustained. At the trial, Williams (P) claimed that Alexander (D) had driven his car through the intersection without slowing down, while Alexander (D) claimed that he had stopped and been run into by another car that caused him to run into Williams (P). Williams (P) introduced a portion of his hospital record to show the extent of his injuries and their treatment. Alexander (D) then introduced the rest of the record containing a statement Williams (P) had made to the doctor in which he stated that the car that hit him was stopped and another car had run into it causing it to hit him. Williams (P) objected on the grounds that this portion of the record was hearsay, but the court overruled the objection. The verdict was for Alexander (D), and Williams appealed.

ISSUE: Is a statement in a hospital report which was not recorded for the purpose of assisting the hospital in carrying on its business admissible under the business records exception?

HOLDING AND DECISION: (Fuld, J.) No. The only information which is admissible in a hospital report under the business reports exception is that which is recorded in the regular course of business and for the purpose of assisting the hospital in carrying on that business. The statement in the report in which Williams (P) related how the accident occurred was made in the regular course of business, but it was not made in order to better carry on the hospital's business. How the accident occurred was not germane to diagnosis or treatment and, therefore, not admissible. For information in a hospital report to be admissible, it must relate to the diagnosis, prognosis, or treatment of the patient or be helpful in understanding the medical or surgical aspects of the patients hospitalization. The judgment of the lower courts is reversed, and the case remanded for a new trial.

DISSENT: (Desmond, J.) Williams's (P) statement to the doctor was properly admitted by the trial court. It was admissible as an extrajudicial declaration against interest and did not need to be admissible under the business reports exception. Also, because Williams (P) introduced part of the hospital report into evidence, he could not object to the rest of the report being introduced.

EDITOR'S ANALYSIS: In most states, statements relating to the history of the patient that are unnecessary to hospital business are inadmissible unless they are admitted under an exception other than the business-records exception. The statements may constitute admissions of a party opponent when offered against the patient, dying declarations, declarations against interest, or excited utterances.

NOTES:

HAHNEMANN UNIVERSITY HOSPITAL v. DUDNICK
Hospital (P) v. Patient (D)
N.J. Super. Ct., 678 A.2d. 266 (1996).

NATURE OF CASE: Appeal from judgment for plaintiff.

FACT SUMMARY: Dudnick (D) alleged that the trial court erred by admitting into evidence computer printout records of the Hospital (P).

CONCISE RULE OF LAW: A computerized business record is considered trustworthy unless the opposing party comes forward with some evidence to question its reliability.

FACTS: The Hospital (P) sued to collect for an outstanding balance due on a hospital bill for treatment. The computer printout of Dudnick's (D) bill was introduced into evidence when it was authenticated by a person who was in charge of the records and personally familiar with them, and was shown to reflect data recorded contemporaneously with the occurrence of the facts recorded in the usual course of the Hospital's (P) usual practice. Dudnick (D) argued that the requisite foundation under the business entry exception to the hearsay rule had not been adequately laid, and appealed.

ISSUE: Is a computerized business record considered trustworthy if the opposing party does not come forward with some evidence to question its reliability?

HOLDING AND DECISION: (Villanueva, J.) Yes. A computerized business record is considered trustworthy unless the opposing party comes forward with some evidence to question its reliability. The Hospital (P) clearly established the reliability of the bill. The burden then shifted to Dudnick (D) to offer some evidence that the bill was not reliable. Dudnick (D) failed to do so. Therefore, the bill was properly admitted. Affirmed.

EDITOR'S ANALYSIS: The court in this case specifically disapproved of an outdated six-prong test for the admission of computer printouts. The New Jersey Rules of Evidence which became effective in 1993 relaxed the standard for admission of such business records. Expert testimony as to the reliability of the programs the computer uses or other technical aspects of its operation are now unnecessary to find computer-generated records circumstantially reliable.

NOTES:

PALMER v. HOFFMAN
Railroad trustee (D) v. Injured claimant (P)
318 U.S. 109 (1943).

NATURE OF CASE: Action for personal injuries arising out of a railroad accident.

FACT SUMMARY: The engineer of a train involved in an accident, who died before trial, made a statement to the railroad company regarding the accident. This statement was not allowed in evidence.

CONCISE RULE OF LAW: A record is considered to be "in the regular course of business" if made systematically or as a matter of routine to reflect events or transactions of the business.

FACTS: Hoffman (P) was injured in an accident with a railroad train and brought suit against Palmer (D), a trustee of the railroad. Shortly after the accident, the engineer of the train made a statement to the superintendent of the railroad and to a representative of the public utilities commission. It was the custom of the railroad to record such statements whenever there was an accident. The engineer died before the trial, and Palmer (D) attempted to introduce the statement into evidence. A statute allowed business records to be admitted if made in the course of regular business, but the court would not allow it into evidence.

ISSUE: Is a record considered to be "in the regular course of business" if made systematically or as a matter of routine to reflect events or transactions of the business?

HOLDING AND DECISION: (Douglas, J.) Yes. A record is considered to be "in the regular course of business" if made systematically or as a matter of routine to reflect events or transactions of the business. The keeping of accident reports, while customary, is not essential to the efficient operation of a railroad. If the mere custom of making a record of non-essential activity could bring that record within the meaning of "regular course" of business, then any company could bring any type of record into court. The primary purpose of the record in this case was not for the efficient management of a railroad, but for litigation. Therefore, the record was not within the regular course of business and was properly excluded.

EDITOR'S ANALYSIS: This is the leading case recognized for records that are kept in the regular course of business. Many scholars have criticized the decision as being contrary to the statute, and therefore lower courts have dealt with the case in varying ways. Current analysis of this case does not create a blanket rule of exclusion for "self serving" accident reports or other such records kept by businesses. Instead, it gives trial courts the discretion to exclude evidence which falls under the business-records exception to the hearsay rule. The motive and the opportunity to falsify are the primary factors in using this case to exclude records.

NOTES:

LEWIS v. BAKER
Brakeman (P) v. Railroad company employer (D)
526 F.2d 470 (2d Cir. 1975).

NATURE OF CASE: Appeal from denial of damages for personal injuries.

FACT SUMMARY: In Lewis' (P) suit against Baker (D) and the Penn Central Railroad for injuries suffered while employed by Penn Central, Lewis (P) contended that accident reports of his injury were improperly admitted into evidence, and therefore, he should be granted a new trial.

CONCISE RULE OF LAW: A writing or record, whether in the form of an entry in a book or otherwise, made as a memorandum or record of any act, occurrence, or event and pursuant to regular business procedure, is admissible.

FACTS: In Lewis's (P) suit against Baker (D) and the Penn Central Railroad for injuries received while Lewis (P) was employed by Penn Central, Lewis (P) alleged that the brake on a railroad car he was working on was faulty and that he was injured as a result of the faulty brake. Evidence that the brake had functioned properly immediately prior to the accident and immediately after the accident when it was checked was admitted in the form of an accident report. Lewis (P) objected to admission of the accident report, stating that the report had not been prepared for the systematic conduct of the business as business of Penn Central. The jury returned a verdict for Baker (D), and Lewis (P) appealed.

ISSUE: Is a writing or record, whether in the form of an entry in an book or otherwise, made as a memorandum or record of any act, occurrence, or event and pursuant to regular business procedure, admissible?

HOLDING AND DECISION: (Waterman, J.) Yes. A writing or record, whether in the form of an entry in a book or otherwise, made as a memorandum or record of any act, occurrence, or event and pursuant to regular business procedure, is admissible. Here, the report in question was made pursuant to regular procedure at Penn Central's yard. Following every accident involving injury to an employee, Penn Central was required to complete inspection reports, and such reports were regularly kept in the course of business. Also, the ICC required Penn Central to prepare and file monthly reports of all accidents involving railroad employees. These reports were undoubtedly of utility to the employer in ascertaining whether equipment involved in accidents was defective so that future accidents could be prevented. These factors are sufficient indicia of trustworthiness to establish the admissibility of the reports into evidence under the Federal Business Records Act. Affirmed.

EDITOR'S ANALYSIS: The hearsay exception for regularly kept records is justified on grounds analogous to those underlying other exceptions to the hearsay rule. Unusual reliability is regarded as furnished by the fact that, in practice, regularly kept records have a very high degree of accuracy. The very regularity and continuity of the records are calculated to train the recordkeeper in habits of precision and most records are also periodically checked by balance-striking and audits.

NOTES:

YATES v. BAIR TRANSPORT, INC.
Injured claimant (P) v. Transport company (D)
249 F.Supp. 681 (1965).

NATURE OF CASE: Action to recover damages for personal injuries received in an accident.

FACT SUMMARY: Yates (P) attempted to have reports of several doctors admitted into evidence.

CONCISE RULE OF LAW: A doctor's report prepared in anticipation of litigation is admissible under the business records exception if the court finds that the reports have an inherent probability of trustworthiness.

FACTS: Yates (P) was injured in an accident involving Bair Transport, Inc. (D) and brought this action to recover his damages. Yates (P) also filed a workmen's compensation claim for the same injuries that were the subject of the action. The Liberty Mutual Insurance Company was the insurance carrier for one of the parties involved in the workmen's compensation claim and was also the insurance carrier for Knickerbocker Despatch, Inc., one of the defendants in this action. In processing the workmen's compensation claim, five doctors submitted reports to Liberty Mutual. Two of these doctors, Guthrie and Youmans, examined Yates (P) on behalf of Liberty Mutual. Richman examined Yates (P) on behalf of Interboro Mutual Indemnity Insurance Co. Fleck and Lewis were Yates's (P) treating physicians. Yates (P) wanted to introduce all of the reports of these doctors and made a pretrial motion to that effect.

ISSUE: Is a doctor's report prepared in anticipation of litigation admissible under the business records exception if the court finds that the reports have an inherent probability of trustworthiness?

HOLDING AND DECISION: (Tenney, J.) Yes. A doctor's report prepared in anticipation of litigation is admissible under the business records exception if the court finds that the reports have an inherent probability of trustworthiness. The reports in this case were prepared in anticipation of litigation, and therefore the court must find that the reports have an inherent probability of trustworthiness. The reports of doctors Guthrie and Youmans were prepared for Liberty Mutual, who is insuring one of the defendants in this action, and since it is Yates (P) who wants to admit these reports, the reports have an inherent probability of trustworthiness. The reports of doctors Fleck and Lewis were prepared for Yates (P) in anticipation of litigation, and therefore they do not have an inherent probability of trustworthiness. It is not clear for whom the report of doctor Richman was prepared, and so it is not deemed trustworthy. The reports of doctors Guthrie and Youmans are therefore admissible and the rest are not.

EDITOR'S ANALYSIS: The modern evidence codes require the judge to determine that the information, method, and time of preparation of a report were such as to indicate its trustworthiness. This is a small minority view, however. One of the leading cases in this area is *Palmer v. Hoffman*, 318 U.S. 109 (1943), which held that records made in anticipation of litigation were untrustworthy and inadmissible. This is the majority view. Under the minority view, if the court finds that there is some reason to believe that the information is trustworthy as in the above case where the reports were prepared by the defendants and offered by the plaintiff, then the evidence will be admitted.

NOTES:

BEECH AIRCRAFT CORP. v. RAINEY
Aircraft manufacturer (D) v. Surviving spouses (P)
488 U.S. 153 (1988).

NATURE OF CASE: Review of reversal of order admitting evidence.

FACT SUMMARY: In a product liability action, Beech Aircraft Corp. (D) sought to introduce a governmental investigative report containing opinions favorable to its case.

CONCISE RULE OF LAW: The public records and reports exception to the hearsay rule permits introduction of opinions and conclusions contained in public records and reports.

FACTS: During a military training exercise, an aircraft manufactured by Beech Aircraft Corp. (D) crashed, killing all aboard. Survivors of the decedents brought a wrongful death/ products liability action. At trial, Beech (D) sought admission of a governmental report generated pursuant to the incident in which blame was generally laid on pilot error. The district court admitted the report, and Beech (D) prevailed. The court of appeals reversed, holding that the public records and reports exception to the hearsay rule, found at Fed. R. Evid. v. 803(8), only permitted the introduction of "facts," not "opinions" or "conclusions." The Supreme Court granted certiorari.

ISSUE: Does the public records and reports exception to the hearsay rule permit introduction of opinions and conclusions contained in public records and reports?

HOLDING AND DECISION: (Brennan, J.) Yes. The public records and reports exception to the hearsay rule permits introduction of opinions and conclusions contained in public records and reports. The rule permits the introduction of opinions, not merely facts contained therein. This implies that portions of the reports other than raw data may be admitted. Moreover, as a policy matter, it can be difficult to tell when data or facts stop and opinions begin. Finally, there is no legislative history tending to show Congress intended the rule to be more restrictive than its language indicated. In light of this, the district court properly admitted the report. Reversed.

EDITOR'S ANALYSIS: Legislative history from the House of Representatives tended to demonstrate a restrictive intent behind the rule. Senate reports indicated the opposite view. The Court took this to mean the legislative histories essentially canceled each other out and, therefore, construed the Rule's language exclusively.

NOTES:

UNITED STATES v. OATES
Federal government (P) v. Drug dealer (D)
560 F.2d 45 (2d Cir. 1977).

NATURE OF CASE: Appeal from a conviction for drug-related offenses.

FACT SUMMARY: Oates (D) claimed that the chemist's report and worksheet identifying the substance seized from him as heroin should have been excluded from evidence as hearsay.

CONCISE RULE OF LAW: Evaluative and law enforcement reports which fail to qualify under the "public records" exception to the hearsay rule cannot be admitted as "business."

FACTS: Oates (D) was convicted of possession of heroin with intent to distribute and conspiracy to commit that substantive offense. On appeal he charged the trial judge erred in admitting into evidence the official report and worksheet of a U.S. Customs Service chemist identifying the substance seized from Oates (D) as heroin. The chemist who wrote the documents was "unavailable," so the government (P) called another Customs Service chemist to testify to the regular procedures and practices used by Customs Service chemists in analyzing unknown substances. She claimed to be able to ascertain from the worksheet the various steps the other chemist had used to determine if the substance was heroin. When Oates (D) made a convincing argument that such documents were not admissible under Fed. R. of Evid. 803(8)'s "public records" exception to the hearsay rule, the government (P) claimed they were nonetheless admissible under the "business records" exception of Rule 803(6).

ISSUE: Are evaluative and law enforcement reports which fail to qualify under the "public records" exception to the hearsay rule admissible as "business"?

HOLDING AND DECISION: (Waterman, J.) No. Evaluative and law enforcement reports which fail to qualify under the "public records" exception to the hearsay rule cannot be admitted as "business." In passing the Federal Rules of Evidence, Congress made clear its intent that evaluative and law enforcement reports be absolutely inadmissible against defendants in criminal cases. So, letting them in as "business records" when they are explicitly precluded from coming in under the more fitting "public records" exception is improper. Fed. R. Evid. 803(8)(C) specifically states that "factual findings resulting from an investigation made pursuant to authority granted by law" are not shielded from the exclusionary effect of the hearsay rule by the "public records" exception if the government seeks to admit them against the accused in a criminal trial. Fed. R. Evid. 803(8)(B) creates a "public records" exception that specifically excludes "matters observed by police officers and other law enforcement personnel" (which means any officer or employee of a governmental agency who has law enforcement responsibilities). The documents introduced at trial in this case should thus not have been admitted. Reversed and remanded for a new trial.

EDITOR'S ANALYSIS: Fear that interference with the accused's right to confront the witnesses against him led Congress to conclude that evaluative and law enforcement reports should not be admissible against a criminal defendant under any exception to the hearsay rule. However, they can be used in civil cases and proceedings and against the government in criminal cases, unless they are untrustworthy.

NOTES:

UNITED STATES v. GRADY
Federal government (P) v. Firearms law violator (D)
544 F.2d 598 (2d Cir. 1976).

NATURE OF CASE: Appeal from a conviction for conspiracy to violate federal firearms law.

FACT SUMMARY: Grady (D) contended that error had been committed at his trial in admitting into evidence under the "public records" exception to the hearsay rule certain Irish records.

CONCISE RULE OF LAW: While Federal Rule of Evidence 803(8)(B) does exclude records and reports setting forth "matters observed by police officers and other law enforcement personnel" from its "public records" exception to the hearsay rule, this exclusionary language covers only police officers' reports of their contemporaneous observations of crime.

FACTS: Grady (D) appealed his convictions for federal firearms law violations by charging that the trial judge had erred in admitting into evidence Irish documents showing that certain rifles with particular serial numbers, purchased in the United States, had been found in Northern Ireland. Grady (D) was a sympathizer with the Catholic minority in Ulster. At any rate, the documents were admitted under the "public records" exception to the hearsay rule, codified in Fed. R. Evid. 803(8)(B). It allows admission of records and reports of public officials or agencies setting forth "matters observed pursuant to duty imposed by law as to which matters there was a duty to report," but is subject to an exception for "matters observed by police officers and other law enforcement personnel."

ISSUE: Does Fed. R. Evid. 803(8)(B) exclude from consideration as a "public record" only those police officers' reports which contain their contemporaneous observations of crime?

HOLDING AND DECISION: (Oakes, J.) Yes. Fed. R. Evid. 803(8)(B) does exclude from its "public records" exception to the hearsay rule records and reports setting forth "matters observed by police officers and other law enforcement personnel," but this exclusionary language covers only police officers' reports of their contemporaneous observations of crime and not the type of reports which were properly admitted in this case. In adopting the exception, Congress was concerned about prosecutors attempting to prove their cases "in chief" simply by putting into evidence police officers' reports of their contemporaneous observations of crime. The reports at issue here are not of that nature. They simply related to the routine function of recording serial numbers and receipt of certain weapons found in Northern Ireland. These strictly routine records were properly admitted under 803(8)(B). Affirmed.

EDITOR'S ANALYSIS: This case is a good example of the liberal attitude courts have generally taken in determining admissibility under Rule 803(8). That rule has its historical underpinnings in the common-law exception to the hearsay rule for written statements of public officials made upon firsthand knowledge.

NOTES:

STROUD v. COOK
Injured motorist (P) v. Automobile driver (D)
931 F. Supp. 733 (D. Nev. 1996).

NATURE OF CASE: Motion in limine to exclude evidence of conviction in negligence action.

FACT SUMMARY: The car driven by Stroud (P) collided with the car driven by Cook (D). Stroud (P) brought a civil action in federal court against Cook (D), who sought to exclude from evidence a criminal misdemeanor judgment of failing to use due care in the operation of his car immediately before the accident.

CONCISE RULE OF LAW: A prior state misdemeanor conviction is admissible in a subsequent federal court action to establish civil liability for the conduct that resulted in the conviction.

FACTS: The car driven by Stroud (P) collided with the car driven by Cook (D). Immediately after the accident, Cook (D) was cited by a highway patrolman for the misdemeanor of failing to use due care in the operation of a motor vehicle right before the accident occurred. Cook (D) was found guilty and was fined $35. Stroud (P) brought a civil action in federal court sounding in negligence against Cook (D), and sought to introduce the judgment as evidence of Cook's (D) negligence. Stroud (P) had sought summary judgment on the issue, arguing that Cook's (D) conviction under state law established Cook's (D) civil liability as a matter of law. The state statute provided that a criminal conviction is conclusive evidence of all facts necessary to impose civil liability for the injury. The court ruled that the judgment of conviction could be admitted in evidence, but that it would constitute only prima facie evidence of the facts of Cook's (D) negligence, subject to rebuttal evidence. Cook (D) moved in limine to exclude the criminal judgment from evidence.

ISSUE: Is a prior state misdemeanor conviction admissible in a subsequent federal court action to establish civil liability for the conduct that resulted in the conviction?

HOLDING AND DECISION: (Reed, Jr., J.) Yes. A prior state misdemeanor conviction is admissible in a subsequent federal court action to establish civil liability for the conduct that resulted in the conviction. The judgment is hearsay. Under the Federal Rules of Evidence, a felony conviction is exempt from the hearsay rule, but here, Cook's (D) conviction was a misdemeanor. Therefore, unless there is another exception applicable to the conviction, it must be excluded. The only other hearsay exception arguably applicable is the exception for "public records" under Fed. R. Evid. 803(8). A judgment of conviction does meet the definition of a public record insofar as it sets forth the activities of the court issuing the judgment. Although the drafters of the Federal Rules of Evidence did not refer to judicial records, but only to the activities of executive agencies and offices, the court of appeals, which binds this court, has ruled that misdemeanor convictions are admissible under the "public records" exception. Therefore, Cook's (D) conviction is admissible under this exception to the hearsay rule. Even absent the court of appeals' ruling in this area, the existence of a state statute that not only authorizes admission of a prior criminal conviction in a subsequent related civil action, but compels it, counsels in favor of admitting the conviction. This is a diversity case. Under *Erie R.R. v. Tompkins,* 304 U.S. 64 (1938), a federal court sitting in diversity normally applies the substantive law of the forum state and federal procedural rules, including the federal evidence rules. However, where a state statute superficially resembles a rule of evidence but is in fact a substantive statute, the federal court must apply the state statute. Here, the state statute is substantive. It is not part of the state's evidence code, and it appears in a chapter limiting liability of certain persons and preserving causes of action for other persons. Even under the law of the case (whereby the conviction constitutes only prima facie evidence of negligence), the state statute alters the burden of proof by creating a presumption that Cook (D) is liable to Stroud (P). State statutes that alter burdens of proof are expressions of public policy, and, therefore, are substantive. For these reasons, Cook's (D) motion is denied.

EDITOR'S ANALYSIS: There is a split in the circuits on the issue of whether a misdemeanor conviction is admissible as a "public record." The district court deciding this case was in the Ninth Circuit, which, as the court noted, has ruled that such convictions are admissible under the "public records" exception to the hearsay rule. The Fourth Circuit, on the other hand, has ruled that they are inadmissible on the grounds that advisory committee notes to the Federal Rules of Evidence and the Rules' legislative history indicate that the drafters intended only felony convictions to qualify for the exception, and declined to do so for misdemeanors. The court in this case, which found the Fourth Circuit's reasoning "unassailable," found a way around this split through use of the *Erie* doctrine.

TURBYFILL v. INTERNATIONAL HARVESTER CO.
Injured driver (P) v. Manufacturer (D)
486 F.Supp. 232 (E.D. Mich. 1980).

NATURE OF CASE: Motion for a new trial upon denial of damages for personal injuries.

FACT SUMMARY: Turbyfill (P) contended the trial court erred in admitting into evidence the handwritten, unsworn account of an accident made by International Harvester's (International) (D) late employee on the basis it was inadmissible hearsay.

CONCISE RULE OF LAW: Under Federal Rule of Evidence 804(b)(5), a statement not specifically covered by a hearsay exception may be admitted if (1) it is made under equivalent guarantees of trustworthiness; (2) it is offered to prove a material fact; (3) it is more probative than other reasonably obtained evidence; and (4) the general purposes of the hearsay exceptions and the interests of justice will be served by its admission into evidence.

FACTS: Turbyfill (P) was severely burned when he attempted to start a truck on International's (D) used car lot. At the time of the accident, International's (D) mechanic, Anderson, was attempting to aid Turbyfill (P) in getting the truck started. After the accident, Brown, Anderson's supervisor, instructed Anderson to go into a room and fill out a statement describing the accident and not to confer with anyone. Anderson did so and signed the handwritten account in Brown's presence, although he wrote it while alone. Turbyfill (P) sued for damages, and Anderson died prior to trial. Turbyfill (P) was denied a recovery and moved for a new trial, contending the court erred in admitting Anderson's handwritten, unsworn account because it was hearsay not within any exception.

ISSUE: Can a hearsay statement not specifically covered by an exception be admitted if (1) it is made, under equivalent guarantees of trustworthiness; (2) it is offered to prove a material fact; (3) it is more probative than other reasonably obtained evidence; and (4) the general purpose of the hearsay exceptions and the interests of justice will be served by its admission into evidence?

HOLDING AND DECISION: (Joiner, J.) Yes. Under Fed. R. Evid. 804(b)(5), a statement not specifically covered by a hearsay exception may be admitted if (1) it was made under equivalent guarantees of trustworthiness; (2) it is offered to prove a material fact; (3) it is more probative than other reasonably obtainable evidence; and (4) the general purpose of the hearsay exceptions and the interests of justice will be served by admitting it. In this case, the statement was made while the events were fresh in Anderson's mind, alone in a room without the pressure of his employer. These facts support its trustworthiness as equivalent to that obtainable under a hearsay exception. Also, it was offered to prove fault—clearly a material fact—and was more probative than any other evidence International (D) could reasonably have obtained. Finally, justice was served by its admission. Therefore, it was properly admitted. Motion denied.

EDITOR'S ANALYSIS: The Federal Rules of Evidence were adopted to provide a broad catch-all exception to the hearsay rule. This exception is illustrated by this case. Even though a statement may be admissible under this exception, the proponent must give adequate notice to the adverse party that the exception will be invoked. He must inform the adverse party of the particulars of the statement including the name and address of the declarant.

NOTES:

UNITED STATES v. DENT
Federal government (P) v. Passenger (D)
984 F.2d 1435 (7th Cir. 1993).

NATURE OF CASE: Review of a criminal conviction for possession of a loaded firearm.

FACT SUMMARY: Dent (D) contended that the trial court erred in admitting grand jury testimony under the residual hearsay exception.

CONCISE RULE OF LAW: Hearsay evidence of an unavailable witness that does not fall within a specific hearsay exception may be admitted if there are particularized guarantees of trustworthiness shown to satisfy Federal Rule of Evidence 804(b)(5) and the Confrontation Clause.

FACTS: A police officer stopped a car driven by Tucker (D) in which Dent (D) was a passenger. Inside the car the police found a loaded weapon. During the grand jury investigation, Elayyan, a car salesman, testified that he sold the car to a woman, who was accompanied by Tucker (D). At trial, the grand jury testimony was read into evidence because Elayyan was out of the country and there was no other way to admit the evidence. Elayyan was considered a disinterested witness who had testified under oath. In addition, the court found corroboration in that Tucker (D) had been driving the car when stopped by police. Dent (D) and Tucker (D) were convicted and appealed.

ISSUE: May hearsay evidence of an unavailable witness that does not fall within a specific hearsay exception be admitted where there are particularized guarantees of trustworthiness drawn from the totality of the circumstances?

HOLDING AND DESIGN: (Wood, Jr., J.) Yes. Hearsay evidence of an unavailable witness that does not fall within a specific hearsay exception may be admitted where particularized guarantees of trustworthiness drawn from the totality of the circumstances are shown to satisfy Fed. R. Evid. 804(b)(5) and the Confrontation Clause. In this case, however, the guarantee of trustworthiness requirements are not satisfied based on the totality of the circumstances. Due to the fact that there was minimal corroboration of Elayyan's grand jury testimony and the identification of Tucker (D), the trial court erred in admitting the grand jury testimony. However, the error was harmless beyond a reasonable doubt because the grand jury testimony was tangential to the issue of Tucker's (D) possession of the loaded firearm. There is still sufficient evidence regarding that issue to uphold the jury's guilty verdict. Affirmed.

CONCURRENCE: (Easterbrook, J.) The court should not have applied Fed. R. Evid. 804(b)(5), the residual exceptions to the hearsay rule, to grand jury testimony in the first place since Fed.

R. Evid. 804(b)(5) is limited to statements not specifically covered by any other exceptions, and grand jury testimony is covered by Fed. R. Evid. 804(b)(1), the prior testimony exception.

EDITOR'S ANALYSIS: Most circuits are in accord with Dent and endorse a case-by-case approach to determine trustworthiness before approving use of the "catchall" exception to admit grand jury testimony by unavailable witnesses. The two most persuasive factors appear to be extensive and convincing corroboration and a suspicion that the defense somehow made the witness unavailable at trial. Murder or intimidation of a witness will occasionally waive the right to exclude hearsay altogether, if proven.

NOTES:

OHIO v. ROBERTS
State (P) v. Convicted forger (D)
448 U.S. 56 (1980).

NATURE OF CASE: Appeal from conviction for forgery and receiving stolen property.

FACT SUMMARY: Roberts (D) contended that the trial court denied him his right to confront a witness when it admitted into evidence the witness' testimony in the form of a transcript from the preliminary hearing.

CONCISE RULE OF LAW: The right to confrontation is not violated by the presentation of the transcript testimony where there was an adequate opportunity to cross-examine the witness at the official proceeding where the testimony was given.

FACTS: Roberts (D) was charged with forgery of a check in the name of Bernard Isaacs and possession of stolen credit cards belonging to Isaac's wife, Amy. At the preliminary hearing, Roberts's (D) counsel saw Anita Isaacs, Bernard's daughter, in the hallway and called her to testify. He vigorously attempted to get her to admit that she had given Roberts (D) her father's checkbook, her mother's credit cards and told him he had permission to use them. She denied this, and the prosecution did not question her. Roberts (D) was indicted, and at trial, the prosecution, after showing Anita was unavailable, was allowed to introduce the transcript from the preliminary hearing. He was convicted and appealed, contending the admission of the transcript denied him his right to confrontation. The Ohio Supreme Court reversed, holding the mere opportunity to cross-examine did not satisfy the Confrontation Clause. The State (P) appealed.

ISSUE: Is the right to confrontation violated by the presentation of transcript testimony where there was an adequate opportunity for cross-examination?

HOLDING AND DECISION: (Blackmun, J.) No. The right to confrontation is not violated by the presentation of the transcript testimony where there was an adequate opportunity to cross-examine the witness at the official proceeding where the testimony was given. Prior testimony is admissible as an exception to the hearsay rule if it bears adequate indicia of reliability. Anita's testimony was given under oath, and Roberts's (D) attorney had an adequate opportunity, through the use of leading questions, to effectively cross-examine her. Therefore, the testimony in fact bore adequate indicia of reliability and was admissible. Reversed and remanded.

EDITOR'S ANALYSIS: Because of the fact that the declarant was under oath at the time, prior testimony is admitted as an exception to the hearsay rule. The introduction of this type of evidence requires that the proponent prove its necessity. Such necessity is shown by the declarant's unavailability. This requirement of necessity is in conformance with the framer's objective in creating the Confrontation Clause in the Sixth Amendment.

NOTES:

UNITED STATES v. INADI
Federal government (P) v. Drug conspirator (D)
457 U.S. 387 (1986).

NATURE OF CASE: Appeal from conviction of conspiracy to manufacture and distribute methamphetamine.

FACT SUMMARY: In the government's (P) action against Inadi (D) for conspiring to manufacture and distribute methamphetamine, Inadi (D) contended that the trial court erroneously admitted a co-conspirator's out-of-court statements without requiring that the government (P) show that the nontestifying co-conspirator was unavailable to testify, and that the court thus violated Inadi's (D) rights under the Confrontation Clause of the Sixth Amendment.

CONCISE RULE OF LAW: The Confrontation Clause does not require that a nontestifying co-conspirator be unavailable to testify as a condition for admission of the co-conspirator's out-of-court statements into evidence.

FACTS: Inadi (D) was involved with three other persons in the manufacture and distribution of methamphetamine. The police lawfully intercepted and recorded five telephone conversations between various participants in the conspiracy to produce and distribute the drug. The conspirators were apprehended and charged with conspiracy to manufacture and distribute methamphetamine. At trial, the tapes of the conversations among the co-conspirators were played for the jury. The conversations dealt with various aspects of the conspiracy, including planned meetings. Inadi (D) sought to exclude the recorded statements of one of the co-conspirators, Lazaro, on the grounds that the statements did not satisfy the requirements of Fed. R. Evid. 801(d)(2)(E) governing admission of co-conspirator declarations. The trial court admitted the evidence, finding that the statements had been made by co-conspirators during the course of and in furtherance of the conspiracy, thereby satisfying Rule 801(d)(2)(E). Inadi (D) was convicted and appealed, contending that the trial court erroneously admitted Lazaro's statements and that Inadi's (D) rights under the Confrontation Clause of the Sixth Amendment had been violated. The Court of Appeals reversed and the U.S. Supreme Court granted certiorari.

ISSUE: Does the Confrontation Clause require that a non-testifying co-conspirator be unavailable to testify as a condition for admission of that co-conspirator's out-of-court statements into evidence?

HOLDING AND DECISION: (Powell, J.) No. The Confrontation Clause does not require that a nontestifying co-conspirator be unavailable to testify as a condition for admission of that co-conspirator's out-of-court statements into evidence. Because co-conspirator statements are made while the conspiracy is in progress, such statements provide evidence of the conspiracy's

context that cannot be replicated, even if the declarant testifies to the same matters in court. When the government (P), as here, offers the statement of one drug dealer to another in furtherance of an illegal conspiracy, the statement will often derive its significance from the circumstances in which it was made. Even when a declarant, such as Lazaro, takes the stand, his in-court testimony seldom will reproduce a significant portion of the evidentiary value of his statements during the course of the conspiracy. An unavailability rule cannot be supported when a defendant himself can call and cross-examine co-conspirator declarants. Reversed.

EDITOR'S ANALYSIS: The Confrontation Clause is applicable only to criminal prosecutions or investigative proceedings criminal in nature. It may be invoked only by the accused. Thus, it is unavailable to the prosecution in a criminal proceeding or to either party in a civil proceeding. So basic are the values served by the Clause, however, that it is occasionally extended to persons other than criminal defendants, such as those who have passed the bar exam but have been denied admission to the bar, as a due process protection.

NOTES:

BOURJAILY v. UNITED STATES

Convicted drug distributor (D) v. Federal government (P)

483 U.S. 171 (1987).

NATURE OF CASE: Appeal from conviction for conspiracy to distribute cocaine and possession of cocaine with intent to distribute.

FACT SUMMARY: In the government's (P) conspiracy case against Bourjaily (D), an out-of-court telephone statement by his alleged coconspirator Lonardo was admitted to show that Bourjaily (D) had participated in the conspiracy. Bourjaily (D) claimed, among other things, that the Confrontation Clause of the U.S. Constitution required that the court independently examine the reliability of the statement before admitting it as an exception to the hearsay rule pursuant to Federal Rule of Evidence 801(d)(2)(E).

CONCISE RULE OF LAW: The Confrontation Clause does not require a court to make an independent inquiry into the reliability of out-of-court statements made by an alleged co-conspirator that otherwise satisfy the requirements of Federal Rule of Evidence 801(d)(2)(E).

FACTS: Bourjaily (D) was charged with conspiring to distribute cocaine and with possession of cocaine with intent to distribute. Over Bourjaily's (D) objection at trial, the government (P) introduced the telephone statement of Lonardo, one of Bourjaily's (D) coconspirators, which implicated Bourjaily (D) in the crimes. The court decided that the government (P) had established, by a preponderance of the evidence, that a conspiracy involving Lonardo and Bourjaily (D) existed and the Lonardo's statements over the phone had been made in the course of and in furtherance of the conspiracy. Thus, the statements satisfied Fed. R. Evid. 801(d)(2)(E) and were not hearsay. Bourjaily (D) was convicted on both counts and appealed. The court of appeals affirmed, rejecting Bourjaily's (D) contention that because he could not cross-examine Lonardo, the admission of Lonardo's statement violated Bourjaily's (D) constitutional right to confront the witnesses against him. The Supreme Court granted certiorari.

ISSUE: Does the Confrontation Clause require a court to make an independent inquiry into the reliability of out-of-court statements made by an alleged co-conspirator that otherwise satisfy the requirements of Fed. R. Evid. 801(d)(2)(E)?

HOLDING AND DECISION: (Rehnquist, C.J.) No. The Confrontation Clause does not require a court to make an independent inquiry into the reliability of out-of-court statements made by an alleged co-conspirator that otherwise satisfy the requirements of Fed. R. Evid. 801(d)(2)(E). The Court has not taken a literal approach to the Confrontation Clause. Such an approach could bar the use of any out-of-court statement, and is too extreme. Instead, the Court has required the prosecution to demonstrate both the unavailability of the declarant and the "indicia of reliability" surrounding the out-of-court statement. As with the unavailability requirement, the "independent indicia of reliability" requirement is not mandated by the Constitution. This is because the hearsay rules and the Confrontation Clause protect similar values and "stem from the same roots." Therefore, no independent inquiry into reliability is required when the evidence falls within a well-established hearsay exception, such as the co-conspirator exception—which is "steeped in our jurisprudence."

EDITOR'S ANALYSIS: Under Fed. R. Evid. 801(d)(2)(E), the existence of a conspiracy in fact is sufficient to support admissibility of evidence. A conspiracy count in the indictment is not required nor does the declarant need be indicted. The evidence is similarly admissible in civil cases, where the conspiracy rule applies to tortfeasors acting in concert.

NOTES:

IDAHO v. WRIGHT
State (P) v. Sexual abuser (D)
497 U.S.. 805 (1990).

NATURE OF CASE: Appeal from reversal of conviction for sexual abuse of a minor.

FACT SUMMARY: Wright's (D) 2½-year-old daughter told her pediatrician that Wright (D) had sexually abused her and her 5½-year-old sister, and the trial court admitted this hearsay under the "residual" exception to the hearsay rule in part because it was corroborated by actual physical evidence of abuse of the two girls.

CONCISE RULE OF LAW: An out-of-court statement of an unavailable declarant which does not fall within a "firmly rooted" hearsay exception is not admissible under the "residual" hearsay exception as particularly trustworthy merely because other evidence corroborates the statement.

FACTS: Wright (D) had two daughters, aged 2½ and 5½ years. She assisted Giles in sexually abusing them. After the adults were apprehended for the abuse, the children were medically examined and physical evidence of the abuse obtained. Further, during an interview with a pediatrician, the younger daughter volunteered that Giles "does do this with me, but he does it a lot more with my sister than with me." At the trial of Wright (D) and Giles, the younger daughter was found incapable of communicating with a jury, and thus unavailable. The trial judge then admitted the 2½-year-old's statement to the pediatrician under the Idaho equivalent of the "residual" exception to the hearsay rule, even though there was some evidence that the pediatrician's interview manner was suggestive and leading. On Wright's (D) appeal from the conviction involving her younger daughter, the Idaho Supreme Court held that admission of the testimony violated the federal Confrontation Clause. The Supreme Court granted certiorari.

ISSUE: Is an out-of-court statement of an unavailable declarant which does not fall within a firmly rooted hearsay exception made admissible under the "residual" hearsay exception as particularly trustworthy merely because other independent evidence corroborates the statement?

HOLDING AND DECISION: (O'Connor, J.) No. An out-of-court statement of an unavailable declarant which does not fall within a "firmly rooted" hearsay exception is not admissible under the "residual" hearsay exception as particularly trustworthy merely because other evidence corroborates the statement. An out-of-court statement of an unavailable declarant has sufficient "indicia of reliability" to be admitted only if it falls within a firmly-rooted hearsay exception or whether it is supported by a showing of particularized guarantees of trustworthiness. The "residual" hearsay exception, which accommodates ad hoc instances in which statements not otherwise falling within a recognized exception might nevertheless be sufficiently reliable to be admissible, does not qualify as a "firmly rooted" hearsay exception, and therefore must meet the latter test. "Particularized guarantees of trustworthiness" is determined by consideration of the circumstances that surround the making of the statement and that render the declarant particularly worthy of belief. Corroborating evidence to support "particularized guarantees" would be presumptively unreliable, however, because it would have the effect of "bootstrapping" on the trustworthiness of other evidence at trial. Here, for example, the government attempted to corroborate Wright's (D) daughter's description of sexual abuse by medical evidence of abuse, but this sheds no light on the childs allegations regarding the identity of the abuser. Nor should the government have tried to show the trustworthiness of the daughter's statement by evidence of Wright's (D) opportunity to commit the abuse and the older daughter's confirming testimony. Instead, the only proper factors considered were whether the child had a motive to make up a story of this nature and whether, given the child's age, the statements are of the type that one would expect a child to fabricate. The mere fact that a 2½-year-old probably would not make up a story of abuse or have a motive for doing so is insufficient standing on its own to guarantee the trustworthiness of her statement. Affirmed.

EDITOR'S ANALYSIS: The Supreme Court here also found that the younger daughter's statements did not meet the strict admissibility standard of trustworthiness because her pediatrician was suggestive and leading in his questioning of the girl. Accordingly, the fact that the girl, after "clamming up," suddenly blurted out her incriminating statement, was not necessarily indicative of trustworthiness because spontaneity following prior interrogation, manipulation, or prompting is inherently suspect. But see J. Myers, Child Witness Law and Practice § 4.6, 129-134 (1987) (use of leading questions with children, when appropriate, does not necessarily render responses untrustworthy).

WHITE v. ILLINOIS
Criminal convict (D) v. State (P)
502 U.S. 346 (1992).

NATURE OF CASE: Appeal from denial of motion for a mistrial.

FACT SUMMARY: In a criminal action in Illinois (P) against White (D), the appellate court, affirming the trial court's ruling, denied White's (D) motion for a mistrial based on the admissibility of out-of-court testimony, even though his accuser was present during trial.

CONCISE RULE OF LAW: The Sixth Amendment Confrontation Clause does not prohibit the admission of testimony under the "spontaneous declaration" and "medical examination" exceptions to the hearsay rule.

FACTS: After White (D) was convicted by a jury for aggravated criminal sexual assault, residential burglary, and unlawful restraint, the appellate court, affirming the trial court's ruling, denied his motion for a mistrial in light of the trial court's determination that out-of-court accusatory statements by S.G., his four-year-old alleged victim, were admissible under the spontaneous declaration and medical examination exceptions to the hearsay rule, despite her presence and failure to testify at trial.

ISSUE: Does the Sixth Amendment Confrontation Clause prohibit the admission of testimony under the "spontaneous declaration" and "medical examination" exceptions to the hearsay rule?

HOLDING AND DECISION: (Rehnquist, C.J.) No. The Sixth Amendment Confrontation Clause does not prohibit the admission of testimony under the "spontaneous declaration" and "medical examination" exceptions to the hearsay rule. The Confrontation Clause and the hearsay rule generally conform to the same purpose, which is the promotion of fact-finding integrity. In this end, certain "firmly rooted" exceptions to the hearsay rule carry sufficient corroborative weight so as to satisfy the reliability requirement posed by the Confrontation Clause. In the instant case, since the trial court determined that the statements S.G. made triggered the application of the spontaneous declaration and medical examination exceptions to the hearsay rule, and since these exceptions are "firmly rooted" in this country's jurisprudence, White's (D) motion for a mistrial is denied. Affirmed.

CONCURRENCE: (Thomas, J.) The Confrontation Clause is implicated by extrajudicial statements only insofar as they are contained in formalized testimonial materials, such as affidavits, depositions, prior testimony, or confessions.

EDITOR'S ANALYSIS: Despite having no textual basis in the Sixth Amendment to reach its result, the majority above assumes that the Confrontation Clause limits admission of hearsay evidence insofar as it does not bear a particularized guarantee of trustworthiness. Notwithstanding this ostensibly evenhanded rule, however, courts accordingly will have wide discretionary latitude in determining a statement's trustworthiness.

LILLY v. VIRGINIA
Convicted robber (D) v. State (P)
527 U.S. 116 (1999).

NATURE OF CASE: Appeal from convictions for robbery, abduction, carjacking, possession of a firearm by a felon, four charges of illegal use of a firearm, and capital murder.

FACT SUMMARY: Over Benjamin Lee Lilly's (D) objection, the trial court allowed the Commonwealth (P) to introduce statements made by codefendant Mark Lilly after his arrest.

CONCISE RULE OF LAW: A confession by a non-testifying accomplice to a crime that shifts or spreads blame is presumptively unreliable, and therefore violates the criminal defendant's rights under the Confrontation Clause.

FACTS: Benjamin Lee Lilly (D), his brother Mark Lilly, and Gary Barker were arrested for a string of robberies, a carjacking, and the murder of Alex DeFilippis. The police questioned each of the three men separately after taking them into custody. Benjamin Lilly (D) did not mention the murder and stated that the other two men forced him to participate in the robberies. Benjamin's (D) brother, Mark, and Barker both maintained that Benjamin (D) masterminded the robberies and killed DeFillippis. The Commonwealth (P) charged Benjamin (D) with several offenses, including the murder of DeFilippis, and tried him separately. At trial, the Commonwealth (P) called Mark as a witness, but he invoked the Fifth Amendment. Thus, the Commonwealth (P) offered the statements Mark made to police after his arrest, arguing they were admissible as declarations of an unavailable witness against his penal interest. Benjamin (D) objected to the admission of these statements on the grounds that they were not statements against interest, as Mark took no responsibility for the crimes, but merely implicated others, and on the grounds that their admission would violate his Sixth Amendment right to confront witnesses against him. The trial court overruled Benjamin's (D) objections and admitted the statements. The jury convicted him on all counts and the Supreme Court of Virginia (P) affirmed.

ISSUE: Is a confession by a non-testifying accomplice to a crime that shifts or spreads blame presumptively unreliable, and therefore in violation of the criminal defendant's rights under the Confrontation Clause?

HOLDING AND DECISION: (Stevens, J.) Yes. A confession by a non-testifying accomplice to a crime that shifts or spreads blame is presumptively unreliable, and therefore violates the criminal defendant's rights under the Confrontation Clause. Accomplices confessions that shift or spread blame are presumptively unreliable. In this case, the Commonwealth (P) was allowed to present Mark's statements shifting blame to his brother and

Barker. Such statements must be subjected to testing under the adversarial process. The trial court erred in allowing these statements and violated Benjamin's (D) Sixth Amendment rights. Reversed and remanded.

CONCURRENCE: (Breyer, J.) The hearsay-based Confrontation Clause test is of recent vintage, whereas the right to confront one's accuser has ancient origins that predate the hearsay rule. Some argue that the recent test is too narrow insofar as it authorizes the admission of out-of-court statements prepared as testimony for a trial when such statements happen to fall within some hearsay rule exception. Others argue the test is too broad insofar as it would make a constitutional issue out of the admission of any relevant hearsay statement, even if that statement is only tenuously related to the elements in dispute or was made long before the crime occurred. However, in this case, there is no need to evaluate these arguments or the connection between the hearsay rule and the Confrontation Clause test because the statements here violated the Clause regardless. Merely because this case does not require such a reevaluation does not mean that there will not be occasion to do so in the future.

CONCURRENCE: (Scalia, J.) The prosecution introduced a tape recording of Mark's statements without making Mark available for cross-examination, and as such committed a paradigmatic Confrontation Clause violation.

CONCURRENCE: (Thomas, J.) The Confrontation Clause extends to any witness who actually testifies at trial and is implicated by extrajudicial statements only insofar as they are contained in formalized testimonial material.

CONCURRENCE: (Rehnquist, C.J.) The Confrontation Clause does not impose a blanket ban on the government's use of accomplice statements to incriminate a defendant. The plurality erroneously addressed an issue not passed upon by the lower courts in its analysis of whether a declaration against interest is a firmly rooted exception to the hearsay rule.

EDITOR'S ANALYSIS: The plurality in *Lilly* left it up to the state courts to determine whether the Sixth Amendment error was harmless beyond a reasonable doubt.

CHAMBERS v. MISSISSIPPI
Convicted murderer (D) v. State (P)
410 U.S. 284 (1973).

NATURE OF CASE: Appeal from conviction for murder.

FACT SUMMARY: Chambers (D) was convicted of murder after not being allowed to show that a witness whom he called to testify confessed to the killing to three of his friends on the ground that such confessions were hearsay.

CONCISE RULE OF LAW: Where constitutional rights directly affecting the ascertainment of guilt are implicated, the hearsay rule may not be applied mechanically so to defeat the ends of justice.

FACTS: Chambers (D) was tried and convicted of murdering a policeman during a confrontation between a few policemen and several townspeople when the former were attempting to arrest one of the latter. McDonald, a town resident, after talking to Rev. Stokes, agreed to see Chambers's (D) lawyers and confess to the killing. He did so, was jailed, but was later released upon repudiating his confession, which he claimed was prompted by a promise of a share in a tort recovery which Chambers (P) would get from the town. At trial, Chambers (D) tried to show that McDonald committed the crime. Hardin testified that he saw McDonald, his long-time friend, shoot the officer. Additionally, Chambers (D) sought to show that McDonald not only confessed to his lawyers, but that he confessed to three of his friends. Chambers (D) called McDonald to testify when the State (P) failed to do so. McDonald again repudiated his confession. The court denied Chambers's (D) motion that McDonald be declared an adverse witness. It also prevented three of McDonald's friends from testifying that he confessed to them on the ground that such a confession was hearsay. Under Mississippi (P) law, a person who presents a witness vouches for his credibility, and the hearsay exception for declarations against interest applies only when that interest is pecuniary, while here it was not. Chambers (D) appealed his conviction on due process grounds.

ISSUE: Where constitutional rights directly affecting the ascertainment of guilt are implicated, may the hearsay rule be applied mechanically so to defeat the ends of justice?

HOLDING AND DECISION: (Powell, J.) No. Where constitutional rights directly affecting the ascertainment of guilt are implicated, the hearsay rule may not be applied mechanically to defeat the ends of justice. Chambers (D) was not allowed to subject McDonald's repudiation and alibi to cross-examination. Cross-examination is fundamental to assuring the accuracy of the truth-determining process. The voucher rule, which does not allow a party to impeach his own witness, bears little usefulness to the criminal process. Here, it not only precluded cross-examination, it restricted the scope of direct examination. The right to confront and cross-examine has never depended on who put the witness on the stand. As for declarations against interest, most states will not admit them even when they are against a penal interest. But here, several circumstances assured the declaration's reliability: (1) Each of McDonald's confessions was spontaneous and made shortly after the killing; (2) each one was corroborated by some other evidence; (3) each was unquestionably against interest; and (4) McDonald was present in the courtroom to explain under oath his declaration. The testimony was absolutely critical to Chambers' (D) defense. Reversed and remanded.

EDITOR'S ANALYSIS: The Court specifically noted that by this case it was not creating any new principles in constitutional law. Rather, the trial rules in question were not "in accord with traditional and fundamental standards of due process." Further, the decision was not intended to diminish each state's ability to create its own trial rules. It would appear arguable, however, that the Court believes hearsay statements should be admitted when trustworthy. The Court does not require the states to go that far as long as their rules do not offend notions of due process.

NOTES:

GREEN v. GEORGIA
Convicted murderer (D) v. State (P)
442 U.S. 95 (1979).

NATURE OF CASE: Appeal from a murder conviction.

FACT SUMMARY: The trial court refused to admit Pasby's testimony that Moore said to him he had committed the murder after sending Green (D) away on an errand, holding it was inadmissible hearsay.

CONCISE RULE OF LAW: The hearsay rule will not apply where exclusion of the evidence would deny a criminal defendant due process of law.

FACTS: Green (D) and Moore were indicted together for rape and murder, yet were tried separately. At Moore's trial, the State (P) introduced testimony of Pasby, who said Moore had confided in him that he killed the victim after ordering Green (D) to run an errand. The statement had been made spontaneously, and Pasby was a close friend of Moore's. After Moore's conviction, Green (D) was tried and prohibited from introducing Pasby's testimony by the trial court, which held it was inadmissible hearsay. Green (D) was convicted of murder and received a capital sentence. He appealed, but the Supreme Court of Georgia upheld the conviction and sentence. Green (D) appealed to the U.S. Supreme Court.

ISSUE: Will the hearsay rule apply, even where exclusion of the evidence would constitute a denial of due process to a criminal defendant?

HOLDING AND DECISION: (Per curiam) No. The hearsay rule will not apply where exclusion of the evidence would constitute a denial of due process to the criminal defendant. In this case, the testimony was highly relevant to a critical issue in the case. Its spontaneous nature and the fact it was spoken to a close friend support its reliability. Furthermore, the statements were against Moore's interest, indicating he had nothing to gain by lying in this way. Finally, the State (P) considered the testimony sufficiently reliable to use it to convict Moore of a capital crime. As a result, under these circumstances, it would defeat the ends of justice and deny Green (D) due process of law to apply the hearsay rule to exclude the testimony. Reversed and remanded.

DISSENT: (Rehnquist, J.) The Court's ruling is without constitutional justification. It is a maxim of evidence law that certain items are admissible against one party but not another.

EDITOR'S ANALYSIS: This case applies the rule articulated in *Chambers v. Mississippi*, 410 U.S. 284 (1973). In that case, the Court held that the hearsay rule could not be invoked to exclude evidence in a criminal trial if the result of the exclusion would be the denial of a fair trial. This exception is therefore constitutionally based and applies only in criminal trials. Its application is rare, and generally a criminal defendant is limited in his use of hear-say to specific exceptions.

NOTES:

CHAPTER FOUR
A RETURN TO RELEVANCE

QUICK REFERENCE RULES OF LAW

1. **Scientific Evidence.** Applications of mathematical techniques in the proof of facts in a criminal case must be critically examined in view of the substantial unfairness to the defendant which may result. (People v. Collins)

2. **Admissibility of Blood Type Evidence.** Evidence that an assailant's semen contains type A blood is admissible unless it can be shown such evidence has prejudiced the defendant. (People v. Mountain)

3. **Scientific Evidence and Expert Witnesses.** The admission of statistical or mathematical evidence substantiated by expert witnesses, when relevant to prove the ultimate issue in a case, does not violate the due process rights of the defendant. (Kammer v. Young)

4. **Habit Evidence.** Evidence of a person's intemperate habits is admissible in an action against the person's employer for the purpose of proving that the employer knew of his intemperate habits and to support a claim for exemplary damages. (Cleghorn v. New York Central & H. River Ry. Co.)

5. **"Michelson Dodge."** When a defendant puts his character at issue through the introduction of reputation evidence, the prosecution may ask these witnesses if they have heard of specific acts of bad conduct relating to the defendant. (Michelson v. United States)

6. **Other Crimes, Wrongs or Acts.** Although Federal Rule of Evidence 404(b) prohibits evidence of other crimes, wrongs, or acts to prove the character of a person, extrinsic acts may be admissible for other purposes, such as identity, if the extrinsic acts bear a high degree of similarity to mark them as the handiwork of the accused. (United States v. Carrillo)

7. **Character to Prove Conduct.** Evidence of other crimes, wrongs, or acts is not admissible to prove the character of a person in order to show that he acted in conformity therewith. (United States v. Beasley)

8. **Prior Conduct Evidence.** Evidence of prior conduct may be introduced to show the defendant's motive for committing the crime for which she is charged. (United States v. Cunningham)

9. **Evidence of Earlier Crime.** Evidence of a prior crime for which the criminal defendant was never convicted is inadmissible. (Tucker v. State)

10. **Character as Circumstantial Evidence.** A court need not make, prior to admitting post acts introduced to show motive or knowledge, a preliminary finding that the acts occurred. (Huddleston v. United States)

11. **Forms of Proof of Character.** When character evidence is used circumstantially, only reputation and opinion are acceptable forms of proof. (Perrin v. Anderson)

12. **Routine Practice.** At least where the issue involves proof of a deliberate and repetitive practice, a party should be able to introduce evidence of habit or regular usage to allow the inference of its persistence, and hence negligence, on a particular occasion. (Halloran v. Virginia Chemicals, Inc.)

13. **Rape Shield Laws.** Evidence of a rape victim's prior sexual conduct, other than that between the victim and the defendant, is inadmissible. (State v. Cassidy)

14. Prior Sexual Conduct. The Confrontation Clause mandates that a defendant be permitted to cross-examine a witness on any relevant matter. (Olden v. Kentucky)

15. Conditional Relevancy of Evidence. If the relevancy of the evidence that the accused seeks to offer depends upon the fulfillment of a condition of fact, it is for the jury to determine whether such condition of fact is fulfilled. (United States v. Platero)

16. Admission of Prior Sexual Misconduct. Evidence of prior sexual misconduct may be excluded where a jury could not reasonably conclude by a preponderance of the evidence that the past act was a sexual assault, or, even where the jury could reasonably find that the prior act was a sexual assault, where the evidence's probative value is substantially outweighed by the danger of unfair prejudice, confusion of the issues, misleading of the jury, or by considerations of undue delay, waste of time, or needless presentation of cumulative evidence. (Johnson v. Elk Lake School District)

17. Information on Absence of Mistaken Accident. Evidence of other similar accidents or occurrences that is relevant circumstantially to show a defective or dangerous condition, notice thereof, or causation on the occasion in question, is admissible. (Simon v. Kennebunkport)

18. Subsequent Remedial Measures. Evidence of subsequent remedial measures is not admissible to prove culpability. (Tuer v. McDonald)

19. Compromise and Settlement Negotiations. Offers to compromise made in the course of settlement negotiations are not admissible to prove liability for or invalidity of the claim or its amount. (Davidson v. Prince)

20. Admissibility of Pleas. Evidence of a guilty plea entered in a traffic court is admissible in a subsequent suit for damages. (Ando v. Woodberry)

PEOPLE v. COLLINS
State (P) v. Robbery convict (D)
Cal. Sup. Ct., 68 Cal. 2d 319, 438 P.2d 33 (1968).

NATURE OF CASE: Appeal from conviction of second-degree robbery.

FACT SUMMARY: In the People's (P) suit against Collins (D) for second-degree armed robbery, Collins (D) contended that testimony admitted into evidence at trial as to the mathematical probability that Collins (D) committed the crime unduly influenced the jury and infected the case with fatal error.

CONCISE RULE OF LAW: Applications of mathematical techniques in the proof of facts in a criminal case must be critically examined in view of the substantial unfairness to the defendant which may result.

FACTS: In the People's (P) suit against Collins (D) for second-degree robbery, the prosecution experienced some difficulty in establishing the perpetrators of the robbery. In order to bolster the identification of Collins (D) as the perpetrator, the prosecutor called a mathematics instructor from a state college who testified about the mathematical probability that persons who possessed the various characteristics possessed by Collins (D) and his wife, a co-defendant, existed. The witness inferred that there could be but one chance in twelve million that Collins (D) and his wife were innocent and that another equally distinctive couple actually committed the robbery. Collins (D) objected to the witness's testimony on the grounds that it was based on unfounded assumptions. Collins (D) was convicted and appealed on the grounds that the mathematician's testimony infected the case with fatal error.

ISSUE: Must applications of mathematical techniques in the proof of facts in a criminal case be critically examined in view of the substantial unfairness to the defendant which may result?

HOLDING AND DECISION: (Sullivan, J.) Yes. Application of mathematical techniques in the proof of facts in a criminal case must be critically examined in view of the substantial unfairness to the defendant which may result. Here, the prosecution's theory of probability rested on the assumption that the witness called by the People (P) had conclusively established that the guilty couple possessed the precise characteristics relied upon by the prosecution. But no mathematical formula could ever establish beyond a reasonable doubt that the prosecution's witness correctly observed and accurately described the distinctive features which were employed to link the Collinses (D) to the crime. The most a mathematical computation could ever yield would be a measure of the probability that a random couple would possess the distinctive features in question. Reversed.

DISSENT: (McComb, J.) The judgment should be affirmed in its entirety.

EDITOR'S ANALYSIS: It appears that the explicit use of theories of probability and statistical inference remains controversial. This is true whether the theories serve either as a basis for the opinions of the experts themselves or as a course of education for jurors in how to think about scientific identification evidence. However, as long as counsel and the experts don't try to place a scientific seal of approval on results not shown to be grounded in science, there is probably room for judicious use of these theories to put identification evidence in perspective.

NOTES:

PEOPLE v. MOUNTAIN
State (P) v. Convicted criminal (D)
N.Y. Ct. App., 486 N.E.2d 802 (1985).

NATURE OF CASE: Appeal from criminal conviction.

FACT SUMMARY: Mountain (D) claimed that it was error to admit evidence that the assailant's sperm contained a certain blood type and to allow references to Mountain's (D) blood type.

CONCISE RULE OF LAW: Evidence that an assailant's semen contains type A blood is admissible unless it can be shown such evidence has prejudiced the defendant.

FACTS: Mountain (D) was convicted of a crime. He claimed that it was error to admit evidence that the assailant's sperm contained type A blood and to allow references to Mountain's (D) blood type. He relied on *People v. Robinson* (27 NY2d 864), where the court held that proof that semen found in and on the victim came from a man with a certain blood type was not probative in the case against the defendant in view of the large proportion of the general population having that blood type.

ISSUE: Is evidence that an assailant's semen contains type A blood admissible unless it can be shown such evidence has prejudiced the defendant?

HOLDING AND DECISION: [Judge not stated in casebook excerpt.] Yes. Evidence that an assailant's semen contains type A blood is admissible unless it can be shown such evidence has prejudiced the defendant. Noted scholars have criticized the *Robinson* rule because although blood grouping may only show that defendant and the assailant are part of a large group having that particular characteristic, it does not follow that such proof completely lacks probative value. When identity is in issue, proof that the defendant and the perpetrator share similar physical characteristics (e.g., race, gender) is not rendered inadmissible simply because those characteristics are also shared by large segments of the population. Proof of such common characteristics may acquire great probative value when considered cumulatively. *Robinson* is, therefore, overruled. Any undue prejudice may be avoided by proper instructions. If the defendant can show that the potential prejudice outweighs the probative value, the court may in its discretion exclude the evidence. Here, there was no showing that Mountain (D) was prejudiced. Affirmed.

EDITOR'S ANALYSIS: Instructions that can avoid prejudice regarding blood-type evidence must emphasize, among other things, that the evidence is only circumstantial, and should note the percentage of the population involved. For example, people with blood type A comprise 40% of the population.

NOTES:

KAMMER v. YOUNG
Biological mother (P) v. Biological father (D)
Md. Ct. Spec. App., 73 Md. App. 565, 535 A.2d 936 (1988).

NATURE OF CASE: Appeal from judicial determination of paternity.

FACT SUMMARY: Kammer (D) was judicially determined to be the father of a child borne by Young (D) after a blood test provided the basis for the estimation that the statistical probability of Kammer's (P) paternity was 99.78%.

CONCISE RULE OF LAW: The admission of statistical or mathematical evidence substantiated by expert witnesses, when relevant to prove the ultimate issue in a case, does not violate the due process rights of the defendant.

FACTS: Young (P) bore a child and claimed that Kammer (D) was the father because he was the only man with whom she had had sex in the year prior to the child's birth. Kammer (D), in turn, claimed that he had stopped having sex with Young (P) fifteen months before the child's birth. In Young's (P) paternity suit against Kammer (P), Kammer (D) was required by Maryland law to submit to a blood test. The test produced a paternity index, or the ratio expressing the odds that the accused is the father of a child based on his chance of producing a sperm with the genetic information found in the child compared to finding such a sperm in the general population. Kammer's (D) paternity index was 460 to 1. Using a mathematical technique known as Bayes's Theorem, the statistical probability of Kammer's (D) paternity was calculated based on this paternity index to be 99.78%. Maryland law allowed receipt of evidence in paternity suits of testing which resulted in a probability of at least 97.3%; accordingly, the court admitted the evidence of Kammer's (D) statistical probability of being the father of Young's (P) child. Kammer (D) was formally adjudged the father, but he appealed, asserting that the admission of opinion evidence on his "statistical probability" of paternity violated his due process rights and prevented him from getting a fair trial.

ISSUE: When relevant to prove an ultimate issue in a case, does the admission of statistical or mathematical evidence substantiated by expert witnesses violate the due process rights of the defendant?

HOLDING AND DECISION: (Bishop, J.) No. The admission of statistical or mathematical evidence substantiated by expert witnesses, when relevant to prove an ultimate issue in a case, does not violate the due process rights of a defendant. Here, all experts agreed on the final calculation of Kammer's (D) statistical probability of being the father of Young's (P) child as 99.78%, using the widely established mathematical technique of Bayes's Theorem as applied to the paternity index. This methodology was not invalidated by the use of a "prior probability" figure of 0.5, which is the standard used in such tests and represents the accumulated non-genetic evidence that tends to indicate the accused man's paternity. Kammer (D) was free to present non-genetic evidence which disputed his paternity and to present opposing witnesses to discredit Bayes's Theorem, the paternity index, and the 0.5 prior probability factor. Affirmed.

EDITOR'S ANALYSIS: In this case, the Maryland court declined to reconsider a previous case, *Haines v. Shanholtz*, 57 Md.App. 92, 468 A.2d 1365, cert. denied 300 Md. 90, 475 A.2d 1201 (1984), in which it held that blood test results which met certain threshold requirements were admissible. See Md.Fam.Law § 5-1029 (relied on in the principal case). Other examples of widely used statistical evidence which are routinely received are blood traces or hair samples used to identify an accused as a criminal at the scene of the crime, and fingerprints (which is really identification evidence the reliability of which is so high that its statistical base is disregarded entirely).

NOTES:

CLEGHORN v. NEW YORK CENTRAL & H. RIVER RY. CO.

Injured claimant (P) v. Common carrier (D)

N.Y. Ct. App., 56 N.Y. 44 (1874).

NATURE OF CASE: Action to recover damages for negligence.

FACT SUMMARY: The accident in which Cleghorn (D) was injured was caused by the carelessness of New York Central's (D) switchman. Evidence of the switchman's intemperate habits was admitted.

CONCISE RULE OF LAW: Evidence of a person's intemperate habits is admissible in an action against the person's employer for the purpose of proving that the employer knew of his intemperate habits and to support a claim for exemplary damages.

FACTS: The accident in which Cleghorn (P) was injured was caused by the negligence of New York Central's (D) switchman. New York Central (D) contended that the trial court erred in admitting evidence of the intemperate habits of the switchman. The evidence was admitted to show that New York Central (D) knew of the switchman's intemperance with a view toward claiming exemplary damages.

ISSUE: Can evidence of a person's intemperate habits be introduced in an action against the person's employer for the purpose of proving that the employer knew of his intemperance to support a claim for exemplary damages?

HOLDING AND DECISION: (Church, C.J.) Yes. Evidence of a person's intemperate habits is admissible in an action against the person's employer for the purpose of proving that the employer knew of his intemperate habits and to support a claim for exemplary damages. In *Warner v. N.Y.C.R.R. Co.*, 44 N.Y. 465, there was an injury at a road crossing. It was proved that the flagman neglected to give the customary signal and was intoxicated at the time. It was held that it was error to allow evidence of previous habits of intemperance known to the officers of the company upon the ground that such evidence had no bearing upon the question of negligence at the time of the evidence. Here, however, the evidence of the switchman's intemperance was introduced to prove not only that he was intoxicated at the time of the accident, but also that his employer knew of his intemperance with a view toward claiming exemplary damages. For this purpose the evidence was competent.

EDITOR'S ANALYSIS: The phrase, "habits of intemperance" may denote a general disposition for excessive drinking or may amount to a specific habit of drinking a certain number of glasses of whiskey every day on going home from work. The probative force of such habits to prove drunkenness on a specific occasion depends on the degree of regularity of the practice and its coincidence with the occasion. On the other hand, "habits" of sobriety may well point to unvarying temperance or abstention and would seem to be highly probative on the question of sobriety on the particular occasion. Evidence of a habit of being drunk has sometimes been considered probative enough to be admissible when there is other evidence but not sufficient standing alone to be admissible to show a drunken condition at a particular time.

NOTES:

MICHELSON v. UNITED STATES
Bribery defendant (D) v. Federal government (P)
335 U.S. 469 (1948).

NATURE OF CASE: Appeal from a conviction of bribery.

FACT SUMMARY: Michelson (D) claimed that he had been entrapped by the official he had allegedly bribed. He introduced testimony as to his good reputation.

CONCISE RULE OF LAW: When a defendant puts his character at issue through the introduction of reputation evidence, the prosecution may ask these witnesses if they have heard of specific acts of bad conduct relating to the defendant.

FACTS: Michelson (D) was accused of bribing an official. Michelson (D) claimed that the official had demanded the money and had threatened to use his official power against Michelson (D) if the money was not paid. Michelson (D) claimed this was entrapment. The trial revolved upon who the jury chose to believe, the official or Michelson (D). Michelson (D) introduced reputation evidence as to his own good reputation in the community. The prosecutor asked these witnesses if they had heard that Michelson (D) had been arrested for buying stolen goods some 20 years earlier. These questions were allowed over Michelson's (D) objection. The jury found him guilty.

ISSUE: May witnesses testifying to defendant's reputation in the community be asked if they have heard of specific bad acts committed by the defendant?

HOLDING AND DECISION: (Jackson, J.) Yes. Where a defendant puts his reputation at issue through the introduction of reputation evidence, the prosecution may ask these witnesses if they have heard of specific acts of bad conduct relating to the defendant. This includes specific acts of misconduct. The acts need not be identical to the charges raised against the defendant. It is sufficient that they cast doubt upon his truth, veracity, or reputation in the community. The law in this area is convoluted and archaic. The prosecution may not attempt to prove the defendant's bad character. However, the defendant may introduce evidence as to his good general reputation in the community. No specific acts may be testified to by these witnesses. Once the defendant has placed his reputation in issue the witnesses may be cross-examined as to specific acts of misconduct. These may include arrests where there was no conviction or even no indictment. These test the witnesses' knowledge of the defendant's reputation. A twenty-seven-year-old conviction may be excluded at the judge's discretion since the defendant may have been rehabilitated. Here, however, Michelson's (D) attorney mentioned a twenty-year-old conviction of a misdemeanor for trading in counterfeit watch dials. It was within the court's discretion to allow the admission of the earlier

crime. The earlier crimes tended to diminish Michelson's (D) reputation evidence. The fact that they were old merely goes to the weight that the jury wishes to place upon these specific acts. Judgment affirmed.

CONCURRENCE: (Frankfurter, J.) Rigid evidentiary rules should be discouraged. I would reserve the decision to the sound discretion of the district courts.

EDITOR'S ANALYSIS: The prosecution may introduce specific acts of misconduct where they show an ongoing conspiracy, establish a common plan, or establish the defendant's modus operandi. In *Hamilton v. State*, the Florida Supreme Court allowed the defendant to introduce reputation testimony from her fellow workers, even though she lived in a different area of the city and they never saw her socially.

NOTES:

UNITED STATES v. CARRILLO
Federal government (P) v. Drug dealer (D)
981 F.2d 772 (5th Cir. 1993).

NATURE OF CASE: Review of criminal conviction for distribution of heroin and cocaine.

FACT SUMMARY: Carrillo (D) contended that the court erred in admitting evidence of extrinsic acts.

CONCISE RULE OF LAW: Although Federal Rule of Evidence 404(b) prohibits evidence of other crimes, wrongs, or acts to prove the character of a person, extrinsic acts may be admissible for other purposes, such as identity, if the extrinsic acts bear a high degree of similarity to mark them as the handiwork of the accused.

FACTS: Carrillo (D) was arrested and charged with distribution of cocaine and heroin. Prior to trial, Carrillo (D) attempted to exclude the introduction of evidence of two extrinsic acts of selling heroin. The court ruled that if Carrillo (D) raised the issue of identity at trial, then the United States (P) could use the extrinsic evidence to prove identity. At trial, Carrillo (D) claimed he was not at the scene of the crime, thereby raising the issue of identity, and the United States (P) called a police officer to testify about Carrillo's (D) prior offenses. Carrillo (D) was found guilty, and he appealed.

ISSUE: Under Fed. R. Evid. 404(b), are extrinsic acts admissible for other purposes such as identity, if the extrinsic acts bear a high degree of similarity to mark them as the handiwork of the accused?

HOLDING AND DECISION: (DeMoss, J.) Yes. Although Fed. R. Evid. 404(b) prohibits evidence of other crimes, wrongs, or acts to prove the character of a person, extrinsic acts may be admissible for other purposes, such as identity, if the extrinsic acts bear a high degree of similarity to mark them as the handiwork of the accused. In this case, the government (P) did not prove that Carrillo's (D) prior offenses were sufficiently similar to the charges at issue, nor did the government (P) show that the prior offenses were sufficiently unique from the typical drug deal. Thus, testimony regarding the extrinsic acts did not corroborate Carrillo's (D) identity as the drug seller by similar or unique elements of the transaction. Therefore, the court erred in admitting the extrinsic evidence of Carrillo's (D) prior drug offenses. Vacated and remanded.

EDITOR'S ANALYSIS: Character evidence is excluded not because it lacks probative value but because it may cause a jury to convict, regardless of guilt. Although Fed. R. Evid. 404(b) prohibits character evidence to prove the accused acted in conformity therewith, evidence of other crimes, wrongs, or acts can be admitted for other purposes, such as proof of motive, opportunity, intent, preparation, plan, knowledge, identity or

absence of mistake or accident. In order to prevent admitted evidence of extrinsic acts from being misused, the court employs procedural controls such as a limiting instruction to the jury that the evidence should only be used for one of the above stated purposes.

NOTES:

UNITED STATES v. BEASLEY
Federal government (P) v. Scientist (D)
809 F.2d 1273 (7th Cir. 1987).

NATURE OF CASE: Appeal from conviction for obtaining and distributing a controlled substance.

FACT SUMMARY: In the government's (P) case against Beasley (D) for obtaining and distributing a controlled substance, Dilaudid, in violation of 21 U.S.C. § 841 (a)(1), Beasley (D) contended that the prosecution's introduction of evidence of other crimes committed by him violated Federal Rule of Evidence 404(b) and was, therefore, inadmissible.

CONCISE RULE OF LAW: Evidence of other crimes, wrongs, or acts is not admissible to prove the character of a person in order to show that he acted in conformity therewith.

FACTS: Beasley (D), a scientist, was indicted on charges of obtaining and distributing a controlled substance, Dilaudid, in violation of 21 U.S.C. § 841(a)(1). Beasley (D) had told his physician that he needed the drug to conduct experiments on plant growth, and the physician supplied Beasley (D) with prescriptions for the drug. Allegedly, Beasley (D) did not administer the drugs to the plants but instead, sold them on the black market. At trial, the government (P) introduced evidence that Beasley (D) had, in the past, committed crimes other than those charged in this proceeding. Beasley (D) objected to the admission of this evidence, arguing that it was in violation of Fed. R. Evid. 404(b), which does not allow evidence of other crimes to be admitted to prove the character of a person to show that he acted in conformity therewith. The court allowed the evidence to be admitted; Beasley (D) was convicted and appealed.

ISSUE: Is evidence of other crimes, wrongs, or acts admissible to prove the character of a person in order to show that he acted in conformity therewith?

HOLDING AND DECISION: (Easterbrook, J.) No. Evidence of other crimes, wrongs, or acts is not admissible to prove the character of a person in order to show that he acted in conformity therewith. The evidence may, however, be admissible for other purposes, such as proof of motive, opportunity, intent, preparation, plan, knowledge, identity, or absence of mistake or accident. Intent was an issue here. Beasley (D) testified that he obtained the drugs to conduct experiments, fed the drugs to his plants, and never distributed the drugs to anyone. The government (P) contended that Beasley (D) sold the Dilaudid and did not conduct or intend to conduct experiments on the effects of narcotics on plants. Evidence that in the past Beasley (D) bilked other physicians into prescribing Dilaudid, which Beasley (D) then resold, tends to show that Beasley (D) acquired the Dilaudid at issue here with the same intent. The admission of such evidence at trial was not harmless error. The prosecutor's extensive use of other-crimes evidence to show intent weighed heavily against Beasley (D), and Beasley's (D) conviction must therefore be vacated. Reversed in part and remanded.

EDITOR'S ANALYSIS: Introduction of character evidence is strictly limited under the Federal Rules of Evidence. Such evidence is often of slight probative value and may be very prejudicial. It tends to distract the trier of fact from the main question of what happened on a particular occasion. It also subtly permits the trier of fact to reward the good person and punish the bad person because of their respective characters despite what the evidence in the case shows actually happened.

NOTES:

UNITED STATES v. CUNNINGHAM
Federal government (P) v. Accused (D)
103 F.3d. 553 (7th Cir. 1996).

NATURE OF CASE: Appeal from a criminal conviction.

FACT SUMMARY: Cunningham (D) was convicted of tampering with a consumer product with reckless disregard for the risk that another person will be placed in danger of death or bodily injury, after evidence of an earlier theft and drug addiction were admitted.

CONCISE RULE OF LAW: Evidence of prior conduct may be introduced to show the defendant's motive for committing the crime for which she is charged.

FACTS: Cunningham (D), a registered nurse at a hospital, was charged with stealing Demerol and withholding the painkiller from patients. Evidence of prior conduct was introduced to show that she was addicted to Demerol and thus had a motive to steal it. Evidence was also introduced that showed her nurse's license had been suspended and that she had falsified some previous drug tests. Cunningham (D) was convicted an appealed, claiming that the trial court abused its discretion when it allowed the introduction of evidence of her prior conduct.

ISSUE: May evidence of prior conduct be introduced to show the defendant's motive for committing the crime for which she is charged?

HOLDING AND DECISION: (Posner, C.J.) Yes. Evidence of prior conduct may be introduced to show the defendant's motive for committing the crime for which she is charged. The evidence of Cunningham's (D) addiction was thus admissible, unless the judge decided that its prejudicial effect clearly outweighed its probative value. The court decided otherwise, and we cannot say that this was an abuse of discretion. The evidence of her earlier suspension was also admissible because evidence of bad-acts is admissible to provide a contextual framework, and by contextualizing enable the jury to understand the issue, while other evidence continues to be a recognized exception to the prohibition of bad-acts evidence. Affirmed.

EDITOR'S ANALYSIS: The court in this case discussed Rule 404(b), which prohibits the introduction of a person's prior conduct for the purpose of showing a propensity to act in accordance with the character indicated by that conduct. That rule expressly allows evidence of prior wrongful acts to establish motive. The greater the overlap between propensity and motive, the more careful the district judge must be about admitting evidence that a jury is likely to use as a basis for inferring propensity.

NOTES:

TUCKER v. STATE
Murder suspect (D) v. State (P)
Nev. Sup. Ct., 82 Nev. 127, 412 P.2d 970 (1966).

NATURE OF CASE: Prosecution for second-degree murder.

FACT SUMMARY: Tucker (D) woke up to find that Evans was dead on Tucker's (D) sofa, a situation which was quite similar to an event which had happened to Tucker (D) six years earlier.

CONCISE RULE OF LAW: Evidence of a prior crime for which the criminal defendant was never convicted is inadmissible.

FACTS: In 1957, Tucker (D) awoke to find the body of Kaylor in Tucker's (D) dining room. The case was investigated by the police and a grand jury was convened, but no indictment was returned. In 1963, Tucker (D) awoke to find Evans dead on his sofa (shot to death). This time he was indicted. At the trial, evidence was admitted concerning the earlier death of Kaylor because of the striking similarity between the two deaths. Tucker (D) was convicted of second-degree murder.

ISSUE: May evidence of a prior crime be introduced even though the defendant was never convicted of it?

HOLDING AND DECISION: (Thompson, J.) No. Evidence of a prior crime for which the criminal defendant was never convicted is inadmissible. There is nothing in the record to establish that Tucker (D) killed Kaylor. Anonymous crimes have no relevance in deciding whether the defendant committed the crime for which he was charged. The court adopted the rule that, "before evidence of a collateral offense is admissible for any purpose, the prosecution must first establish by plain, clear, and convincing evidence that the defendant committed that offense. Fundamental fairness demands this standard in order to preclude verdicts which might otherwise rest on false assumptions." The prosecution had introduced the evidence because of the parallel circumstances between the deaths of Kaylor and Evans on the assumption that these showed a common scheme or purpose. However, without a showing that Tucker (D) was guilty of the first killing, there is no way in which a jury could draw the common scheme inference. Because of its prejudicial nature, its introduction was reversible error.

EDITOR'S ANALYSIS: Usually, evidence which shows a common plan, design, or system is admissible to show one link in a chain of events which constitutes or at least indicates the commission of the crime charged. There must be a reasonable similarity showing a modus operandi from which the jury could logically infer that the commission of the earlier crime tends to show that the defendant was likely to have committed the crime charged. Therefore, in a case such as *Lyles v. State*, 215 Ga. 229, 109 S.E. 2d 785 (1959), the court allowed evidence to be introduced that the defendant had previously murdered two husbands and a mother-in-law. These three, as well as Lyles's daughter (the crime she was being charged with), were all killed by arsenic poisoning; they were close family members leaving insurance policies naming Lyles as a beneficiary; and Lyles predicted all of their deaths and expressed a dislike of all of them. While nearly a perfect example of prior similar crimes, *Lyles* does point out the type of parallel circumstances the court is looking for. Without them, a jury cannot logically bridge the inferential gap between the proved commission of past misdeeds and current misconduct. And, where the past misconduct has not been proved, any inferences drawn must be based on suspicion and innuendo. These types of inferences will not be allowed because the jury would have to infer the commission of the previous misdeed, a collateral issue not before the court.

NOTES:

HUDDLESTON v. UNITED STATES

Convicted dealer of stolen goods (D) v. Federal government (P)
485 U.S. 681 (1988).

NATURE OF CASE: Review of conviction based on buying and selling stolen goods.

FACT SUMMARY: If a prosecution based on dealing in stolen goods, the trial court did not make a preliminary finding as to the accuracy of evidence of similar acts introduced to show motive and knowledge, prior to admission of the evidence.

CONCISE RULE OF LAW: A court need not make, prior to admitting post acts introduced to show motive or knowledge, a preliminary finding that the acts occurred.

FACTS: Huddleston (D) was indicted on charges of buying and selling stolen goods. At trial, the prosecution sought to introduce evidence of prior similar transactions by Huddleston (D). The court, without making any preliminary findings that the alleged prior acts had occurred, admitted the evidence based on Fed. R. Evid. 404(b), which permits the introduction of evidence of prior acts to show motive or knowledge. Huddleston (D) was convicted, and the court of appeals affirmed. The Supreme Court accepted review.

ISSUE: Must a court make, prior to admitting past acts introduced to show motive or knowledge, a preliminary finding that the acts occurred?

HOLDING AND DECISION: (Rehnquist, C.J.) No. A court need not make, prior to admitting past acts introduced to show motive or knowledge, a preliminary finding that the acts occurred. Fed. R. Evid. 404(b) prohibits the use of evidence of prior acts to prove conduct in conformity therewith, but permits the introduction of such evidence to prove knowledge, motive, opportunity or the like. Huddleston (D) argues that the court must preliminarily find that the prior acts did in fact occur. However, this runs contrary to the structure of the Rules of Evidence. Relevant evidence is to be admitted. Evidence of prior conduct, if relevant to show a legitimate item such as motive or knowledge, is equally admissible. It is for the jury to decide whether the prior act occurred. The only determination the court need make is that the evidence is relevant, which is to say, that a jury could find that the prior acts do in fact show motive or knowledge. Here, the court appears to have done just that. Affirmed.

EDITOR'S ANALYSIS: Fed. R. Evid. 404(b) is essentially an exclusionary section. It prohibits otherwise relevant evidence of prior acts to be introduced to prove conduct in conformity therewith. The rationale behind this is that the possibility of prejudice inherently outweighs whatever probative value exists. However, prior acts introduced to prove other than acts in conformity therewith are admissible.

NOTES:

PERRIN v. ANDERSON
Father of decedent (P) v. Police officer (D)
784 F.2d 1040 (10th Cir. 1986).

NATURE OF CASE: Appeal from denial of damages in a civil rights action.

FACT SUMMARY: In Perrin's (P) suit against Anderson (D) for compensatory and punitive damages in a 42 U.S.C. § 1983 civil rights action arising from the death of Perrin's (P) son, Perrin (P) alleged that Anderson (D) and another Oklahoma Highway Patrol officer deprived his son of his civil rights when they shot and killed him while they were attempting to obtain information about a traffic accident in which he had been involved.

CONCISE RULE OF LAW: When character evidence is used circumstantially, only reputation and opinion are acceptable forms of proof.

FACTS: Perrin's (P) son, Terry, was involved in an auto accident on an Oklahoma highway. Terry went home, but later, when the Oklahoma Highway Patrol officers, Anderson (D) and Von Schriltz, went to Terry's home to obtain information about the accident, Terry wouldn't let them in. After about twenty minutes, Terry finally allowed the officers to enter, but his behavior was erratic and a fight ensued between Terry and officer Anderson (D). Terry kicked Anderson (D) repeatedly in the face and chest, and Anderson (D) shot Terry because he felt that Terry was going to kill him. Perrin (P) brought suit against Anderson (D) under 42 U.S.C. § 1983 for compensatory and punitive damages. At trial, four police officers testified that they had had violent encounters with Terry, and that on earlier occasions, Terry was completely uncontrollable and violent in the presence of police officers. Anderson (D) introduced this evidence to prove that Terry was the first aggressor in the fight and that Anderson (D) had to defend himself. The court admitted the evidence over Perrin's (P) objection under Federal Rules of Evidence provisions treating both character and habit evidence. The jury found in Anderson's (D) favor, and Perrin (P) appealed, contending that admission of the evidence was error.

ISSUE: When character evidence is used circumstantially, are reputation and opinion the only acceptable forms of proof?

HOLDING AND DECISION: (Logan, J.) Yes. When character evidence is used circumstantially, only reputation and opinion are acceptable forms of proof. Rule 404(a) of the Federal Rules of Evidence limits circumstances under which character evidence may be admitted to prove that an individual, at the time in question, acted in conformity with his character. This type of evidence is very prejudicial, and in most instances it is impermissible to allow a jury to infer that an individual performed alleged acts based on a particular trait. Circumstantial use of

evidence regarding a person's character is permissible, but only reputation and opinion are acceptable forms of proof. Here, the district court improperly permitted testimony about specific acts involving Terry. However, the testimony was properly admitted as evidence of habit under Fed. R. Evid. 406. Habit is relevant to prove that the conduct of a person on a particular occasion was in conformity with the habit. Anderson (D) did demonstrate that Terry repeatedly reacted with extreme aggression when dealing with uniformed police officers, and Perrin (P) offered no evidence of any peaceful encounter between Terry and the police. Affirmed.

EDITOR'S ANALYSIS: "Habit" describes one's regular responses to a repeated specific situation. A habit is a person's regular practice of meeting a particular kind of situation with a specific type of conduct, such as the habit of running down a particular stairway two stairs at a time. The doing of the habitual acts may become semi-automatic, and habit evidence is highly persuasive as proof of conduct on a particular occasion.

NOTES:

HALLORAN v. VIRGINIA CHEMICALS INC.
Auto mechanic (P) v. Chemical company (D)
N.Y. Ct. App., 41 N.Y.2d 386, 393 N.Y.S.2d 341, 361 N.E.2d 991 (1977).

NATURE OF CASE: Personal injury product liability action.

FACT SUMMARY: The trial judge refused to allow Virginia Chemicals (D) to introduce evidence that Halloran (P) had previously used an immersion heating coil to heat cans of refrigerant to show that he was acting in such a negligent fashion when one of the cans blew up and injured him.

CONCISE RULE OF LAW: At least where the issue involves proof of a deliberate and repetitive practice, a party should be able to introduce evidence of habit or regular usage to allow the inference of its persistence, and hence negligence, on a particular occasion.

FACTS: Halloran (P), an automobile mechanic, sued Virginia Chemicals (D) for the injuries he sustained when a can of refrigerant they produced exploded while he was using it to service the air-conditioning system in a car. The trial judge refused to permit Virginia Chemicals (D) to introduce evidence that Halloran (P) had, on previous occasions, ignored the label warnings on the can by using an immersion coil to heat the can so the refrigerant would flow more easily. The appellate division agreed that evidence of habit or usage was never admissible to establish that one persisted in such habit and hence acted negligently on a particular occasion.

ISSUE: Where the issue involves proof of a deliberate and repetitive practice, may evidence of habit or regular usage be admitted?

HOLDING AND DECISION: (Breitel, J.) Yes. At least where the issue involves proof of a deliberate and repetitive practice, a party should be able to introduce evidence of habit or regular usage to allow the inference of its persistence, and hence negligence, on a particular occasion. The statement that evidence of habit or regular usage is never admissible to establish negligence is too broad. Of course, conduct which involves other persons or independently controlled instrumentalities cannot produce a regular usage because of the likely variation of the circumstances in which such conduct will be indulged. However, proof of a deliberate repetitive practice by one in complete control of the circumstances, as in this case, is quite another matter and should be admissible because it is so highly probative. Of course, Virginia Chemicals (D) must be able to show on voire dire a sufficient number of instances of the conduct in question to justify introduction of habit or regular usage. Remitted for a new trial on the issue of liability.

EDITOR'S ANALYSIS: Since the days of the common-law reports, habit evidence has generally been admissible to prove conformity on specified occasions. However, where negligence is at issue, many courts have resisted allowing evidence of specific acts of carelessness or carefulness to create an inference that such conduct was repeated when like circumstances were again presented.

NOTES:

STATE v. CASSIDY
State (P) v. Rape convict (D)
Conn. App. Ct., 3 Conn. App. 374, 492 A.2d 1239 (1985).

NATURE OF CASE: Appeal from conviction for rape.

FACT SUMMARY: In the State's (P) action against Cassidy (D) for the rape of a woman, Cassidy (D) contended that evidence of the woman's prior sexual conduct with another man should be admitted to prove a pattern of conduct, and that not admitting the evidence was error.

CONCISE RULE OF LAW: Evidence of a rape victim's prior sexual conduct, other than that between the victim and the defendant, is inadmissible.

FACTS: The victim in this case alleged that Cassidy (D) forced her to submit to sexual intercourse and threatened to kill her. Cassidy (D) contended that the victim consented to sexual intercourse with him, but afterwards became hysterical, said that she wanted to die, assaulted Cassidy (D), and then left Cassidy's (D) house. At trial, Cassidy (D) tried to introduce evidence of a sexual encounter between the victim and another man where the victim also became hysterical after sexual relations. The trial court would not admit the evidence because the Connecticut "rape shield" statute specifically barred the use of prior sexual conduct of an alleged sexual assault victim as too prejudicial. Cassidy (D) was convicted and appealed, arguing that the evidence should have been admitted to prove a pattern of conduct, and that not admitting the evidence was error.

ISSUE: Is evidence of a rape victim's prior sexual conduct, other than that between the victim and the defendant, admissible?

HOLDING AND DECISION: (Borden, J.) No. Evidence of a rape victim's prior sexual conduct, other than that between the victim and the defendant, is inadmissible. Here, Cassidy (D) contended that the evidence of the victim's prior conduct should have been admitted to prove the victim's pattern of sexual conduct, and that the evidence was so relevant and material to a critical issue in the case that excluding it would violate his constitutional rights. However, one similar instance is not sufficient to prove a pattern of conduct. One cannot logically infer that the victim acted in the manner described by Cassidy (D) simply because of a somewhat similar incident one year beforehand. The evidence, therefore, was legally irrelevant and was properly excluded without denying Cassidy (D) his constitutional rights. Affirmed.

EDITOR'S ANALYSIS: Nearly all jurisdictions have enacted "rape shield" laws. The reforms range from barring all evidence of the victim's character for chastity to merely requiring a preliminary hearing to screen out inadmissible evidence on the issue. Fed. R. Evid. 412 lies between the extremes and bars reputation and opinion evidence of the victim's past sexual conduct, but permits evidence of specific incidents if certain substantive and procedural conditions are met.

NOTES:

OLDEN v. KENTUCKY
Sex crime convict (D) v. State (P)
488 U.S. 227 (1988).

NATURE OF CASE: Appeal of conviction for forcible sodomy.

FACT SUMMARY: Olden (D), accused of various sex crimes, was not permitted to cross-examine accusing witness Matthews regarding a relationship Olden (D) claimed Matthews was trying to protect by accusing him of sexual assault.

CONCISE RULE OF LAW: The Confrontation Clause mandates that a defendant be permitted to cross-examine a witness on any relevant matter.

FACTS: Matthews, a white female, met Olden (D), a black male, at a bar. It was disputed as to what transpired thereafter, but Matthews accused Olden (D) of rape. Olden (D) contended that Matthews had consented. Olden (D) attempted to elicit, on cross-examination, an admission from Matthews that she was involved in a relationship with one Russell. It was Olden's (D) contention that Matthews had invited him to have sex with her but, when Russell found out, she accused Olden (D) of rape. The trial court limited the cross-examination, holding that evidence that Matthews had a relationship with Russell, a black, would be prejudicial against Matthews. Olden (D) was convicted of forcible sodomy, and the Kentucky Court of Appeals affirmed. The Supreme Court granted review.

ISSUE: Does the Confrontation Clause mandate that a defendant be permitted to cross-examine a witness on any relevant matter?

HOLDING AND DECISION: (Per curiam) Yes. The Confrontation Clause mandates that a defendant be permitted to cross-examine a witness on any relevant matter. Cross-examination is an integral right under the Confrontation Clause. Any subject matter that tends to demonstrate an improper motive or bias by the witness is a proper subject of cross-examination. The only limit on this is that the court has discretion to limit repetitive or unduly harassing interrogation. Also, cross-examination on matters only marginally relevant is not a right. Here, however, the subject of the cross-examination was a possible motive for Matthews to lie, and this was central to the case against Olden (D). Cross examination should have been permitted in this instance. Reversed and remanded.

DISSENT: (Marshall, J.) The summary disposition per curiam opinion here was improper. The Court should have invited fuller briefing.

EDITOR'S ANALYSIS: Many states have enacted "rape shield" laws, which prevent an alleged rape victim from being cross-examined on prior sexual conduct. It is not clear to what extent the present opinion cuts away at such laws. It appears that laws that per se prohibit such cross-examination would likely conflict with this decision.

NOTES:

UNITED STATES v. PLATERO
Federal government (P) v. Sexual assault convict (D)
72 F.3d 806 (10th Cir. 1995).

NATURE OF CASE: Appeal from an order upholding a conviction for aggravated sexual assault.

FACT SUMMARY: Platero (D) appealed his conviction of sexual assault on Francis, contending that the district court denied his right under the Confrontation Clause of the Sixth Amendment when it refused to submit to the jury the question of whether a sexual relationship existed between Laughlin and Francis to show Francis' motive to fabricate her allegations against him.

CONCISE RULE OF LAW: If the relevancy of the evidence that the accused seeks to offer depends upon the fulfillment of a condition of fact, it is for the jury to determine whether such condition of fact is fulfilled.

FACTS: Susan Francis and her co-worker Vernon Laughlin were drinking at a bar prior to their confrontation with Platero (D). Laughlin was driving Francis home when he was pulled over by Platero (D), a security guard, who threatened to arrest Laughlin for a DWI. Platero (D) told Laughlin to "start walking" and that he was going to arrest Francis. Platero (D) then drove Francis to another location, raped her twice, and forced her to have oral sex in the front seat of his car. After Platero (D) returned Francis to her car, Francis told Laughlin that she had been raped and went to the hospital to receive treatment. At his trial, Platero (D) admitted to having sex with Francis, claiming that it was consensual. However, Platero (D) contended that Francis had fabricated her allegations of sexual assault against him to protect her extra-marital relationship with Laughlin from her husband. Platero (D) filed a motion under Fed.R.Evid. 412(b)(1) to introduce evidence of Francis' relationship with Laughlin at the time of the alleged rape to demonstrate that Francis had a motive to fabricate the rape allegations against Platero (D). Francis and Laughlin testified that their relationship evolved from a friendship to a romantic involvement only after the rape. Laughlin's former girlfriend, however, testified that she believed Francis and Laughlin were having an affair, and a government witness reported that Francis referred to Laughlin as her "boyfriend" in her statement to the police and to the physician who examined her. However, the district court excluded the evidence regarding their relationship. Platero (D) was convicted of sexual assault, and he appealed. On remand, the court concluded that no sexual relationship existed between Francis and Laughlin and let the conviction stand. Platero (D) appealed again, arguing that his constitutional right to trial by jury and his right of confrontation had been infringed.

ISSUE: If the relevancy of the evidence that the accused seeks to offer depends on the fulfillment of a condition of fact, is it for the jury to determine whether such condition is fulfilled?

HOLDING AND DECISION: (Holloway, J.) Yes. If the relevancy of the evidence that the accused seeks to offer depends upon the fulfillment of a condition of fact, it is for the jury to determine whether such condition of fact is fulfilled. In this case, Platero (D) provided sufficient evidence to allow the jury to determine whether a romantic relationship existed between Francis and Laughlin. When the relevancy of evidence depends upon the fulfillment of a condition of fact, the court shall admit it upon the introduction of evidence sufficient to support a finding of the fulfillment of the condition. The preliminary fact can be decided by the judge against the proponent only where the jury could not reasonably find the preliminary fact to exist. The judge's decision under the old version of Rule 412(c)(2), which required the court to determine whether a condition of fact was fulfilled, impinged on Platero's (D) right to trial by jury. The determination of the issue by a trial judge without submission of the issue to the jury and without the defendant's ability to confront and cross-examine his accuser violates the defendant's Sixth Amendment rights. Reversed and remanded.

EDITOR'S ANALYSIS: When the above case was remanded the first time, the district court had upheld the conviction after finding the testimony of Laughlin's girlfriend was not credible. Under Rule 104(a) governing the admissibility of extrinsic offense evidence, the preliminary fact can be decided by the judge against the proponent only where the jury could not reasonably find the fact to exist. Court precedent denies the trial judge the right to decide the preliminary relevancy–conditioned–on–fact issue in all other cases.

NOTES:

JOHNSON v. ELK LAKE SCHOOL DISTRICT
Student (P) v. Guidance counselor (D)
283 F.3d 138 (3d Cir. 2002).

NATURE OF CASE: Appeal from jury verdict for defendant in sexual harassment and abuse case.

FACT SUMMARY: Johnson (P), who alleged that her guidance counselor, Stevens (D), sexually harassed and abused her, claimed that it was error to exclude evidence of Stevens' prior sexual misconduct offered by Radwanski, a teacher's associate in the school.

CONCISE RULE OF LAW: Evidence of prior sexual misconduct may be excluded where a jury could not reasonably conclude by a preponderance of the evidence that the past act was a sexual assault, or, even where the jury could reasonably find that the prior act was a sexual assault, where the evidence's probative value is substantially outweighed by the danger of unfair prejudice, confusion of the issues, misleading of the jury, or by considerations of undue delay, waste of time, or needless presentation of cumulative evidence.

FACTS: Johnson (P) claimed that her guidance counselor, Stevens (D), sexually harassed and abused her while she was a high school student. She alleged that Stevens (D) repeatedly sent her letters, roses, cards, and other suggestive correspondence, attempted on numerous occasions to hug and kiss her without her consent, and at one point fondled her breasts and vagina. At trial, she sought to introduce the testimony of Radwanski, a former co-worker of Stevens (D), regarding a bizarre incident in which Stevens (D) allegedly picked her up off the floor in another teacher's office and, in the course of doing so, touched her in the crotch area. Johnson had sought to present this testimony as evidence of Stevens's (D) propensity for sexual abuse under Fed. R. Evid. 415, which allows for the introduction of evidence of past sexual assaults in civil cases in which the claim for damages is predicated on the defendant's alleged commission of a sexual assault. The district court excluded Radwanski's "other acts" testimony, finding that her testimony was equivocal as to whether the touching was intentional, and that the incident did not qualify as an "offense of sexual assault." A jury found for Stevens (D), and Johnson (P) appealed to the court of appeals.

ISSUE: May evidence of prior sexual misconduct be excluded where a jury could not reasonably conclude by a preponderance of the evidence that the past act was a sexual assault, or, even where the jury could reasonably find that the prior act was a sexual assault, where the evidence's probative value is substantially outweighed by the danger of unfair prejudice, confusion of the issues, misleading of the jury, or by considerations of undue delay, waste of time, or needless presentation of cumulative evidence?

HOLDING AND DECISION: (Becker, C.J.) Yes. Evidence of prior sexual misconduct may be excluded where a jury could not reasonably conclude by a preponderance of the evidence that the past act was a sexual assault, or, even where the jury could reasonably find that the prior act was a sexual assault, where the evidence's probative value is substantially outweighed by the danger of unfair prejudice, confusion of the issues, misleading of the jury, or by considerations of undue delay, waste of time, or needless presentation of cumulative evidence. Fed. R. Evid. 413-15 establish exceptions to the general prohibition on character evidence in cases involving sexual assault and child molestation. Fed. R. Evid. 413-14 apply to criminal proceedings, whereas Fed. R. Evid. 415 applies to civil trials. For evidence of a past act to be admitted under Fed. R. Evid. 415, the trial court need not make a preliminary finding by a preponderance of the evidence under Fed. R. Evid. 104(a) that the act in question qualifies as a sexual assault and that it was committed by the defendant. Rather, the court may admit the evidence so long as it is satisfied that the evidence is relevant, with relevancy determined by whether a jury under Fed. R. Evid. 104(b) could reasonably conclude by a preponderance of the evidence that the past act was a sexual assault and that it was committed by the defendant. However, even when the evidence of a past sexual offense is relevant, the trial court retains discretion to exclude it under Fed. R. Evid. 403 if the evidence's "probative value is substantially outweighed by the danger of unfair prejudice, confusion of the issues, or misleading the jury, or by considerations of undue delay, waste of time, or needless presentation of cumulative evidence." In cases where the past act is demonstrated with specificity and is substantially similar to the act(s) for which the defendant is being sued, it is Congress's intent that the probative value of the similar act be presumed to outweigh Fed. R. Evid. 403's concerns. In a case such as this one, however, in which the evidence of the past act of sexual offense is equivocal and the past act differs from the charged act in important ways, no presumption in favor of admissibility is in order, and the trial court retains significant authority to exclude the proffered evidence under Rule 403. Here, the district court correctly noted that for the Radwanski touching incident to have qualified as an "offense of sexual assault," it would have to have been done intentionally. The district found that Radwanski's equivocal testimony was insufficiently specific as to the intentionality of Stevens' (D) conduct. Therefore, the district court had discretion to exclude the evidence for not being sufficiently relevant under Fed. R. Evid. 104(b). However, the district court

Continued on next page.

did not indicate what standard for admission it was applying to the evidence—nor was it required to do so, as it was not required to hold an in limine hearing or make formal findings. Although it did not explicitly say so, it seems that the court concluded that Radwanski's testimony did not satisfy Fed. R. Evid. 403. Accordingly, it appropriately bypassed the reasonable jury determination. Lacking more specific evidence of intentionality, the court apparently concluded that the probative value of the evidence was slight and was outweighed by Fed. R. Evid. 403's concerns of prejudice, undue delay, waste of time, etc. The district court's judgment was sound given the equivocal nature of Radwanski's testimony. In addition, the exclusion of the testimony was justified because of significant differences between Stevens's (D) alleged assaults of Radwanski and Johnson (P), which further reduced the probative value of the excluded testimony. The fact that the alleged touching of Radwanski was only an isolated incident also is a relevant factor supporting the district court's decision. Given this reduced probative value, any presumption in favor of admissibility was unwarranted, and the district court's exclusion of the evidence can be justified on grounds that its introduction might have prejudiced Stevens (D) unfairly, misled the jury, confused the issues, and wasted valuable trial time. Accordingly, the court did not abuse its discretion in excluding Radwanski's testimony. Affirmed.

EDITOR'S ANALYSIS: The court in this case based a significant portion of its reasoning on *Huddleston v. United States*, 485 U.S. 681 (1988). In *Huddleston*, the U.S. Supreme Court considered the same issue in the context of Fed. R. Evid. 404(b), which allows for the introduction of evidence of "other crimes, wrongs, or acts" to prove issues other than character. The Supreme Court in that case held in a unanimous opinion "that a preliminary finding by the court that the government has proved the act by a preponderance of the evidence is not called for under Rule 104(a)." Instead, the Court identified Rule 104(b), which governs the relevancy of evidence conditioned on fact (the jury gets to decide the issue), as the applicable safeguard against the risk of introducing prejudicial unsubstantiated evidence. *Huddleston* identified Rule 104(b) as appropriate because the question of the defendant's commission of the past act was simply one of conditional relevancy—the relevancy of the bad act is conditioned on the defendant's having committed it. Presumably, this once-removed determination of the trial judge lowers the burden for the party seeking to introduce the prior act evidence.

NOTES:

SIMON v. KENNEBUNKPORT
Injured pedestrian (P) v. Town (D)
Me. Sup. Jud. Ct., 417 A.2d 982 (1980).

NOTES:

NATURE OF CASE: Appeal from denial of damages for personal injuries.

FACT SUMMARY: The Town of Kennebunkport (Town) (D) contended evidence of prior slip-and-fall accidents at the site of Simon's (P) accident was inadmissible to show a defect in the design or construction of the sidewalk.

CONCISE RULE OF LAW: Evidence of other similar accidents or occurrences that is relevant circumstantially to show a defective or dangerous condition, notice thereof, or causation on the occasion in question, is admissible.

FACTS: Simon (P) sued the Town (D), contending she slipped and fell while on a public sidewalk. At trial, she was precluded from offering evidence of prior similar accidents at the same location. The jury rendered a verdict for the Town (D), and Simon (P) appealed.

ISSUE: Is evidence of other similar accidents or occurrences that is relevant circumstantially to show a defective or dangerous condition, notice thereof, or causation on the occassion in question, admissible?

HOLDING AND DECISION: (Glassman, J.) Yes. Evidence of other similar accidents or occurrences that is relevant circumstantially to show a defective or dangerous condition, notice thereof, or causation on the occasion in question, is admissible. While such evidence may have some prejudicial impact on a jury, it is clearly probative to show the area in question may be a causative factor in such accidents and in the accident giving rise to the present litigation. Thus it is admissible. Judgment vacated.

EDITOR'S ANALYSIS: It is necessary to establish that the area in which the accident occurred has not been altered in any material manner to allow evidence of prior accidents to be admissible. Any material changes would render such evidence irrelevant and thus inadmissible.

TUER v. McDONALD
Surviving spouse (P) v. Doctor (D)
Md. Ct. App., 701 A.2d 1101 (1997).

NATURE OF CASE: Appeal from a verdict for defendant in a medical malpractice suit.

FACT SUMMARY: When Tuer's (P) husband went into cardiac arrest and died because it was the policy of the hospital at the time to discontinue the use of a certain drug prior to surgery, she alleged that evidence should have been admitted at trial showing that the hospital changed its policy following her husband's death.

CONCISE RULE OF LAW: Evidence of subsequent remedial measures is not admissible to prove culpability.

FACTS: Tuer (P) sued McDonald (D), the surgeon, and the hospital (D) where her husband died when a certain drug was not administered because he was supposed to go into surgery, accompanied by unforeseen delay of several hours. A new protocol at the hospital (D) now requires that the drug be continuously administered until the patient is taken into the operating room. A jury returned a verdict for McDonald (D), which was affirmed on appeal. Tuer (P) alleged that evidence of the change in procedure adopted after her husband's death was admissible because it controverted the feasibility of using the drug until a patient is taken into the operating room, and also because it impeached McDonald's (D) testimony that restarting the drug would have been unsafe. The Maryland Supreme Court granted certiorari to consider whether the trial court erred in excluding evidence that McDonald (D) and the Hospital (D) changed the protocol regarding the administration of the drug to patients awaiting coronary artery bypass surgery.

ISSUE: Is evidence of subsequent remedial measures admissible to prove culpability?

HOLDING AND DECISION: (Wilner, J.) No. Evidence of subsequent remedial measures is not admissible to prove culpability. McDonald (D) was not asserting that restarting the drug would have been unsafe, but only that, given the complications that could have arisen, there was a relative safety risk that, at the time, he and the Hospital (D) believed was not worth taking. That does not constitute an assertion that restarting the drug at the time was not feasible, but simply that it was not advisable. McDonald (D) made a judgment call based on his knowledge and collective experience at the time. The later re-evaluation of the protocol at the Hospital (D) is precisely what the exclusionary provision of the rule was designed to encourage. Affirmed.

EDITOR'S ANALYSIS: The court in this case discussed the two justifications for excluding evidence of subsequent remedial measures. The subsequent conduct is not in fact an admission, since the conduct is equally consistent with injury by mere accident or through contributing negligence. Also, there is a social policy encouraging people to take steps in furtherance of added safety.

NOTES:

DAVIDSON v. PRINCE
Gored claimant (P) v. Truck driver (D)
Utah Ct. App., 813 P.2d 1225 (1991).

NATURE OF THE CASE: Appeal from the denial of a motion for a new trial in an action to recover damages for personal injury.

FACT SUMMARY: Davidson (P) filed suit to recover damages after he was gored by a steer released onto the highway when Prince (D) negligently overturned a truck he was driving for his employer.

CONCISE RULE OF LAW: Offers to compromise made in the course of settlement negotiations are not admissible to prove liability for or invalidity of the claim or its amount.

FACTS: Davidson (P) was gored by a steer released onto the highway when Prince (D) negligently overturned a truck he was driving for Folkens Brothers Trucking (D). In deposition testimony, Davidson (P) estimated he was about forty feet away from the steer when he was attacked. However, in a letter to Folkens Brothers (D), Davidson (P) stated he was ten feet from the injured animal, a distance that supported Folkens Brothers' (D) claim that Davidson (P) had cornered the animal, making Davidson contributorily negligent. Over Davidson's (P) objections, the trial court allowed the statement from Davidson's (P) letter to be introduced as evidence. Davidson (P) claimed the letter was a "settlement" letter, and thus the evidence should have been excluded. The jury awarded damages to Davidson (P) but reduced those damages by 40%, the amount of his fault. Davidson (P) appealed.

ISSUE: Are offers to compromise made in the course of settlement negotiations admissible to prove liability for or invalidity of the claim or its amount?

HOLDING AND DECISION: (Billings, J.) No. Offers to compromise made in the course of settlement negotiations are not admissible to prove liability for or invalidity of the claim or its amount. Here, the trial judge was correct in admitting the statement from the letter sent by Davidson (P) to Folkens Brothers (D) because the letter was not an offer to compromise Davidson's (P) claim nor was it written as part of settlement negotiations. To the contrary, the letter is merely an attempt to inform Folkens Brothers (D) as to the facts of the incidents. Furthermore, Davidson (P), in the letter, demands payment in full of his claim; the whole tenor of the letter is that he will not compromise one bit. Affirmed.

EDITOR'S ANAYSIS: The court here applied Utah R. Evid. 408, which is based verbatim on Fed. R. Evid. 408. Thus, the court looked to federal law interpreting Rule 408 to define the contours of the Utah Rule. The court noted that even if Davidson's (P) letter were to be construed to have been part of settlement discussions, it could still have been admitted to impeach his prior testimony regarding the distance between himself and the steer prior to the attack which caused his injury.

NOTES:

ANDO v. WOODBERRY
Motorcycle police officer (P) v. Auto owner and driver (D)
N.Y. Ct. App., 8 N.Y.2d 165, 203 N.Y.S.2d 74, 168 N.E.2d 520 (1960).

NATURE OF CASE: Appeal from a judgment denying damages.

FACT SUMMARY: Ando (P) was injured when his motorcycle was struck by a car operated by Nichols (D) and owned by Woodberry (D). Before the traffic court, Nichols (D) pleaded guilty to charges of failing to make a proper turn and failing to signal before turning. At a subsequent trial to recover damages for personal injuries sustained, Ando (P) sought to introduce evidence of Nichols' (D) guilty plea, but the trial court excluded the proffered evidence.

CONCISE RULE OF LAW: Evidence of a guilty plea entered in a traffic court is admissible in a subsequent suit for damages.

FACTS: Robert Ando (P), a police officer, was proceeding north on Fifth Avenue in New York City, when Edward Nichols (D), driving a car owned by Essie Woodberry (D), attempted to make a left turn at 110th Street. His car collided with Ando's (P) motorcycle, injuring the officer. Nichols (D) was issued a summons which charged him with failure to make a proper turn or to signal before turning. In an appearance before the Manhattan Traffic Division of Magistrate's Court, Nichols (D) pleaded guilty to the charges. At the trial of Ando's (P) suit for damages, only Ando (P) and Nichols (D) appeared as witnesses. Ando (P) testified that Nichols (D) had pulled over to the right then made a left turn without signaling and struck Ando's (P) motorcycle, injuring him (P). Nichols (D) denied that he had moved to the right and also claimed that he had signaled before turning. In order to corroborate his testimony, Ando (P) sought to introduce evidence of Nichols's (D) guilty plea before the traffic court, but that evidence was excluded by the trial court. The jury returned a verdict in favor of the defendants, and the appellate division affirmed. Ando (P) appealed, alleging error in the refusal to admit evidence of Nichols's (D) plea of guilty to the traffic violation.

ISSUE: Is a guilty plea entered in a traffic court admissible in a subsequent suit for damages?

HOLDING AND DECISION: (Fuld, J.) Yes. Evidence of a guilty plea entered in a traffic court is admissible in a subsequent suit for damages. A prior plea of guilt constitutes an admission and is therefore not rendered inadmissible by the hearsay rule. However, it is alleged that evidence of the guilty plea should be excluded because of a public policy distinguishing a traffic violation from a crime and recognizing that a plea of guilty to a traffic infraction is not always the result of an admission of guilt. In support of their contentions, defendants cite a portion of the Vehicle and Traffic Law which states that conviction of a traffic offense shall not affect or impair the violator's credibility as a witness. But that section applies only to attempts to discredit a witness and does not preclude facts pertaining to the infraction from being introduced as evidence in chief. The legislature obviously could have forbidden the introduction for all purposes of a plea of guilty to a traffic offense but has declined to do so. An additional argument is made, based on "experience," that alleged traffic offenders often plead guilty as a matter of convenience and do not intend by that plea to admit guilt, having in mind only to enter a plea analogous to one of nolo contendere. However, the nolo contendere plea has been abolished in New York and, while it may be assumed that pleas of guilty to traffic charges are often generated by expediency, it is impossible to state that any particular guilty plea is so motivated, especially when a charge involving injury to a person or property, which carries with it the possibility of suspension or revocation of one's driving privileges, is involved. Any claim that Nichols (D) did not intend to admit responsibility for the accident would therefore pertain not to the admissibility of the evidence of his guilty plea, but to the weight to which such evidence is entitled. Since the evidence was improperly excluded, a new trial must be granted.

DISSENT: (Van Voorhis, J.) The law of evidence is rooted in experience. It should therefore be realized that guilty pleas in traffic court are frequently designed to save the expense of time and money involved in a legal proceeding and are not necessarily indicative of a recognition of guilt. Therefore, evidence of pleas of guilty to traffic offenses cannot fairly be admitted into evidence as admissions of liability in subsequent civil actions.

EDITOR'S ANALYSIS: In recognition of the fact that individuals frequently plead guilty to traffic offenses for reasons of convenience unrelated to guilt, many courts have refused to admit evidence of such pleas in civil actions for damages. In some instances, the admissibility of evidence of guilty pleas under such circumstances has been barred by statute. However, in a significant proportion of cases, evidence of prior pleas of guilt to traffic offenses has been admitted.

NOTES:

CHAPTER FIVE
IMPEACHMENT AND REHABILITATION; CROSS-EXAMINATION

QUICK REFERENCE RULES OF LAW

1. **Impeachment of Witnesses.** The prosecution may not call a witness it knows to be hostile for the primary purpose of eliciting otherwise inadmissible impeachment testimony. (United States v. Hogan)

2. **Impeachment and Collateral Matters.** A witness cannot be impeached upon matters collateral to the principal issues being tried. (State v. Oswalt)

3. **Methods of Impeachment.** Evidence of other crimes, wrongs, or acts may be admissible to impeach through contradiction a defendant acting as a witness. (United States v. Copelin)

4. **Impeachment Methods.** Under Military Rule of Evidence 608(b), counsel may impeach a witness by extracting on cross-examination his admission to a prior act of intentional falsehood under oath. (United States v. Owens)

5. **Cross-examination as Evidence.** Cross-examination questions alone cannot constitute extrinsic evidence. (United States v. Drake)

6. **Unavailable Declarant's Prior Bad Acts.** Extrinsic evidence of a hearsay declarant's prior bad acts is not admissible where the declarant is unavailable. (United States v. Saada)

7. **Methods of Impeachment.** Evidence of prior felony convictions may be used to attack the credibility of a witness only if the probative value of the evidence outweighs its prejudicial effect. (United States v. Sanders)

8. **Admission of Evidence of Prior Crimes.** Federal Rule of Evidence 609 requires the admission of impeachment evidence of prior convictions of crimes involving dishonesty, and a trial court cannot exclude such evidence regardless of its prejudicial effect. (United States v. Wong)

9. **Methods of Impeachment.** Bank robbery is not per se a crime of "dishonesty" as that term is used in Federal Rule of Evidence 609(a)(2). (United States v. Brackeen)

10. **Impeachment by Prior Conviction.** To raise and preserve for review the claim of improper impeachment with a prior conviction, a defendant must testify at trial. (Luce v. United States)

11. **Methods of Impeachment.** Psychiatric evidence regarding a recent history of mental instability may be used to impeach a chief witness. (United States v. Lindstrom)

12. **Impeachment by Prior Inconsistent Statement.** Before a witness can be impeached by evidence of prior inconsistent statements, the statements must be related to him, with the circumstances of times, places, and persons present, and he must be asked whether he has made the statements, and, if so, allowed to explain them. (Coles v. Harsch)

13. **Prior Consistent Statements.** A witness's out-of-court statements consistent with court testimony are admissible to rebut a charge of recent fabrication or improper influence or motive only if made before the charged recent fabrication or improper influence or motive. (Tome v. United States)

14. **Federal Rule 403.** A district court is accorded a wide discretion in determining the admissibility of evidence under the Federal Rules. (United States v. Abel)

UNITED STATES v. HOGAN
Federal government (P) v. Accused drug conspirators (D)
763 F.2d 697 (5th Cir. 1985).

NATURE OF CASE: Appeal from a conviction for importing marijuana and for conspiracy to import and possess it with the intent to distribute it.

FACT SUMMARY: After Carpenter retracted statements he made implicating the Hogan brothers (D) in a drug importation conspiracy, the United States (P) called Carpenter to testify at the Hogans' (D) trial and then proceeded to impeach Carpenter's retraction through the use of inadmissible hearsay evidence.

CONCISE RULE OF LAW: The prosecution may not call a witness it knows to be hostile for the primary purpose of eliciting otherwise inadmissible impeachment testimony.

FACTS: Carpenter, pilot of Barry Hogan's (D) plane, was arrested by Mexican officials after a pouch of money was found on the plane, and about 6,000 pounds of marijuana was found in a truck parked near the landing strip. In statements given to Mexican and United States (P) Drug Enforcement Agency officials, Carpenter implicated the Hogan brothers (D) in a drug conspiracy. The United States filed suit against the Hogans (D). After being given immunity, Carpenter denied that he or the Hogans (D) had any involvement in a drug conspiracy, testifying that his prior confessions were coerced. DEA and embassy officials then testified that they observed no abuse of Carpenter, and at no time had he complained of mistreatment. The trial court allowed this testimony, despite the defense objection that it was hearsay and improper impeachment. The Hogans (D) were convicted. This appeal followed.

ISSUE: May the prosecution call a witness it knows to be hostile for the primary purpose of eliciting otherwise inadmissible impeachment testimony?

HOLDING AND DECISION: (Clark, C.J.) No. The prosecution may not call a witness it knows to be hostile for the primary purpose of eliciting otherwise inadmissible impeachment testimony. Here, the impeachment proof consisted only of out-of-court statements offered to prove the truth thereof and thus were hearsay. Carpenter had testified under oath on three previous occasions, adhering to his account of fabrication each time. Thus, the court of appeals declared that the primary if not sole purpose in calling him to testify again was focused on getting his prior statements before the jury. The danger in this procedure is that the jury will hear the impeachment evidence, which is not otherwise admissible and is not substantive proof of guilt but is likely to be received as such proof. The admission of this evidence constituted plain, not harmless, error. Reversed.

EDITOR'S ANALYSIS: Under common law, parties were not allowed to impeach their own witnesses. This rule was justified by the notion that the party calling the witness vouches for his trustworthiness and thus may not challenge a witness's testimony that turns out to be unfavorable. The other rationalization was that allowing a party to impeach his own witness may coerce the witness to testify untruthfully merely to avoid the impeachment. Neither reason was particularly compelling, and the no-impeachment doctrine was abandoned by federal courts with the enactment of Fed. R. Evid. 607. The exception to the Rule enunciated in *Hogan* is, however, followed by all circuits that have considered the issue.

NOTES:

STATE v. OSWALT

State (P) v. Criminal defendant (D)

Wash. Sup. Ct., 62 Wash.2d 118, 381 P.2d 617 (1963).

NATURE OF CASE: Appeal from a conviction of robbery and burglary.

FACT SUMMARY: Ardiss testified that Oswalt (D), who was accused of a crime in Washington, was in Oregon on the day of the crime and that he had been in Oregon every day for several months. The State (P) attempted to impeach him by means of a police officer's testimony that Oswalt (D) had been in Washington on a day one month before the crime.

CONCISE RULE OF LAW: A witness cannot be impeached upon matters collateral to the principal issues being tried.

FACTS: To support his defense of alibi, Oswalt (D) called Ardiss as a witness. Ardiss testified that Oswalt (D) was in Oregon on the day of the crime, which occurred in Washington. On cross-examination, Ardiss testified that Oswalt (D) had been in Oregon every day for the past few months. The State (P) attempted to impeach Ardiss by means of a police officer's testimony that he had seen Oswalt (D) in Washington on a day one month before the crime. Defendant was convicted of robbery and first-degree burglary.

ISSUE: Can a witness be impeached upon matters collateral to the principal issues being tried?

HOLDING AND DECISION: (Hamilton, J.) No. A witness cannot be impeached upon matters collateral to the principal issues being tried. The purpose of this rule is to avoid undue confusion of the issues and to prevent undue advantage over a witness unprepared to answer concerning matters unrelated or remote to the issues at hand. The test of collateralness is, "Could the fact as to which the error is predicated have been shown in evidence for any purpose independent of the contradiction?" Here, Oswalt (D) attempted to prove through Ardiss that he was not in Washington on the day of the crime. He was not trying to prove that he had not been in Washington prior to that date. Thus, for the purpose of impeaching Ardiss, whether Oswalt (D) was in Washington on a given day one month prior to the crime was irrelevant and collateral. It was error to admit the questioned testimony. Reversed and remanded.

EDITOR'S ANALYSIS: Two general kinds of facts meet the classical test for collateralness enunciated in *Oswalt*. The first are facts that are relevant to the substantive issues in the case. The second are facts which would be independently provable by extrinsic evidence apart from the contradiction to impeach or disqualify the witness. Among these are facts showing bias, interest, conviction of crime, and want of capacity or opportunity for knowledge.

NOTES:

UNITED STATES v. COPELIN
Federal government (P) v. Convicted drug dealer (D)
996 F.2d 379 (D.C. Cir. 1993).

NATURE OF CASE: Appeal from a conviction for unlawful distribution of cocaine.

FACT SUMMARY: During Copelin's (D) trial for selling crack cocaine, the trial court allowed the United States (P) to introduce evidence of Copelin's (D) positive drug tests for cocaine, while on pretrial release, for impeachment purposes without issuing a limiting instruction to the jury.

CONCISE RULE OF LAW: Evidence of other crimes, wrongs, or acts may be admissible to impeach through contradiction a defendant acting as a witness.

FACTS: Copelin (D) was arrested and tried for unlawful distribution of cocaine after he allegedly sold crack cocaine to an undercover police officer. During his trial, Copelin (D) testified that another individual had actually sold the cocaine while that individual, Copelin (D), and other were engaged in a dice game. Copelin (D) further testified that he only saw money exchanged, not the drugs, and that the only time he had seen drugs was on television. The trial court permitted the United States (P) to question Copelin (D) concerning three previous positive drug tests for cocaine as a means of demonstrating that Copelin's (D) statement about his unfamiliarity with drugs was false. However, the trial court failed to issue an immediate cautionary instruction informing the jury as to the permissible uses of that evidence. Copelin (D) contended that the trial court committed reversible error in not issuing a limiting instruction. After the jury found Copelin (D) guilty, he appealed his conviction.

ISSUE: May evidence of other crimes, wrongs, or acts be admissible to impeach through contradiction a defendant acting as a witness?

HOLDING AND DECISION: (Mikva, C.J.) Yes. Evidence of other crimes, wrongs, or acts may be admissible to impeach through contradiction a defendant acting as a witness. Here, the district court correctly permitted the government (P) to cross-examine Copelin (D) as to his positive drug test for impeachment purposes. However, if the jury considered the evidence for other, impermissible purposes, it was likely to be substantially prejudiced against Copelin (D). It was, therefore, imperative for the trial judge to issue an immediate cautionary instruction informing the jury as to the limited allowable uses of the drug test evidence. His failure to do so constituted reversible plain error. Thus, Copelin's (D) conviction is overturned, and the case is remanded to the district court for a new trial. Reversed and remanded.

EDITOR'S ANALYSIS: The information regarding Copelin's (D) positive drug tests was "bad acts" evidence of the most prejudicial sort. Moreover, it tended to bolster the government's (P) contention that Copelin (D) was the man who sold the same drug to the undercover officer. Courts frequently use limiting instructions to temper the potential prejudice caused by marginal evidence admitted for purposes other than establishing the charged crime.

NOTES:

UNITED STATES v. OWENS
Federal government (P) v. Convicted murderer (D)
U.S. Ct. of Military App., 21 M.J. 117 (1985).

NATURE OF CASE: Appeal from conviction of unpremeditated murder.

FACT SUMMARY: In the government's (P) case against Owens (D) for the unpremeditated murder of Owens' (D) wife, Mary, Owens (D) contended that it was improper for the prosecutor to attempt to impeach him by eliciting, on cross-examination, Owens's (D) admission to a prior act of intentional falsehood, and that the impeachment did not constitute harmless error.

CONCISE RULE OF LAW: Under Military Rule of Evidence 608(b), counsel may impeach a witness by extracting on cross-examination his admission to a prior act of intentional falsehood under oath.

FACTS: Owens (D) was apprehended for the murder of his wife, Mary. At trial, the government (P) introduced evidence to show that Owens (D) fired a rifle at his wife in anger following a domestic quarrel, and that Owens (D) intended his wife's death or grievous bodily harm. Owens (D) took the witness stand in his own defense. On cross-examination the prosecutor attempted to impeach Owens (D) by eliciting Owens's (D) admission to a prior act of intentional falsehood. Owens (D) was convicted and appealed, contending that the prosecutor's cross-examination was improper, and that the impeachment did not constitute harmless error.

ISSUE: Under Military Rule of Evidence 608(b), may counsel impeach a witness by extracting on cross-examination his admission to a prior act of intentional falsehood under oath?

HOLDING AND DECISION: (Cox, J.) Yes. Under Military Rule of Evidence 608(b), counsel may impeach a witness by extracting on cross-examination his admission to a prior act of intentional falsehood under oath. Here, the suggested evidence had substantial probative value. First, the issue of the appellant's prior falsehood was clearly a matter contested by the parties. Second, other evidence to show that Owens (D) engaged in an act of deceit was not available to the government (P). Finally, the strength of the suggested evidence to show Owens's (D) prior falsehood was considerable. There existed substantial circumstances indicating deliberate deceit by Owens (D). In view of the considerable probative value of the evidence for a proper purpose, the military judge did not abuse his discretion in admitting the evidence. Affirmed.

EDITOR'S ANALYSIS: Particular instances of conduct, though not the subject of criminal conviction, may be inquired into on cross-examination of the principal witness or of a witness who testifies concerning the character of the principal witness for truthfulness. Effective cross-examination demands that some allowance be made for going into matters of this kind, but the possibilities of abuse are substantial. Consequently, safeguards are set up in the form of specific requirements that the instances inquired into be probative of truthfulness or its opposite.

NOTES:

UNITED STATES v. DRAKE
Federal government (P) v. Fraud convict (D)
932 F.2d. 861 (10th Cir. 1991).

NATURE OF CASE: Appeal from a criminal conviction for fraud.

FACT SUMMARY: Drake (D) alleged that the government (P) in its cross-examination introduced extrinsic evidence of specific instances of conduct in violation of Federal Rule of Evidence 608(b).

CONCISE RULE OF LAW: Cross-examination questions alone cannot constitute extrinsic evidence.

FACTS: Drake (D) was convicted of fraud on the basis of allegations that he sought financing while concealing the existence of a third party's security interest in the collateral. Drake (D) alleged that he was unaware of the security interest because of his lack of formal training in business management. Drake (D) testified that he had majored in psychology in college. On cross-examination, he was impeached on this point by the use of prior inconsistent statements. The government (P) then alleged that his college transcript, which was not in evidence, indicated that he had been dismissed from the University of Illinois for violation of the terms of his probation and for falsification of facts in a disciplinary investigation. Drake (D) alleged that this line of questioning dealt unfairly with prejudicial and irrelevant material, and constituted the introduction of extrinsic evidence of specific instances of conduct offered in violation of Fed. R. Evid. 608 (b), and appealed his conviction.

ISSUE: Can cross-examination questions alone constitute extrinsic evidence?

HOLDING AND DECISION: (Anderson, J.) No. Cross-examination questions alone cannot constitute extrinsic evidence. Though the questions asked did not constitute extrinsic evidence, they were arguably improper because they assumed facts not in evidence. However, no substantial right of Drake (D) was affected, because he had already been impeached by the use of inconsistent statements. The damage had already been done by the time the objection now on appeal was raised. The trial court, therefore, did not abuse its discretion nor thereby commit a harmful error. Affirmed.

EDITOR'S ANALYSIS: The court in this case stated that the prosecution could elicit admissions from Drake (D) that his earlier testimony had been inaccurate. The subject of the cross-examination was thus not inappropriate. Drake (D) alleged that the form of the questions themselves constituted the introduction of extrinsic evidence of specific instances of conduct, but the court found that they did not.

NOTES:

UNITED STATES v. SAADA
Federal government (P) v. Convicted criminal (D)
212 F.3d 210 (3d Cir. 2000).

NATURE OF CASE: Appeal from conviction for fraud.

FACT SUMMARY: Saada (D), who was convicted of various fraud charges, claimed that the trial court erred by admitting evidence of specific instances of misconduct by Yaccarino, who was a witness to the alleged crime and whose statement made at the time of the incident was admitted as hearsay under the excited utterance exception. Yaccarino was dead at the time of trial.

CONCISE RULE OF LAW: Extrinsic evidence of a hearsay declarant's prior bad acts is not admissible where the declarant is unavailable.

FACTS: Saada (D) was convicted of various fraud charges arising out of a scheme to cheat an insurance company, whereby Saada (D) allegedly staged a flooding of a warehouse belonging to his family's business by intentionally breaking a sprinkler head. Yaccarino, a former state judge who had been removed from the bench and disbarred, was a vice president of the business, and was present at the warehouse when the flooding began. Another employee testified that Yaccarino, who was deceased at the time of the trial, had run into the kitchen screaming that Saada (D) had done something stupid and was dumb. Yaccarino said something to the effect of: "[Saada (D) threw] something, now he has got a mess . . . ." Yaccarino's statement purportedly provided contemporaneous evidence that Saada (D) had accidentally broken the sprinkler head. Accordingly, the government (P) sought to attack the statement by impeaching Yaccarino's credibility. The government asked the district court to take judicial notice of two judicial decisions ordering Yaccarino's removal from the bench and disbarment for unethical conduct, as well as the factual details supporting those decisions, which reflected his unethical conduct. Saada (D) objected on the grounds that the credibility of a hearsay declarant may not be impeached with extrinsic evidence of bad acts. The district court granted the government's (P) request, and Saada (D) appealed to the court of appeals.

ISSUE: Is extrinsic evidence of a hearsay declarant's prior bad acts admissible where the declarant is unavailable?

HOLDING AND DECISION: (Harris, J.) No. Extrinsic evidence of a hearsay declarant's prior bad acts is not admissible where the declarant is unavailable. The resolution of this appeal, raising an issue of first impression, requires resolution of the interplay between Fed. R. Evid. 806 and 608(b). Fed. R. Evid. 806 provides for the impeachment of a hearsay declarant, but limits that impeachment to "any evidence which would be admissible for [impeachment purposes] . . . if declarant had testified as a witness." Fed. R. Evid. 608(b) prohibits the use of extrinsic evidence to prove specific instances of conduct of a witness to attack (or support) the witness' credibility. Saada (D) argues that if Yaccarino had testified, Fed. R. Evid. 608(b) would have prevented the government (P) from introducing extrinsic evidence of his unethical conduct, and would have limited the government (P) to questioning him about that conduct on cross-examination. The government (P) argues that because Yaccarino's death foreclosed eliciting the facts of his misconduct on cross-examination, it was entitled to introduce extrinsic evidence of his misconduct. Here, the trial court implicitly interpreted Fed. R. Evid. 806 to modify Fed. R. Evid. 608(b)'s ban on extrinsic evidence. This issue has been decided by only two circuit courts, which are themselves in conflict over this issue. One allowed extrinsic evidence when the hearsay declarant was unavailable, and the other did not. The better approach is to not allow extrinsic evidence when the hearsay declarant is unavailable. Fed. R. Evid. 806 does not modify Fed. R. Evid. 608's ban on extrinsic evidence of prior bad acts in the context of hearsay declarants, even when those declarants are unavailable to testify. This conclusion is dictated by the plain language of both rules. The unavailability of the declarant does not warrant departing from the rules, as such unavailability will not always foreclose using prior misconduct as an impeachment tool because the witness testifying to the hearsay statement may be questioned about the declarant's misconduct—without reference to extrinsic evidence thereof—on cross-examination concerning knowledge of the declarant's character for truthfulness or untruthfulness. And, even if a hearsay declarant's credibility may not be impeached with evidence of prior misconduct, other avenues for impeaching the hearsay statement remain open (e.g., opinion and reputation evidence; prior criminal convictions; prior inconsistent statements). Also, Fed. R. Evid. 806 makes no allowance for the unavailability of a hearsay declarant in the context of impeachment by specific instances of misconduct, but makes such an allowance in the context of impeachment by prior inconsistent statements. The fact that Fed. R. Evid. 806 does not provide a comparable allowance for the unavailability of a hearsay declarant in the context of Fed. R. Evid. 608(b)'s ban on extrinsic evidence indicates that the latter's ban on extrinsic evidence applies with equal force in the context of hearsay declarants. Accordingly, the district court erred in admitting the challenged extrinsic evidence. However, such error was harmless. Affirmed.

Continued on next page.

EDITOR'S ANALYSIS: The consequences of the court's decision is that the party against whom the hearsay statement was admitted may have to call the declarant to testify, even though it was the party's adversary who adduced the statement requiring impeachment in the first place. And, where the declarant is unavailable to testify—as in this case—the ban prevents using evidence of prior misconduct as a form of impeachment, unless the witness testifying to the hearsay has knowledge of the declarant's misconduct; in many instances, the witness may know nothing about the declarant's past. Here, the court has determined that these potential drawbacks do not outweigh the reasons for banning the extrinsic evidence—namely, to avoid having a minitrial on a wholly collateral matter.

NOTES:

UNITED STATES v. SANDERS
Federal government (P) v. Prisoner (D)
964 F.2d 295 (4th Cir. 1992).

NATURE OF CASE: Appeal from convictions for assault with a deadly weapon with intent to do bodily harm and for possession of contraband.

FACT SUMMARY: After the trial court allowed the government (P) to cross-examine Sanders (D) about his prior convictions for assault and possession of a contraband knife, or shank, while incarcerated, the jury convicted Sanders (D) of identical offenses.

CONCISE RULE OF LAW: Evidence of prior felony convictions may be used to attack the credibility of a witness only if the probative value of the evidence outweighs its prejudicial effect.

FACTS: While Sanders (D) and Alston (D) were incarcerated, they were indicted for assault of a fellow prisoner with intent to commit murder and for possession of a contraband knife, or shank. Before trial, Sanders (D) moved to exclude evidence of his prior convictions. The district court allowed the government (P) to cross-examine Sanders (D) about his prior assault and contraband possession convictions. The jury convicted Sanders of possession of a contraband shank but could not reach a verdict on the assault count against him. The court declared a mistrial. Before the second trial, Sanders renewed his motion to exclude his prior convictions. The court denied the motion. After Sanders (D) testified that he had acted in self-defense, the government (P) cross-examined Sanders (D) about his prior convictions. The jury returned a verdict of the lesser included offense of assault with a dangerous weapon with intent to do bodily harm. Sanders (D) appealed both convictions.

ISSUE: May evidence of prior felony convictions be used to attack the credibility of a witness only if the probative value of the evidence outweighs it prejudicial effect?

HOLDING AND DECISION: (Phillips, J.) Yes. Evidence of prior felony convictions may be used to attack the credibility of a witness only if the probative value of the evidence outweighs its prejudicial effect. This balancing is required by Fed. R. Evid. 609(a). In this case, it is unclear whether and how the district court balanced the probative value of this evidence of Sanders' (D) prior convictions against its prejudicial effect. In any event, the evidence is inadmissible because of the high likelihood of prejudice that accompanies it. Neither is the evidence admissible under Fed. R. Evid. 404(b) to show intent since it is a prime example of evidence that proves only criminal disposition. Thus, the district court erred in admitting it. While the error was harmless as to the possession count for which Sanders (D) was convicted

in his first trial, it was not harmless as to his assault conviction. Affirmed in part, reversed in part, and remanded.

DISSENT: (Niemeyer, J.) When Sanders (D) claimed that he stabbed a fellow inmate in self-defense, he placed his intent at issue. Therefore, evidence of a prior assault, which was probative of intent, should have been ruled admissible.

EDITOR'S ANALYSIS: When faced with a *Sanders*-like decision, the Third Circuit has instructed courts to consider the impeachment value of the prior crime, the similarity between it and the charged offense, and the centrality of the impeachment issue. Despite these precautions, admission of evidence of a similar offense often does little to impeach the credibility of a testifying defendant while undoubtedly prejudicing him. The jury, despite limiting instructions, can hardly avoid drawing the inference that the past conviction suggests some probability that the defendant committed the similar offense for which he is currently charged.

NOTES:

UNITED STATES v. WONG
Federal government (P) v. Mail fraud convict (D)
703 F.2d 65 (3d Cir. 1983).

NATURE OF CASE: Appeal from a mail fraud conviction.

FACT SUMMARY: Wong (D) contended the trial court erred in admitting evidence of his prior convictions of crimes involving dishonesty without reference to their prejudicial effect.

CONCISE RULE OF LAW: Federal Rule of Evidence 609 requires the admission of impeachment evidence of prior convictions of crimes involving dishonesty, and a trial court cannot exclude such evidence regardless of its prejudicial effect.

FACTS: Wong (D) was charged with mail fraud. At trial, he moved to preclude use of his prior fraud convictions for impeachment. The court denied the motion, holding that since the prior convictions were crimes involving dishonesty, under Fed. R. Evid. 609(a)(2) no balancing of prejudice against probative value was appropriate, and that it was therefore compelled to admit them. Wong (D) took the stand and was impeached with the prior convictions. He appealed his subsequent conviction, contending that Rule 609 is qualified by the general prejudice-against-probity balancing test in Rule 403, and therefore the trial court erred in failing to consider the prejudicial impact of the convictions.

ISSUE: Under Fed. R. Evid. 609, can a trial court exclude impeachment evidence of prior convictions of crimes involving dishonesty if it finds the prejudicial effect of the evidence substantially outweighs its probative value?

HOLDING AND DECISION: (Per curiam) No. Fed. R. Evid. 609 requires the admission of impeachment evidence of prior convictions of crimes involving dishonesty, and a trial court cannot exclude such impeachment evidence regardless of its prejudicial effect. Rule 403 was not designed to override specific rules. Rather it was enacted as a guide for situations where no specific rule applied. Rule 609 clearly states that impeachment evidence of past convictions of crimes of dishonesty must be admitted. Clearly, then, the trial court was correct in holding that a balance between prejudice and probity was inappropriate, and the evidence was properly admitted. Affirmed.

EDITOR'S ANALYSIS: Any prior felony conviction is admissible in federal court for impeachment purposes. As this case illustrates, if the convictions involve crimes of dishonesty, they must be admitted regardless of their prejudicial effect. If they involve crimes which do not involve dishonesty, such as battery, then the prejudice-against-probity balancing test determines their admissibility. In the case of prior misdemeanor convictions, only those involving dishonesty are inadmissible under all circumstances.

NOTES:

108

UNITED STATES v. BRACKEEN
Federal government (P) v. Convicted bank robber (D)
969 F.2d 827 (9th Cir. 1992).

NATURE OF CASE: Appeal from conviction for aiding and abetting an armed bank robbery.

FACT SUMMARY: Brackeen (D) objected to the trial court's allowing, for impeachment purposes, the use of his prior guilty pleas to two unarmed bank robberies.

CONCISE RULE OF LAW: Bank robbery is not per se a crime of "dishonesty" as that term is used in Federal Rule of Evidence 609(a)(2).

FACTS: Brackeen (D) robbed three different banks. The first robbery was committed with an accomplice, Moore, who used a pistol. In the other two robberies, Brackeen (D) was unarmed and apparently acted alone. Brackeen (D) pleaded guilty to both unarmed bank robberies, then went to trial for aiding and abetting Moore in the armed bank robbery. Before testifying as the sole defense witness, Brackeen (D) objected to the use, for impeachment purposes, of his guilty pleas to the two unarmed bank robberies. The court allowed impeachment with the guilty pleas on cross-examination pursuant to Fed. R. Evid. 609(a)(2), which allows impeachment of a defendant by any crime involving "dishonesty or false statement." Brackeen (D) was convicted and appealed, claiming the impeachment was improper because the guilty pleas were to bank robbery, a crime that does not involve dishonesty or false statement.

ISSUE: Is bank robbery per se a crime of "dishonesty" as that term is used in Fed. R. Evid 609(a)(2)?

HOLDING AND DECISION: (Per curiam) No. Bank robbery is not per se a crime of "dishonesty" as that term is used in Fed. R. Evid. 609(a)(2). Under Fed. R. Evid. 609(a)(2), evidence that any witness has been convicted of a crime shall be admitted to attack credibility if it involved dishonesty or false statement, regardless of the punishment. Brackeen's (D) bank robberies did not involve any "false statement" and were not actually committed by fraudulent or deceitful means. However, "dishonesty" has both a broad and a narrow meaning. In its broader meaning, dishonesty is defined as a breach of trust, which would include bank robbery, while, in its narrower meaning, it is defined as deceitful behavior. While nothing in Rule 609(a)(2) indicates precisely what Congress meant when it used the term "dishonesty," the legislative history of the Rule makes it clear that Congress used the term in the narrower sense to mean only those crimes that involve deceit. Bank robbery is a crime of violent, not deceitful, taking. Brackeen's (D) conviction is thus reversed, and the case is remanded for a new trial.

EDITOR'S ANALYSIS: The House Conference Committee Report on Rule 609 stated that the phrase "dishonesty and false statement" meant crimes that involve some element of deceit, untruthfulness, or falsification bearing on the accused's propensity to testify truthfully. Such crimes would include perjury or subornation of perjury, false statement, criminal fraud, embezzlement, or false pretense, or any other offense in the nature of crimen falsi. In addition to bank robbery, state and federal courts have refused to conclude that larceny, shoplifting, and narcotic violations are per se crimes of "dishonesty."

NOTES:

LUCE v. UNITED STATES

Convicted drug dealer (D) v. Federal government (P)

469 U.S. 38 (1984).

NATURE OF CASE: Appeal from conviction for conspiracy and possession of cocaine with intent to distribute.

FACT SUMMARY: In the government's (P) action against Luce (D) for conspiracy and possession of cocaine with intent to distribute, Luce (D) contended that the district court's ruling denying Luce's (D) motion to forbid the use of a prior conviction to impeach his credibility was an abuse of discretion.

CONCISE RULE OF LAW: To raise and preserve for review the claim of improper impeachment with a prior conviction, a defendant must testify at trial.

FACTS: Luce (D) was indicted on charges of conspiracy and possession of cocaine with intent to distribute in violation of 21 U.S.C. §§ 846 and 841(a)(1). During his trial, Luce (D) moved for a ruling to preclude the government (P) from using a 1974 state conviction to impeach him if he testified. Luce (D) made no commitment that he would testify if the motion was granted and did not make a proffer to the court as to what his testimony would be. In opposing the motion, the government (P) represented that the conviction was for a serious crime-possession of a controlled substance. The district court ruled that the prior conviction fell within the category of permissible impeachment evidence under Fed. R. Evid. 609(a). Luce (D) did not testify, and the jury returned a guilty verdict. The U.S. Court of Appeals for the Sixth Circuit affirmed the district court's decision. The court of appeals refused to consider Luce's (D) contention that the district court abused its discretion in denying Luce's (D) motion in limine without making a specific finding that the probative value of the prior conviction outweighed its prejudicial effect. The court of appeals held that when a defendant does not testify, the court will not review the district court's in limine ruling.

ISSUE: To raise and preserve for review the claim of improper impeachment with a prior conviction, must a defendant testify at trial?

HOLDING AND DECISION: (Burger, C.J.) Yes. To raise and preserve for review the claim of improper impeachment with a prior conviction, a defendant must testify at trial. Under Fed. R. Evid. 609(a)(1), which directs the court to weigh the probative value of a prior conviction against the prejudicial effect to the defendant, to perform such balancing, a court must know the precise natures of the defendant's testimony, which is unknowable when, as here, a defendant does not testify. Were in limine rulings under Rule 609(a) reviewable on appeal, almost any error would result in the windfall of automatic reversal. Requiring Luce (D) to testify in order to preserve Rule 609(a) claims will enable the reviewing court to determine the impact any erroneous impeachment may have had in light of the record as a whole. Affirmed.

CONCURRENCE: (Brennan, J.) A defendant who does not testify at trial may not challenge on appeal for two reasons: the weighing of probative value and prejudicial effect can only be evaluated on appeal in the specific factual context of a trial, and if the defendant does not testify, the reviewing court cannot make the harmless error determination should the lower court's in limine ruling be found incorrect.

EDITOR'S ANALYSIS: As a method of impeachment, evidence of conviction of crime is significant only because it stands as proof of the commission of the underlying criminal act. There is little disagreement from the general proposition that at least some crimes are relevant to credibility. There is, however, much disagreement among cases and commentators about which crimes are usable for this purpose. Traditionally, use of felonies has been accepted for crimes involving dishonesty or false statement without regard to the grade of the offense.

NOTES:

UNITED STATES v. LINDSTROM
Federal government (P) v. Mail fraud conspirators (D)
698 F.2d 1154 (11th Cir. 1983).

NATURE OF CASE: Appeal from convictions for mail fraud.

FACT SUMMARY: Lindstrom (D) and Slater (D) were convicted of mail fraud and conspiracy after the trial court severely limited cross-examination of the government's (P) key witness as to her psychiatric disorders and past manipulative and destructive conduct.

CONCISE RULE OF LAW: Psychiatric evidence regarding a recent history of mental instability may be used to impeach a chief witness.

FACTS: Lindstrom (D) and Slater (D), part-owners of Bay Therapy, Inc., which provided physical therapy to injured people, were accused of inflating medical costs and defrauding insurance companies. They were indicted for mail fraud and conspiracy to commit mail fraud. The government's (P) key witness at trial, an employee of Bay Therapy, testified that she and Lindstrom (D) had altered records, that Lindstrom (D) and Slater (D) ordered her to duplicate billing cards, and that patients signed up for treatment they did not receive. Lindstrom (D) and Slater (D) contended that the witness was carrying out a vendetta against them. They sought to impeach her credibility with evidence of her psychiatric disorders, showing a history of manipulative and destructive conduct. The trial court imposed extremely narrow limits on cross-examination as to the witness's psychiatric history. The jury found Lindstrom (D) and Slater (D) guilty, and they appealed.

ISSUE: May psychiatric evidence regarding a recent history of mental instability be used to impeach a chief witness?

HOLDING AND DECISION: (Vance, J.) Yes. Psychiatric evidence regarding a recent history of mental instability may be used to impeach a chief witness. A criminal defendant has the right to be confronted with the witnesses against him. The right of confrontation includes the right to cross-examination, one goal of which is to impeach the credibility of opposing witnesses. Certain forms of mental disorder have a high probative value on the issue of credibility. Here, the medical records of the government's (P) chief witness suggested a history of psychiatric disorders manifested by violent threats and manipulative and destructive conduct relevant to the witness's motivation in this case. She initiated and pursued the investigation of Bay Therapy, was an insider to the fraud scheme, and testified in detail about the operation and activities of Lindstrom (D) and Slater (D). The district court thus committed reversible error in depriving Lindstrom (D) and Slater (D) of their Sixth Amendment right to confrontation and cross-examination.

EDITOR'S ANALYSIS: Mental illness may bear on credibility in a variety of ways. I may produce bias, impair veracity because of an inability to observe or recollect actual events, or distort reactions to events. A paranoid person, for example, may interpret a reality skewed by suspicious fantasies, while a schizophrenic may have a memory distorted by delusions and hallucinations.

NOTES:

COLES v. HARSCH
Husband (P) v. Alleged adulterer (D)
Or. Sup. Ct., 129 Or. 11, 276 P. 248 (1929).

NATURE OF CASE: Action for alienation of spouse's affections.

FACT SUMMARY: Thompson was one of Harsch's (D) principal witnesses, who testified that Harsch's (D) conduct towards Coles' (P) wife was proper and harmless. Coles (P) testified that Thompson told him on one occasion that the conduct of Harsch (D) and Coles' (P) wife toward each other was disgraceful.

CONCISE RULE OF LAW: Before a witness can be impeached by evidence of prior inconsistent statements, the statements must be related to him, with the circumstances of times, places, and persons present, and he must be asked whether he has made the statements, and, if so, allowed to explain them.

FACTS: Thompson was one of Harsch's (D) principal witnesses, and he testified that Harsch's (D) conduct towards Coles's (P) wife, whose affections Harsch (D) was accused of alienating, was proper and harmless. On cross-examination, Thompson was asked whether he recalled talking to Coles (P) about a picnic. He replied in the negative. Coles (P) then testified that Thompson had told him that at a certain picnic the conduct of Harsch (D) and Coles's (P) wife toward one another had been disgraceful. Harsch (D) had objected to the inquiry which elicited this response, but Coles's (P) counsel stated that the answer was sought for the sole purpose of impeaching Thompson. Judgment was made in favor of Coles, and Harsch appealed.

ISSUE: Before a witness can be impeached by evidence of prior inconsistent statements, must he be told the statements and the surrounding circumstances and be allowed to explain them, if he acknowledges them as his?

HOLDING AND DECISION: (Rossman, J.) Yes. Before a witness can be impeached by evidence of prior inconsistent statements, the statements must be related to him, with the circumstances of times, places, and persons present, and he must be asked whether he made the statements and, if so, allowed to explain them. Here, the only foundation laid for the impeaching testimony was the question of whether Thompson remembered talking to Coles (P) about a picnic. The alleged statement was never related to Thompson, nor were the accompanying circumstances. Hence, it was error to admit the impeaching evidence. Reversed.

EDITOR'S ANALYSIS: The purposes of the "foundation requirement" are to avoid unfair surprise to the adversary, to save time (as an admission by the witness may make the extrinsic proof unnecessary), and to give the witness, in fairness to him, a chance to explain the discrepancy. McCormick points out that the requirement may work unfairly for the impeacher. He may only learn of the inconsistent statement after he has cross-examined, and after the witness, by leaving the courtroom, has made it impracticable to recall him for further cross-examination to lay the foundation belatedly.

NOTES:

TOME v. UNITED STATES
Sexual assault convict (D) v. Federal government (P)
513 U.S. 150 (1995).

NATURE OF CASE: Appeal from an order upholding a sexual assault conviction.

FACT SUMMARY: Tome (D) appealed his conviction for sexually assaulting his daughter, A.T., contending that the statements made by A.T. regarding the sexual abuse were made after a motivation to fabricate those statements arose and should therefore be excluded under the hearsay rule.

CONCISE RULE OF LAW: A witness's out-of-court statements consistent with court testimony are admissible to rebut a charge of recent fabrication or improper influence or motive only if made before the charged recent fabrication or improper influence or motive.

FACTS: Tome (D) was charged with sexually abusing his daughter, A.T., while she was in his custody. Tome (D) had been granted primary physical custody of A.T. after he divorced A.T.'s mother. A.T.'s mother had been unsuccessful in obtaining primary custody of A.T., and Tome (D) contended that the allegations of the sexual abuse were fabricated so that A.T.'s mother could obtain custody of A.T. The government (P) produced six witnesses who recounted statements made by A.T. which implicated Tome (D) in the sexual abuse. The statements were admitted in court to rebut Tome's (D) charge that A.T.'s testimony was motivated by her desire to live with her mother. The trial court convicted and sentenced Tome (D) to twelve years imprisonment. On appeal, the court affirmed, holding that all of A.T.'s out-of-court statements were admissible even though they had been made after A.T.'s alleged motive to fabricate. The Supreme Court granted review.

ISSUE: Are a witness's out-of-court statements consistent with court testimony admissible to rebut a charge of recent fabrication or improper influence or motive only if made before the charged recent fabrication or improper influence or motive?

HOLDING AND DECISION: (Kennedy, J.) Yes. A witness's out-of-court statements consistent with court testimony are admissible to rebut a charge of recent fabrication or improper influence or motive only if made before the charged recent fabrication or improper influence or motive. Reversed.

CONCURRENCE: (Scalia, J.) The Advisory Committee's Notes are not authoritative and cannot be used to change the meaning of the Rules.

DISSENT: (Breyer, J.) The issue in this case concerns relevance, not hearsay. Fed. R. Evid. 801(d)(1)(B) has nothing to do with relevance and does not codify the common law absolute timing

requirement. Hearsay law turns on an out-of-court declarant's reliability and timing does not affect reliability. There is no strong reason for making the premotive rule an absolute condition of admissibility here.

EDITOR'S ANALYSIS: The court mentions the possible application of Fed. R. Evid. 803(24) in this case as an alternative. The history of the rule at common law was also reviewed by the Court. The Notes are used to confirm the holding.

NOTES:

UNITED STATES v. ABEL
Federal government (P) v. Convicted bank robber (D)
469 U.S. 45 (1984).

NATURE OF CASE: Appeal from reversal of conviction for bank robbery.

FACT SUMMARY: In the government's (P) action against Abel (D) for bank robbery, Abel (D) contended that the district court improperly admitted testimony which impeached one of Abel's (D) witnesses, and that this was reversible error.

CONCISE RULE OF LAW: A district court is accorded a wide discretion in determining the admissibility of evidence under the Federal Rules.

FACTS: Abel (D) and two cohorts were indicted for robbing a savings and loan in violation of 18 U.S.C. §§ 2113(a) and (d). The cohorts decided to plead guilty, but Abel (D) went to trial. One of the cohorts, Ehle, agreed to testify against Abel (D) and identify him as a participant in the robbery. Abel (D) objected to this testimony, but the district court held that the probative value of Ehle's testimony outweighed its prejudicial effect, and that Abel (D) might be entitled to a limiting instruction if his counsel would submit one to the court. After Ehle's testimony, Abel's (D) counsel did not request a limiting instruction and did not get one. Abel (D) was convicted and appealed, contending that the court improperly admitted Ehle's testimony, impeaching Abel's (D) witness, Mills, and that this was reversible error. The court of appeals reversed, holding that Ehle's testimony was admitted to show that because Mills belonged to a secret, allegedly perjurious organization, he must be lying on the stand. This suggestion of perjury should not have been permitted. The government (P) appealed.

ISSUE: Is a district court accorded a wide discretion in determining the admissibility of evidence under the Federal Rules?

HOLDING AND DECISION: (Rehnquist, J.) Yes. A district court is accorded a wide discretion in determining the admissibility of evidence under the Federal Rules. Assessing the probative value of common membership in any particular group and weighing any factors counseling against admissibility is a matter first for the district court's sound judgment under Rules 401 and 403, and ultimately, if the evidence is admitted, for the trier of fact. Here, before admitting Ehle's testimony, the district court gave heed to the extensive arguments of counsel both in chambers and at the bench. The court also offered to give a limiting instruction concerning the testimony. These precautions may not have prevented all prejudice to Abel (D) from Ehle's testimony, but they did ensure that the admission of this highly probative evidence did not unduly prejudice Abel (D). There was no abuse of discretion under Rule 403 in admitting Ehle's testimony. Reversed.

EDITOR'S ANALYSIS: Case law recognizes that certain circumstances call for the exclusion of evidence which is of unquestioned relevance. These circumstances involve risks which range all the way from inducing decision on a purely emotional basis at one extreme, to nothing more harmful than just wasting time at the other extreme. Situations in this area call for balancing the probative value of and need for the evidence against the harm likely to result from its admission.

NOTES:

CHAPTER SIX
CONFIDENTIALITY AND CONFIDENTIAL COMMUNICATION

QUICK REFERENCE RULES OF LAW

1. **Attorney-Client Privilege.** Communications between an attorney and client concerning the time, date, and place of trial are not privileged. (United States v. Woodruff)

2. **"Client" in the Attorney-Client Privilege.** The attorney-client privilege extends to communications between corporate counsel and lower echelon employees who make the communications at the direction of their superiors. (Upjohn Co. v. United States)

3. **Holder of the Attorney-Client Privilege.** A person who acts as an intermediate agent for communication between an attorney and client may invoke the attorney-client privilege and refuse to reveal the communication. (City and County of San Francisco v. Superior Court)

4. **"Confidentiality" Requirement for the Attorney.** The attorney-client privilege may not be invoked as a bar to the testimony of an eavesdropper, and does not apply to communications which are in furtherance of criminal activity. (Clark v. State)

5. **The Attorney-Client Privilege.** A district court is not obligated to hold, upon request, an in camera review of the validity of a claimed crime-fraud exception to the attorney-client privilege. (United States v. Zolin)

6. **Psychotherapist-Patient Privilege.** If the death for which a wrongful death action is brought occurred under circumstances consistent with either negligence of the defendant or suicide, so that the mental condition of the deceased is at issue, the psychotherapist-patient privilege will not prevent disclosure of relevant communications between the deceased and his psychotherapist. (Prink v. Rockefeller Center, Inc.)

7. **Scope of Psycotherapist-patient Privilege.** Confidential communications between a licensed social worker and a patient should be protected from compelled disclosure under the psychotherapist-patient privilege. (Jaffee v. Redmond)

8. **Exceptions to the Privilege.** A psychotherapist's warning to the patient's intended victim is not privileged, even if it relates an otherwise protected communication, where there is reasonable cause to believe that the patient is dangerous and disclosure is necessary to prevent any harm. (Menendez v. Superior Court)

9. **Spousal Privileges.** A criminal defendant cannot prevent his spouse from voluntarily offering adverse testimony against him because the privilege against adverse spousal testimony belongs to the testifying spouse. (Trammel v. United States)

10. **Parent-child Privilege.** Federal law does not recognize a parent-child privilege. (In re Grand Jury)

11. **Media Privilege.** Newspeople and other media representatives are not constitutionally privileged to withhold duly subpoenaed documents that may be highly relevant to a criminal proceeding, even though confidential sources may be publicly divulged if the documents are not withheld. (Matter of Farber)

UNITED STATES v. WOODRUFF
Federal government (P) v. Bail jumper (D)
383 F.Supp. 696 (E.D. Pa. 1974).

NATURE OF CASE: Motion to compel testimony of defense counsel.

FACT SUMMARY: The government (P) moved to the district court to order the public defender representing Woodruff (D) to respond to questions relating to whether he advised Woodruff (D), who failed to appear for trial, of the time and place scheduled for trial.

CONCISE RULE OF LAW: Communications between an attorney and client concerning the time, date, and place of trial are not privileged.

FACTS: Woodruff (D) was free on bail and failed to appear for trial. The government (P), seeking an indictment for bail jumping, moved the district court to compel the public defender representing Woodruff (D) to answer its questions relating to whether the attorney advised Woodruff (D) of the time and date set for the trial. The public defender contended the information was protected under the attorney-client privilege.

ISSUE: Are communications between an attorney and client concerning the time, date, and place of trial protected under the attorney-client privilege?

HOLDING AND DECISION: (Green, J.) No. Communications between an attorney and client relating to the time, date, and place of trial are not protected under the attorney-client privilege. Communications are covered only if they were made by the client or the attorney relating to the client's legal problem. In this case, the communication did not relate to Woodruff's (D) legal problem. Further, the information concerning the time and date of trial was gained by the attorney from the court and not from Woodruff (D). The attorney acted as a mere messenger in relation to this information. As a result, it cannot be considered privileged. Motion granted.

EDITOR'S ANALYSIS: A communication is privileged under the attorney-client privilege only if its purpose is related to consultation for legal advice. The person seeking advice need not ultimately hire the attorney to invoke the privilege; therefore preliminary discussions are protected. No privilege exists when the lawyer acts in any capacity, other than as attorney. Further, the client is the holder of the privilege, and it does not terminate upon the death of the client. His estate or personal representative may assert it.

NOTES:

116

UPJOHN CO. v. UNITED STATES
Corporation (D) v. Federal government (P)
449 U.S. 383 (1981).

NATURE OF CASE: Appeal from an order enforcing a summons to produce corporate records.

FACT SUMMARY: Upjohn Co. (D) refused to produce documents prepared by its employees during its in-house investigation of potential bribery payments, contending they were protected by the attorney-client privilege.

CONCISE RULE OF LAW: The attorney-client privilege extends to communications between corporate counsel and lower echelon employees who make the communications at the direction of their superiors.

FACTS: Upjohn Co. (D) decided to conduct an internal investigation to find out if any of its foreign subsidiaries had made illegal payments to foreign governments. Upjohn's (D) chairman of the board sent out a letter to its subsidiaries to prepare reports containing information from any employee concerning whether any such payments were made. The reports were to be sent directly to the corporate counsel who was conducting the investigation. Subsequently, Upjohn (D) voluntarily submitted a preliminary report to the Securities and Exchange Commission (SEC) disclosing certain questionable payments. The SEC turned the report over to the Internal Revenue Service (IRS) to investigate the tax consequences. The IRS issued a summons requiring Upjohn (D) to turn over its subsidiaries reports. Upjohn (D) refused, contending the reports were protected by the attorney-client privilege. The government (P) petitioned the district court to enforce the summons. The court held that because the communications were made outside the "control group" of the corporation, they were not covered by the attorney-client privilege. Upjohn (D) appealed.

ISSUE: Does the attorney-client privilege extend to communications between corporate counsel and lower echelon employees who make the communications at the direction of their superiors?

HOLDING AND DECISION: (Rehnquist, J.) Yes. The attorney-client privilege extends to communications between corporate counsel and lower echelon employees who make the communications at the direction of their superiors. The control group test frustrates the purpose of the privilege by discouraging the communication of relevant information by employees of the corporate client to attorneys seeking to render advice to the corporation. In this case, the reports were made to the corporate counsel to allow him to assess Upjohn's (D) legal position. As a result, the reports were privileged. Reversed and remanded.

CONCURRENCE: (Burger, C.J.) The court was correct in its holding, yet it should have formulated a standard applicable in other cases concerning whether particular discussions will be protected.

EDITOR'S ANALYSIS: As this case illustrates, a problem arises in the application of the attorney-client privilege to corporations. As a legal entity, a corporation is entitled to invoke the privilege. However, the problem arises in identifying who the client is. Formerly the client was considered to be that group of key officers actually in control of the corporation. This was known as the control group test. The Court in this case, although refusing to confine the privilege to the control group, specifically stated that the application of the privilege would have to be determined with respect to corporations on a case by case basis.

NOTES:

CITY AND COUNTY OF SAN FRANCISCO v. SUPERIOR COURT
Municipality (D) v. Injured plaintiff (P)
Cal. Sup. Ct., 37 Cal. 2d 227, 231 P.2d 26 (1951).

NATURE OF CASE: Petition for writ of mandamus to compel testimony.

FACT SUMMARY: San Francisco (D) contended that Dr. Catton could be compelled to testify concerning Hession's (P) neurological condition because he admitted no physician-patient privilege existed.

CONCISE RULE OF LAW: A person who acts as an intermediate agent for communication between an attorney and client may invoke the attorney-client privilege and refuse to reveal the communication.

FACTS: Hession (P) sued San Francisco (D) for personal injuries, contending he suffered neurological damage due to the City's (D) actions. At the request of Hession's (P) attorney, Dr. Catton, a physician specializing in nervous diseases, examined Hession (P) twice. In his deposition, Dr. Catton testified there was no physician-patient relationship between him and Hession (P), and the sole purpose of the examinations was to aid Hession's (P) attorneys in preparing the lawsuit. Dr. Catton refused to answer the City's (D) questions concerning Hession's (P) condition, contending he was an agent of Hession's (P) attorneys and the information was protected under the attorney-client privilege. San Francisco (D) petitioned the California Supreme Court for a writ of mandamus to compel the superior court to order Dr. Catton to testify.

ISSUE: May a person who acts as an intermediary agent for communication between an attorney and client invoke the attorney-client privilege and refuse to reveal the communication?

HOLDING AND DECISION: (Traynor, J.) Yes. A person who acts as an intermediate agent for communication between an attorney and client may invoke the attorney-client privilege and refuse to reveal the communication. It is clear that if Hession (P) had communicated his condition directly to his attorneys, neither he nor his attorneys could be compelled to reveal it. The communication is no less one between Hession (P) and his attorneys merely because of the existence of the intermediate agent Dr. Catton. This would be true if the agent were an interpreter, a messenger, or any other agent of transmission. The same policies aimed at promoting full disclosure between clients and attorneys apply where there exists an intermediate agent. Therefore, Dr. Catton could properly invoke the privilege. Petition denied.

EDITOR'S ANALYSIS: The rationale behind the recognition of the attorney-client privilege is that adequate legal representation depends upon the client revealing all relevant facts to his attorney. The failure to fully disclose such facts renders any advice given by the attorney useless. Therefore, to promote full disclosure, a client is able to refuse to reveal any communication between himself and his attorney, or his attorney's agent, and he can prevent the attorney or agent from so revealing.

NOTES:

CLARK v. STATE
Convicted murderer (D) v. State (P)
Tex. Ct. Crim. App., 159 Tex. Cr. R. 187, 261 S.W.2d 339 (1953).

NATURE OF CASE: Appeal from a conviction for murder.

FACT SUMMARY: Bartz, a telephone operator, eavesdropped during a telephone conversation between Clark (D) and his attorney in which he (D) admitted to the murder of his wife and was advised to dispose of the murder weapon. At trial, Bartz' testimony was admitted despite the objection that it was precluded by application of the attorney-client privilege.

CONCISE RULE OF LAW: The attorney-client privilege may not be invoked as a bar to the testimony of an eavesdropper and does not apply to communications which are in furtherance of criminal activity.

FACTS: On the evening that she had obtained a divorce from her husband, Clark's (D) wife was found murdered. The findings of a firearms expert indicated she had been killed by the same type of gun as was owned by Clark (D). Other evidence at trial included the testimony of Marjorie Bartz, a telephone operator who testified that she had placed a call from Clark (D) to his attorney on the evening of Mrs. Clark's murder. Bartz admitted that she eavesdropped during the conversation, and heard Clark (D) admit to the murder of his wife. She testified that he was then advised by his attorney to "get rid of the weapon." Clark (D) was convicted of murder, but argued on appeal that Bartz's testimony should have been excluded since it related to a privileged communication between a lawyer and his client.

ISSUE: Does the attorney-client privilege bar the testimony of an eavesdropper and apply to communications which are in furtherance of criminal activity?

HOLDING AND DECISION: (Morrison, J.) No. The attorney-client privilege may not be invoked as a bar to the testimony of an eavesdropper and does not apply to communications which are in furtherance of criminal activity. Evidence, even if obtained by eavesdropping, is admissible provided that it is relevant. And, since the eavesdropper occupies no confidential relationship to either party, such evidence may not be excluded by invocation of the attorney-client privilege, notwithstanding that the testimony relates to a conversation which both the client and his attorney believed was confidential. Therefore, Bartz's testimony was properly admitted, and Clark's (D) conviction must be affirmed.

ON MOTION FOR REHEARING: (Woodley, J.) The attorney-client privilege is justified by the public's interest in encouraging disclosure to an attorney of all facts material to a client's case. But this laudable interest may not be abused by parties who would invoke the privilege to protect against communications in which a client is advised of ways in which to avoid apprehension for a crime. When an attorney advises his client of how best to avoid prosecution, he becomes an accessory to his client's crime. Since such conduct is not within the realm of legitimate professional employment, communications of this type are not entitled to the protection afforded by the attorney-client privilege.

EDITOR'S ANALYSIS: Courts permitting an eavesdropper to disclose the contents of a conversation between an attorney and his client generally justify their narrow application of the privilege by pointing out that rules of evidence which tend to frustrate truth ascertainment are entitled to strict construction. The Clark court's holding that the privilege may not be asserted to protect against disclosure of communications in furtherance of a crime is in accord with the weight of authority.

NOTES:

UNITED STATES v. ZOLIN
Federal government (P) v. Church
491 U.S. 554 (1989).

NATURE OF CASE: Review of tax evasion action.

FACT SUMMARY: The Internal Revenue Service (IRS) (P) contended that a district court was obligated, upon request, to hold an in camera review on the validity of a claimed crime-fraud exception to the attorney-client privilege.

CONCISE RULE OF LAW: A district court is not obligated to hold, upon request, an in camera review of the validity of a claimed crime-fraud exception to the attorney-client privilege.

FACTS: The IRS (P) brought a tax evasion action against the Church of Scientology (D). The IRS (P) sought production of certain tapes of conversations between Church (D) officials and legal counsel. The Church (D) claimed attorney-client privilege. The IRS (P) claimed a crime-fraud exception to the privilege and contended that the district court was obligated, upon request, to hold an in camera review on the validity of a claimed crime-fraud exception to the attorney-client privilege. The district court held itself not so obligated, and denied review. The Supreme Court granted certiorari.

ISSUE: Is a district court obligated to hold, upon request, an in camera review of the validity of a claimed crime-fraud exception to the attorney-client privilege?

HOLDING AND DECISION: (Blackmun, J.) No. A district court is not obligated to hold, upon request, an in camera review of the validity of a claimed crime-fraud exception to the attorney-client privilege. To so hold would place the policy of protecting legitimate disclosure between counsel and client at risk. Disclosure of communications, even if to a court in camera, presents a danger to the confidentiality of attorney-client communications. Moreover, the rule urged by Zolin (D) would place an undue burden on district courts. Rather, this Court believes that the better rule is to require a party claiming the exception to show an adequate factual basis for a good faith belief that the exception applies. [The Court then remanded for such a hearing as to whether such a factual basis existed.]

EDITOR'S ANALYSIS: The Church (D) contended that in camera review was flatly prohibited in circumstances such as those presented here. The Court disagreed. The Court was of the opinion that neither the Federal Rules of Evidence nor common law established a firm rule.

NOTES:

PRINK v. ROCKEFELLER CENTER INC.
Wife of decedent (P) v. Office center (D)
N.Y. Ct. App., 48 N.Y.2d 309, 422 N.Y.S.2d 911, 398 N.E.2d 517 (1979).

NATURE OF CASE: Action for damages for wrongful death.

FACT SUMMARY: Mrs. Prink's (P) husband died after a fall from his Rockefeller Center (D) office window. Rockefeller Center (D) claimed it had been a suicide and sought to delve into what Mr. Prink's psychiatrist had told Mrs. Prink (P) about her husband's condition in a conversation after his death.

CONCISE RULE OF LAW: If the death for which a wrongful death action is brought occurred under circumstances consistent with either negligence of the defendant or suicide, so that the mental condition of the deceased is at issue, the psychotherapist-patient privilege will not prevent disclosure of relevant communications between the deceased and his psychotherapist.

FACTS: In a wrongful death action brought by Mrs. Prink (P), it was claimed her husband fell from his Rockefeller Center (D) office window by accident because he was forced to kneel on his desk to open the jammed window. Rockefeller Center (D) claimed that Mr. Prink had committed suicide by jumping from the window and successfully moved for an order compelling Mrs. Prink to testify as to the content of a conversation she had with her husband's psychiatrist after his death. On appeal, Mrs. Prink (P) continued to argue that the information the psychiatrist imparted to her was covered by her husband's patient-physician privilege.

ISSUE: Does the psychotherapist-patient privilege prevent disclosure of relevant communications between the deceased and his psychotherapist in a wrongful death action where mental condition is at issue?

HOLDING AND DECISION: (Meyer, J.) No. If the death for which a wrongful death action is brought occurred under circumstances consistent with either negligence of the defendant or suicide, so that the mental condition of the deceased is at issue, the psychotherapist-patient privilege will not prevent disclosure of relevant communications between the deceased and his psychotherapist. In a wrongful death action where mental condition is an issue, e.g., whether the circumstances of death are consistent with either negligence on the defendant's part or suicide, the psychotherapist-patient privilege will not prevent disclosure of relevant communications between the deceased and his psychotherapist. While the privilege is not terminated by death alone, it is effectively waived when the patient brings or defends a personal injury action in which his mental condition is affirmatively put in issue. By analogy, it is similarly waived by the bringing of a wrongful death action putting the client's mental condition at issue. Thus, the order requiring the psychiatrist to testify was proper. Affirmed.

EDITOR'S ANALYSIS: Frequently, statutes provide that the patient-physician or patient-psychotherapist privileges are not operative or are curtailed in certain types of proceedings. These include criminal prosecutions, workmen's compensation proceedings, malpractice suits, and will contests, among others.

NOTES:

JAFFEE v. REDMOND
Executor of estate (P) v. Former police officer (D)
518 U.S. 1 (1996).

NATURE OF CASE: Review of reversal of award of damages for violation of constitutional rights and wrongful death.

FACT SUMMARY: The administrator of Allen's estate (P) filed suit against Officer Redmond (D) for use of excessive force which resulted in Allen's death and sought the notes from the social worker who counseled Redmond (D) regarding Allen's death.

CONCISE RULE OF LAW: Confidential communications between a licensed social worker and a patient should be protected from compelled disclosure under the psychotherapist-patient privilege.

FACTS: Redmond (D) was a police officer on patrol duty when she responded to a "fight in progress" call involving Allen. Redmond (D) shot and killed Allen because she believed he was about to stab the man he was chasing. After the shooting, Redmond (D) participated in about fifty counseling sessions with Beyer, a clinical social worker licensed by the State of Illinois. The administrator of Allen's estate (P) filed suit in federal district court, alleging that Redmond (D) had used excessive force, and sought access to Beyer's notes concerning the sessions. Both Redmond (D) and Beyer resisted the order of the district judge to disclose Beyer's notes. In his jury instructions, the judge advised the jury that it could presume that the contents of the notes would have been unfavorable to Redmond (D). The jury returned a verdict for Allen's estate (P). The Court of Appeals reversed and remanded for a new trial, stating that the psychotherapist-patient privilege should be recognized if the patient's privacy interests outweighed evidentiary need.

ISSUE: Should confidential communications between a licensed social worker and a patient be protected from compelled disclosure under the psychotherapist-patient privilege?

HOLDING AND DECISION: (Stevens, J.) Yes. Confidential communications between a licensed social worker and a patient should be protected from compelled disclosure under the psychotherapist-patient privilege. The psychotherapist privilege is rooted in the notion that effective psychotherapy requires an atmosphere of trust and confidence in which the patient is able provide information without fear that it will be disclosed. This privilege serves both private and public interests by promoting the treatment of mental health problems. The denial of this privilege will both inhibit disclosure of important information between psychotherapist and patient and impede the effective treatment of mental health problems without the concomitant evidentiary benefit. Furthermore, the need to recognize this privilege at common law is evidenced by state legislation in all fifty states and the District of Columbia protecting the psychotherapist privilege. This psychotherapist privilege should also extend to confidential communications made to licensed social workers engaged in psychotherapy, since they serve the same public goals as those of psychologists and psychiatrists. Affirmed.

DISSENT: (Scalia, J.) The Court's analysis is misdirected to a general question, i.e., should there be a psychotherapist privilege, that can only be answered in the affirmative, which it then applies to the issue without giving it full consideration. It is unlikely that fear of disclosure would produce a chilling effect upon psychotherapy since it was a thriving practice before the protection of the psychotherapist privilege. It would be irresponsible to extend the psychotherapist privilege to all licensed social workers without first exploring the scope of the protection.

EDITOR'S ANALYSIS: The psychotherapist-patient privilege as applied to licensed social workers and, in some states, marital counsellors, was one that was extended through common law principles interpreted in the light of reason and experience under Rule 501 of the Federal Rules of Evidence. Even though consideration of testimony protected by the privilege would aid in the determination of truth in most cases, the interests or relationships fostered by the confidential communications are considered to be of sufficient social importance that nondisclosure is an acceptable cost.

NOTES:

MENENDEZ v. SUPERIOR COURT
Murdering brothers (D) v. Court (P)
Cal. Sup. Ct., 3 Cal. 4th 435, 834 P.2d 786 (1992).

NATURE OF CASE: Appeal from the denial of a petition for a writ of mandate regarding the admissibility of privileged communications in a murder prosecution.

FACT SUMMARY: The trial court ruled in a pretrial hearing that the cassette tapes obtained from the psychotherapist treating the Menendez brothers (D) were not privileged as the tapes fell within the "dangerous patient" exception.

CONCISE RULE OF LAW: A psychotherapist's warning to the patient's intended victim is not privileged, even if it relates an otherwise protected communication, where there is reasonable cause to believe that the patient is dangerous and disclosure is necessary to prevent any harm.

FACTS: In investigating the murders of Jose and Mary Louise Menendez, three audiocassette tapes were obtained from Dr. Oziel, psychotherapist for sons Lyle and Erik Menendez (D). Oziel claimed the psychotherapist-patient privilege on behalf of the brothers. The tapes contained notes relating to sessions with the Menendezes (D) on October 31 and November 2, 1989, notes relating to a session with Erik (D) on November 28, and an actual session with Lyle and Erik (D) on December 11. The brothers (D) were subsequently arrested and placed in custody. Because they had made threats of harm, in the first two sessions, to Oziel, his wife, and his lover, Oziel disclosed these communications to the two women. The superior court rejected the privilege claim as to all of the tapes under the "dangerous patient" exception. The court of appeals twice denied the brothers' (D) petition for a writ of mandate, and they petitioned for review.

ISSUE: Is a psychotherapist's warning to the patient's intended victim privileged, if it relates an otherwise protected communication, where there is reasonable cause to believe that the patient is dangerous and disclosure is necessary to prevent any harm?

HOLDING AND DECISION: (Mosk, J.) No. A psychotherapist's warning to the patient's intended victim is not privileged, even if it relates an otherwise protected communication, where there is reasonable cause to believe that the patient is dangerous and disclosure is necessary to prevent any harm. In this case, the "dangerous patient" exception was applicable to the sessions on October 31 and November 2 after Oziel, having reasonable cause to believe that the Menendezes (D) were dangerous and that disclosure was necessary to prevent harm, disclosed to his wife and his lover all the communications made at those sessions. The requirements for the exception were not met, however, for the November 28 and December 11 sessions because there was insufficient evidence that Oziel had reasonable cause for belief

that disclosure was necessary. Affirmed in part, reversed in part, and remanded.

EDITOR'S ANALYSIS: California Evidence Code has codified the exception in § 1024. Other exceptions to the psychotherapist-patient privilege include communications made to court-appointed psychotherapists who breach the therapist-patient relationships and to psychotherapists who have cause to believe that a patient under the age of sixteen is the victim of a crime.

NOTES:

TRAMMEL v. UNITED STATES

Co-conspirator spouse (D) v. Federal government (P)
445 U.S. 40 (1980).

NATURE OF CASE: Appeal from convictions for conspiracy to import and importing heroin.

FACT SUMMARY: Trammel's (D) wife agreed to testify against her husband in return for lenient treatment for herself, but Trammel (D) argued he had the right to prevent her from testifying against him.

CONCISE RULE OF LAW: A criminal defendant cannot prevent his spouse from voluntarily offering adverse testimony against him because the privilege against adverse spousal testimony belongs to the testifying spouse.

FACTS: In return for lenient treatment for herself, Mrs. Trammel, an unindicted co-conspirator, agreed to testify against her husband at his trial for conspiracy to import and importing heroin. The district court ruled she could testify to any act she observed during the marriage and to any communication made in the presence of a third person but not as to confidential communications between herself and her husband because they fell within the privilege attaching to confidential marital communications. On appeal, Trammel (D) contended that he was entitled to invoke the privilege against adverse spousal testimony so as to exclude the voluntary testimony of his wife. The court of appeals rejected this contention and affirmed the convictions.

ISSUE: Can a criminal defendant invoke the privilege against adverse spousal testimony so as to prevent his spouse from voluntarily offering adverse testimony against him?

HOLDING AND DECISION: (Burger, C.J.) No. A criminal defendant cannot prevent his spouse from voluntarily offering adverse testimony against him because the privilege against adverse spousal testimony belongs to the testifying spouse. The *Hawkins* case left the federal privilege for adverse spousal testimony where it found it at the time thus continuing a rule which barred the testimony of one spouse against the other unless both consented. However, since that 1958 decision, support for that conception of the privilege has eroded further and the trend in state law is toward divesting the accused of the privilege to bar adverse spousal testimony. The ancient foundations for so sweeping a privilege involved a conception of the wife as her husband's chattel to do with as he wished, and they have long since disappeared. Nor is the desire to protect the marriage a valid justification for affording an accused such a privilege. If his spouse desires to testify against him, simply preventing her from doing so is not likely to save the marriage. Affirmed.

EDITOR'S ANALYSIS: The Model Code of Evidence and the Uniform Rules of Evidence completely abolished the notion of a privilege against adverse spousal testimony and limited themselves to recognizing a privilege covering confidential marital communications. Several state legislatures have followed suit.

NOTES:

IN RE GRAND JURY
Federal government (P) v. Parents (D)
103 F. 3d 1140 (3d Cir. 1997).

NATURE OF CASE: Consolidated appeals from criminal convictions.

FACT SUMMARY: Cases from the Virgin Islands and Delaware were consolidated on appeal. In the Virgin Islands case, a father was subpoenaed to testify against his son. In the Delaware case, a minor daughter was subpoenaed to testify against her father. A parent-child privilege was claimed in both.

CONCISE RULE OF LAW: Federal law does not recognize a parent-child privilege.

FACTS: Appeals concerning a parent-child privilege were consolidated into one hearing. One appeal originated in the Virgin Islands, and the other originated in Delaware. In the Virgin Islands' case, the father of the target of a grand jury investigation was subpoenaed as a witness, and moved to quash the subpoena by asserting privilege under Federal Rule of Evidence 501. The father argued that he had a close, loving relationship with his son and, should he be forced to testify, he would not be able to talk with his son without the son's attorney present for the entire investigation. The father's motion to quash was denied because the Third Circuit had not addressed the issue of whether the federal court recognized a parent-child privilege, and all other circuits had refused to recognize the privilege. In the Delaware case, a minor daughter was subpoenaed to testify to the grand jury regarding charges against her father for the interstate kidnapping of a woman. She refused to testify and was found in contempt of court. The contempt order was stayed pending appeal.

ISSUE: Does federal law recognize a parent-child privilege?

HOLDING AND DECISION: (Garth, J.) No. Federal law does not recognize a parent-child privilege. Although legal academicians seem to favor adoption of a parent-child privilege, there are several reasons for not adopting such a privilege. First, the overwhelming majority of all federal and state courts have rejected such a privilege, and only lower courts in four states have recognized it. Second, Fed. R. Evid. 501, which allows adoption of all common law privileges, does not support the creation of a parent-child privilege. This is because privileges are generally disfavored, and, in this case, because no common law principles have been adduced that support a parent-child privilege. Finally, adopting a parent-child privilege would be inconsistent with U.S. Supreme Court precedent and with this court's precedent. The Supreme Court has emphasized that in determining whether a particular privilege "promotes sufficiently important interests to outweigh the need for probative evidence," a court must be guided by reason and experience. Given that only four states have provided some limited parent-child privilege, the "experience" of the state courts (to which the federal courts are to look) is overwhelmingly to reject such a privilege. This court has also previously looked to the experience of other jurisdictions in determining whether to create a privilege. In addition, the parent-child privilege has no long history in American common law. Instead, it is or relatively recent vintage and is essentially the product of legal academicians. Such a privilege also does not rest on confidentiality as an essential element of the full and satisfactory maintenance of the relationship between the parties. A privilege should only be recognized where such a privilege would by indispensable to the survival of the relationship that society deems should be fostered. It is not clear whether children would be more likely to discuss private matters with their parents if the privilege was recognized, or whether a child would know of the privilege's existence, unlike a lawyer or other professional, or whether, even knowing of the privilege, the child would enter into the decision to confide in the parent. An even more compelling reason to reject a parent-child privilege stems from the fact that the parent owes a duty to the child. Sometimes, that duty requires the parent to reveal the child's confidences. If the privilege were to be recognized, it would be dependent on both the parent and the child asserting it. But, because of the parent's duty, the parent may not be able to keep parent-child conversations confidential, thus vitiating the privilege. An effective parent-child privilege would require "that the parent's lips be sealed but such a sealing would be inexcusable in the parent-child relationship. No government should have that power." Affirmed.

EDITOR'S ANALYSIS: In his concurring and dissenting opinion, Judge Mansmann argued that because Fed. R. Evid. 501 already grants congressional authority to recognize a parent-child privilege, given that such a privilege exists in the common law of four states, the court should have recognized a limited privilege.

MATTER OF FARBER
[Parties not listed.]
N.J. Sup. Ct., 78 N.J. 259, 394 A.2d 330 (1978).

NATURE OF CASE: Appeal from judgments for civil and criminal contempt.

FACT SUMMARY: Farber (D), a reporter, and his employer, The New York Times Company (New York Times) (D), refused to disclose investigative reporting documents for *in camera* inspection in a murder trial, and were cited for criminal and civil contempt. They claimed a news reporting privilege to refrain from revealing investigative information.

CONCISE RULE OF LAW: Newspeople and other media representatives are not constitutionally privileged to withhold duly subpoenaed documents that may be highly relevant to a criminal proceeding, even though confidential sources may be publicly divulged if the documents are not withheld.

FACTS: The New York Times Company and Myron Farber, a reporter employed by the newspaper, challenged judgments of civil and criminal contempt entered against them. The proceedings were instituted in an ongoing murder trial of Dr. Mario E. Jascalevich, as a result of their failure to comply with two subpoenas duces tecum, directing them to produce certain documents and materials compiled by one or both of them in the course of Farber's (D) investigative reporting of certain allegedly criminal activities. Farber (D) claimed a First Amendment privilege to refrain from revealing information sought by the subpoenas duces tecum, for *in camera* inspections, for the reason that, if the material were divulged, confidential sources of such information would be made public. The state also had a "shield law," which granted newspeople and other media representatives the privilege of declining to reveal confidential sources of information.

ISSUE: Are newspeople and other media representatives constitutionally privileged to withhold duly subpoenaed documents that may be highly relevant to a criminal proceeding, even though confidential sources may be publicly divulged if the documents are not withheld?

HOLDING AND DECISION: (Mountain, J.) No. Newspeople and other media representatives are not constitutionally privileged to withhold duly subpoenaed documents that may be highly relevant to a criminal proceeding, even though confidential sources may be publicly divulged if the documents are not withheld. The U.S. Supreme Court, in *Branzburg v. Hayes*, 408 U.S. 665 (1972), held that the First Amendment affords no privilege to a newsman to refuse to appear before a grand jury and testify as to relevant information he possesses, even though in so doing he may divulge confidential sources. Thus, there is no authority for the proposition that newsmen are constitutionally privileged to withhold duly subpoenaed documents material to the prosecution or defense of a criminal case. Although *Branzburg* did not involve a shield law, as this case does, it is clear from the legislative intent behind the state's shield law that the statute seeks to protect confidential sources of the press to the greatest extent permitted by the federal and state constitutions. Facially, the shield law is constitutional. However, where the constitutions and the shield law collide, the latter must yield. Further, the Sixth Amendment and the New Jersey constitution afford a defendant in a criminal prosecution the right to compel the attendance of witnesses and the production of documents and other material for which he may have, or may believe he has, a legitimate need in preparing or undertaking his defense. It also means that witnesses properly summoned will be required to testify, and that material demanded by a properly phrased subpoena duces tecum will be forthcoming and available for appropriate examination and use. These constitutional provisions override any state laws designed to protect the confidentiality of a reporter's sources of information. However, in light of the strongly expressed legislative intent to favor confidentiality, certain safeguards must be observed. There must be a full threshold hearing on the issues of relevance, materiality, and overbreadth of the subpoena. Here, Farber (D) and the New York Times (D) have aborted that hearing by refusing to submit the requested documents. The *in camera* hearing is not in itself an invasion of the shield law privilege. Rather, it is a preliminary step in determining whether, and to what extent, the statutory privilege must yield to a defendant's constitutional rights. Any attempt to make such determinations prior to an *in camera* inspection would stultify the judicial criminal process. The threshold determination would normally follow the service of a subpoena on the newsperson or media representative, and the defense would have to show by a preponderance of the evidence that the material sought was relevant and material to the defense, could not be obtained in a less intrusive way, and was needed by the defense. Here, the record would inescapably lead to a conclusion of materiality, relevancy, unavailability of another source, and need. Affirmed.

EDITOR'S ANALYSIS: In this case, Farber (D) and the New York Times argued that the New Jersey "shield" law protected against the disclosure of confidential sources of information. That statute read in part "a person engaged in the gathering or procuring . . . of news for the general public . . . has a privilege to refuse to disclose, in any legal or quasi-legal proceeding . . . the source, author, means, agency, or person from or through whom any information was procured." N.J.S.A. 2A: 84A-21 and 21a.

CHAPTER SEVEN
GOVERNMENTAL PRIVILEGES

QUICK REFERENCE RULES OF LAW

1. **"Secrets of State" Privilege.** Where the court finds, from all the circumstances, that there is a reasonable danger that compulsion of evidence will risk national security, the court may not require the U.S. government to produce the evidence. (United States v. Reynolds)

2. **Executive Privilege.** While all private presidential communications are presumptively privileged, the fundamental demands of due process of law in the fair administration of criminal justice take precedence where the privilege is invoked on only a generalized interest in confidentiality. (United States v. Nixon)

3. **"Informer's" Privilege.** The informer's privilege may not be invoked when the identity and testimony of the informer are relevant and helpful to the defense of the accused or are essential to the just determination of a particular cause. (Roviaro v. United States)

4. **"Informer's" Privilege.** The government has no right to withhold the identity of an informer where such information is material to the question of guilt or innocence, but where only the preliminary issue of probable cause is in question, the informer's identity may be withheld if the testimony of the officers involved sets forth the underlying circumstances of the tip with sufficient specificity to permit the court to determine "what the informer actually said, and why the officer thought the information was credible." (McCray v. Illinois)

UNITED STATES v. REYNOLDS
Federal government (D) v. Wrongful death claimant (P)
345 U.S. 1 (1953).

NATURE OF CASE: Appeal of an order to disclose military information.

FACT SUMMARY: Reynolds (P) sought discovery of an Air Force accident report, containing classified military information.

CONCISE RULE OF LAW: Where the court finds, from all the circumstances, that there is a reasonable danger that compulsion of evidence will risk national security, the court may not require the U.S. government to produce the evidence.

FACTS: Reynolds (P) brought a wrongful death action under the Federal Tort Claims Act to recover damages for the death of her husband, who was killed in a plane crash while acting as a civilian observer on an Air Force test flight. At pretrial, she moved to discover (per Fed. R. Civ. P. 34) the official Air Force Accident Report. Over government objections, the judge found "good cause" for the discovery. Following this, the Secretary of the Air Force filed a formal "Claim of Privilege," asserting that the flight was involved in a "secret mission," the disclosure of which would not be in the national interest. The court rejected this claim and ordered the government to produce the report. When the government refused, the court ordered (per Fed. R. Civ. P. 37b) that the facts on the issue of negligence would be taken as established in Reynolds's (P) favor. From judgment for Reynolds (P), the government appealed.

ISSUE: May the U.S. government be required to produce evidence where the court finds, from all the circumstances, that there is a reasonable danger that compulsion of the evidence will risk national security?

HOLDING AND DECISION: (Vinson, C.J.) No. It is well settled that a privilege to protect military and State secrets belongs to the government, and where the court may find, from all the circumstances, that there is a reasonable danger that compulsion of evidence formally claimed to be so privileged would be contrary to the interests of national security, no disclosure may be required. It is true that judicial control over evidence in a case may not be abdicated to the mere caprice of judicial officers. This does not mean, however, that the court becomes automatically entitled to receive and review any and all evidence, regardless of the nature and extent of any privilege which it may be subject to. Here, the trial court was justified in finding "good cause" for discovery upon the showing of necessity by Reynolds (P). Once the Secretary filed his formal claim of privilege, however, the court should have taken judicial notice of contemporary national defense needs and granted the claim. Reversed and remanded.

EDITOR'S ANALYSIS: This case points up the general and common-law rule that the government has a right to protect military and state secrets for the public interest. Note that this rule survives *U.S. v. Nixon*, 418 U.S. 683 (1974).

NOTES:

UNITED STATES v. NIXON
Federal government (P) v. President (D)
418 U.S. 683 (1974).

NATURE OF CASE: Motion to quash subpoena duces tecum.

FACT SUMMARY: Incident to a federal trial of seven individuals for various violations of federal law, a subpoena duces tecum was issued for certain presidential documents and tapes. The President (D) resisted the subpoena on a claim of privilege.

CONCISE RULE OF LAW: While all private presidential communications are presumptively privileged, the fundamental demands of due process of law in the fair administration of criminal justice take precedence where the privilege is invoked on only a generalized interest in confidentiality.

FACTS: In connection with the federal criminal trials of seven individuals for conspiracy to defraud the United States (P) and to obstruct justice, a subpoena duces tecum was issued for certain presidential documents and tapes. The President (D) had been named as an unindicted co-conspirator in the original indictments. The President (D) resisted the subpoena by claiming the materials requested were constitutionally protected confidential communications.

ISSUE: Must the President of the United States honor a subpoena for documents relating to private presidential communications issued in connection with a criminal trial where the communications involved do not pertain to military or diplomatic secrets or otherwise involve national security?

HOLDING AND DECISION: (Burger, C.J.) Yes. While all private presidential communications are presumptively privileged, the fundamental demands of due process of law in the fair administration of criminal justice take precedence where the privilege is invoked on only a generalized interest in confidentiality. Not withstanding the deference each branch of our government must show to the independent acts of the other branches, it is emphatically the province and the duty of this Court to say what the law is with respect to the claim of privilege asserted in this case. While there is no explicit constitutional reference to presidential privilege in the area of confidential communications, it is clear that the privilege devolves from the necessary implementation of his enumerated powers. However, the privilege is not absolute as regards nonmilitary and nondiplomatic discussions. It cannot be asserted in a manner that would unduly disrupt the workings of another branch. Because the President (D) and his advisors must feel free in their private

discussions to speak candidly and bluntly, any private presidential communications are presumptively privileged. This presumptive privilege must be weighed in this case against the constitutional mandate that an accused shall have the right "to be confronted with the witnesses against him" and "to have compulsory process for obtaining witnesses in his favor." Further, no man is to be deprived of liberty without due process of law. In the face of these constitutional requirements, a claim of privilege based on a generalized claim of confidentiality cannot prevail. The fundamental demands of due process of law in the fair administration of criminal justice require that the privilege must give way. The President (D) and his advisors cannot be affected in the candor of their remarks merely because there may be infrequent disclosures in the context of a criminal trial. It has been said by Chief Justice Marshall that "in no case of this kind would a court be required to proceed against the President (D) as against an ordinary individual." This is not to be read as placing the President (D) above the law, but as a recognition of the unique position of the office and its related duties. The trial judge correctly recognized that the requested material must be handled with the greatest care so that only the most relevant portions are produced at trial. All deliberations prior to selection of usable evidence must be made in camera, and any unused portions returned undisclosed with the balance returned when their purpose is served.

EDITOR'S ANALYSIS: The Court, in a footnote, made clear that this decision had no application to civil litigation or to the requests for information made by the Congress to the President (D). The case was limited to the conflict of a generalized assertion of confidentiality against the constitutional need for relevant evidence in criminal trials. The decision would appear to be in accord with Rule 508 of the 1974 Approved Draft of the Uniform Rules of Evidence relating to State secrets and governmental privilege. Rule 509 of the same Uniform Rules would have required dismissal of the charges against the defendants if the privilege were upheld.

ROVIARO v. UNITED STATES

Narcotics law violator (D) v. Federal government (P)

353 U.S. 53 (1957).

NATURE OF CASE: Appeal from a conviction for violation of the Narcotic Drugs Import and Export Act.

FACT SUMMARY: Roviaro (D) was convicted of two violations of the federal narcotics laws. On appeal, he alleged reversible error in the court's refusal to compel disclosure of the identity of an undercover informer who had played a material part in Roviaro's (D) arrest.

CONCISE RULE OF LAW: The informer's privilege may not be invoked when the identity and testimony of the informer are relevant and helpful to the defense of the accused or are essential to the just determination of a particular cause.

FACTS: Roviaro (D) was indicted on two counts of violating the Narcotic Drugs Import and Export Act. Count 1 charged him with the sale of heroin, Count 2 with knowingly transporting and concealing it after its importation. He was arrested after federal narcotics agents and Chicago policemen observed his sale of quantities of heroin to an individual whom the government (P) later identified only as "John Doe." Before trial, Roviaro (D) moved for a bill of particulars requesting disclosure of "Doe's" identity, but the motion was denied when the government (P) objected that "Doe" was an informer and that his identity was therefore privileged. The court also refused to permit cross-examination of government (P) witnesses concerning "Doe's" identity. Roviaro (D) was found guilty on both counts, and was fined and sentenced to two-year prison sentences for each conviction, the sentences to run concurrently. The court of appeals, upholding the conviction on Count 2, held that there had been no abuse of discretion in denying Roviaro's (D) requests for disclosure of "Doe's" identity.

ISSUE: May the government refuse to disclose the identity of an anonymous informer who played a material role in the events which resulted in the defendant's arrest for violation of the federal narcotics laws?

HOLDING AND DECISION: (Burton, J.) No. The informer's privilege may not be invoked when the identity and testimony of the informer are relevant and helpful to the defense of the accused or are essential to the just determination of a particular cause. The informer's privilege is designed to preserve the anonymity of citizens who report their knowledge of the commission of crimes, and thus to encourage their performance of that duty. However, the scope of the privilege is limited by the requirements of fundamental fairness. Thus, the privilege must yield in those cases in which the informer's identity would be relevant and helpful to the defendant, or is essential to the fair

determination of a case. In deciding whether or not the privilege may be sustained, the court must balance the public's interest in insuring that information will be reported against the individual's right to prepare an effective defense. In the present case, the charge in Count 2 involves "Doe" to such an extent that his identity and testimony are highly material. "Doe" was the one witness through whom Roviaro (D) could have shown facts which negated the charge that he (D) had knowledge of the contents of the package which he (D) transported and, through "Doe's" testimony, Roviaro (D) might have been able to demonstrate that entrapment had occurred. It was, therefore, error for the court to refuse to compel disclosure of "Doe's" identity and, this error being prejudicial to Roviaro (D), his conviction must be reversed.

DISSENT: (Clark, J.) The undisputed evidence indicates that "Doe's" identity was already known to Roviaro (D). Therefore, the dictates of fairness were not violated by refusing to compel the fruitless act of disclosing his identity at trial.

EDITOR'S ANALYSIS: One reason that the court in *Roviaro* required disclosure of the identity of the government's informer may be that his participation went beyond the act of mere informing. The fact that one serves as an informer should not insulate him from revelation of his identity where his supplying of information is only incidental to a more active role in effecting the arrest of the accused. The limitations which *Roviaro* imposes upon the informer's privilege are less frequently applied in civil cases than in criminal matters.

NOTES:

McCRAY v. ILLINOIS
Heroin possessor (D) v. State (P)
386 U.S. 300 (1967).

NATURE OF CASE: Appeal of possession of heroin conviction.

FACT SUMMARY: McCray (D) was arrested (without a warrant) and heroin found on his person based on an informer's tip.

CONCISE RULE OF LAW: The government has no right to withhold the identity of an informer where such information is material to the question of guilt or innocence, but where only the preliminary issue of probable cause is in question, the informer's identity may be withheld if the testimony of the officers involved sets forth the underlying circumstances of the tip with sufficient specificity to permit the court to determine "what the informer actually said, and why the officer thought the information was credible."

FACTS: McCray (D) was arrested for possession of heroin by officers acting on a tip. At pretrial, both officers testified to (1) what the informer had said (McCray [D] was selling heroin in the vicinity of 47th and Calumet); (2) how long they had known the informer (one and two years); (3) how often he had supplied them reliable information (15-16 and 20-25 times); and, (4) that such information had previously resulted in convictions. Before trial, McCray (D) moved to suppress the heroin on the grounds that no probable cause for arrest was established (no warrant had been obtained). In furtherance of this motion, McCray (D) moved to discover the name of the informer. Both motions were denied, and McCray (D) was convicted. He appealed.

ISSUE: May probable cause for an arrest based on an informer's tip be established without disclosing the identity of the informer?

HOLDING AND DECISION: (Stewart, J.) No. The government has no right to withhold the identity of an informer where such information is material to the question of guilt or innocence, but, where only the preliminary issue of probable cause is in question, the informer's identity may be withheld if the testimony of the officers involved sets forth the underlying circumstances of the tip with sufficient specificity to permit the court to determine "what the informer actually said, and why the officer thought the information was credible." The fourth amendment requirement of probable cause is served if a "judicial mind passes upon the existence of probable cause." The fact that no warrant is obtained does not substantially alter the court's inquiry into this question, either. All that need be determined is whether there is reason to believe that the officer (whether seeking a warrant or explaining a warrantless arrest) has told the truth about what he was told. Here, the officers testified with precision. The conviction must be affirmed.

EDITOR'S ANALYSIS: This case points up the general rule that the government may invoke its privilege to protect the identity of an informer, even where no judicial scrutiny was exercised over the police, prior to the arrest based on such informer's tip. It is enough if the trial court can discern a sufficient basis for probable cause at the time of trial (i.e., that the officers acted with probable cause based on the information given to them by the informer). Note, however, that there are generally two exceptions to the rule. The first, mentioned in the case, is where the informer's identity is relevant to guilt or innocence (cf. *Roviaro v. U.S.*). The second arises when the purpose of the privilege (i.e., protecting the informer) has been frustrated because those who are a danger to him already know who he is. In such a case, the government cannot use the privilege merely to prevent the accused from reaching the informer.

NOTES:

CHAPTER EIGHT
THE BEST EVIDENCE RULE

QUICK REFERENCE RULES OF LAW

1. **Best Evidence Rule.** Under the best evidence rule, a party who seeks to prove the content of a document must offer in evidence the original copy of the document, but if secondary evidence is offered, the proponent must explain his failure to offer the original in order to proceed. (Sirico v. Cotto)

2. **"Proving Contents of Writing" Requirement.** The best evidence rule (secondary evidence of a writing is inadmissible unless adequate explanation for not producing the original is given) does not apply to testimony describing nonwritten transactions. (Herzig v. Swift & Co.)

3. **"Proof of Contents of Writing" Requirement.** In the federal courts, the "best evidence rule" ("where the content of a writing is sought to be proved, secondary evidence is inadmissible unless failure to offer the original writing as primary evidence is satisfactorily explained") is limited to cases where the contents of a writing are to be proved. (Meyers v. United States)

4. **What Constitutes a "Writing."** The best evidence rule (unless otherwise explained, secondary evidence of the contents of a writing is inadmissible in the absence of the original writing) applies to motion pictures. (People v. Enskat)

5. **Authentication of Documents.** As a condition precedent to admissibility, documents that are not self-authenticating require authentication or identification by evidence sufficient to show they are what their proponent claims. (United States v. Dockins)

6. **Admission of Evidence of Telephone Calls.** Under Federal Rule of Evidence 901(b)(6), when a person places a telephone call to a listed number and the answering party identifies himself as the expected party, the call is properly authenticated. (First State Bank of Denton v. Maryland Casualty Co.)

SIRICO v. COTTO
X-ray patient (P) v. Civil defendant (D)
Civ. Ct. N.Y.C., 67 Misc.2d 636, 324 N.Y.S.2d 483 (1971).

NATURE OF CASE: Action for damages for personal injuries.

FACT SUMMARY: Sirico's (P) attorney called Dr. Wolfson, who had x-rayed Sirico (P), to testify, but he no longer had the x-rays, which were not produced at trial, so his testimony was excluded upon Cotto's (D) objection.

CONCISE RULE OF LAW: Under the best evidence rule, a party who seeks to prove the content of a document must offer in evidence the original copy of the document, but if secondary evidence is offered, the proponent must explain his failure to offer the original in order to proceed.

FACTS: Sirico (P) sought damages for personal injury. She was x-rayed by Dr. Wolfson who sent the x-ray plates and his report to the treating physician. The treating physician was not called to testify. Dr. Wolfson was called to testify by Sirico's (P) attorney. The x-ray plates were not introduced, and Dr. Wolfson refreshed his memory from a copy of his report. Cotto (D) objected, invoking the best evidence rule. The objection was sustained, and the trial judge filed this memorandum, explaining the basis for his ruling.

ISSUE: Under the best evidence rule, must a party who seeks to prove the content of a document offer in evidence the original copy of the document, unless he explains his failure to offer the original when offering secondary evidence instead?

HOLDING AND DECISION: (Younger, J.) Yes. Under the best evidence rule, a party who seeks to prove the content of a document must offer in evidence the original copy of the document, but if secondary evidence is offered, the proponent must explain his failure to offer the original in order to proceed. When Dr. Wolfson was asked to describe what he saw on the x-ray plates, secondary evidence of their contents was asked for. The x-ray plates were the original "document." Sirico's (P) counsel failed to explain the absence of the x-ray plates.

EDITOR'S ANALYSIS: A "document" within the meaning of the best evidence rule includes any physical embodiment of information from letters and contracts, to books and receipts, and to blueprints, photographs, and x-ray plates. Some believe that the rule was to discourage fraud while others claim it recognizes the central position which the written word occupies in the law. A problem with copies as evidence is more the chance of error than anything else. The mistransmittal of words in a contract, deed, or will can be crucial to the outcome of a case. One very recent view of the rule sees its purpose as protecting "against intentional or unintentional misleading through introduction of selected portions of a comprehensive set of writings to which the opponent has no access."

NOTES:

HERZIG v. SWIFT & CO.
Wife of decedent (P) v. Company (D)
146 F.2d 444 (2d Cir. 1945).

NATURE OF CASE: Wrongful death action.

FACT SUMMARY: Herzig (P) sought to introduce testimony on her deceased husband's earnings from his partnership without having to present the firm's books.

CONCISE RULE OF LAW: The best evidence rule (secondary evidence of a writing is inadmissible unless adequate explanation for not producing the original is given) does not apply to testimony describing nonwritten transactions.

FACTS: On the issue of damages in wrongful death suit, Herzig (P) offered testimony on the amount of earnings her deceased husband derived from a partnership. The trial court ruled the testimony inadmissible since the books of the partnership were not presented nor any explanation given for not doing so. The action was dismissed.

ISSUE: Does the best evidence rule apply to testimony describing nonwritten transactions?

HOLDING AND DECISION: (Frank, J.) No. The best evidence rule (secondary evidence of a writing is inadmissible unless adequate explanation for not producing the original is given) does not apply to testimony describing nonwritten transactions. There is no attempt here to prove the contents of a writing. The only issue is the deceased husband's earnings. While the earnings were recorded, this was only for convenience after the transactions had already occurred. The books only prove the testimony, and not the other way around. Herzig (P) does not have to produce the books. Reversed and remanded.

EDITOR'S ANALYSIS: Testimony as to earnings or profits has been held not to fall within the scope of the best evidence rule. However, courts have also exempted from the rule's operation testimony an company policy, and testimony by a police officer on conversations overheard by him which were tape-recorded.

MEYERS v. UNITED STATES

Perjurer (D) v. Federal government (P)

171 F.2d 800 (D.C. Cir. 1948).

NATURE OF CASE: Appeal from conviction of perjury and subornation.

FACT SUMMARY: Trial court permitted the chief counsel to a senate committee to testify on the testimony given by Lamarre (D) before that body, and later in the trial permitted the government to introduce into evidence a stenographic transcript of Lamarre's (D) testimony.

CONCISE RULE OF LAW: In the federal courts, the best evidence rule ("where the content of a writing is sought to be proved, secondary evidence is inadmissible unless failure to offer the original writing as primary evidence is satisfactorily explained") is limited to cases where the contents of a writing are to be proved.

FACTS: Lamarre (D) was indicted for perjuring his testimony before a U.S. Senate subcommittee, and for suborning the perjuries of Meyers (D). The words and expressions charged to Lamarre (D) in the indictment did not appear in the transcript, but were, the government argued, to be inferred from his answers to the many questions put to him. Rogers, chief counsel to the committee, had heard all of Lamarre's (D) testimony before the Senate body. Rogers was permitted to testify early in the trial as to what Lamarre had sworn to the subcommittee. Towards the close of the trial, the government introduced into evidence a stenographic transcript of Lamarre's (D) testimony at the hearing. Lamarre (D) objected to this staggered introduction of the oral testimony as a "bizarre procedure."

ISSUE: Does the best evidence rule apply to cases where the contents of nonwritten testimony are to be proved?

HOLDING AND DECISION: (Miller, J.) No. In the federal courts, the best evidence rule ("where the content of a writing is sought to be proved, secondary evidence is inadmissible unless failure to offer the original writing as primary evidence is satisfactorily explained") is limited to cases where the contents of a writing are to be proved. The prosecution, by having Rogers testify, did not attempt to prove the contents of a writing; the issue was what Lamarre had said, not what the transcript contained. Hence, the best evidence rule is inapplicable here. Rogers's testimony was equally competent and was admissible, whether it was given before or after the transcript was received in evidence. Statements alleged to be perjured may be proved by any person who heard them, as well as by a reporter who recorded them in shorthand. Since both methods of proving the perjury were permissible, the prosecution could present its proof in any order it chose. Lamarre's (D) and Meyers's (D) counsel had full opportunity to study the transcript and to cross-examine Rogers

in light of that study. There is no indication that Meyers's (D) position before the jury would have been more favorable had the transcript been offered on an earlier day of the trial.

DISSENT: (Prettyman, J.) The prosecutor could not have first put into evidence the transcript of Lamarre's (D) testimony and thereafter have produced Rogers to give the jury from the witness box his own summation, since this would have been met with a ruling that "the transcript speaks for itself." Summation and interpretation are aspects of argument, and not evidence. The impression given by a succinct summation by a live witness on the stand cannot be corrected or offset by the later reading of a long, cold record. Stenographic recording has become highly developed and should be considered the best evidence of testimony when presented.

EDITOR'S ANALYSIS: In substantiating the former testimony of a party or defendant, four methods are generally approved: (1) a first-hand observer may testify from his memory without use of any aids. The observer need not give a word-by-word account, but may give the purport of the former testimony; (2) a first-hand observer may refresh his present memory by use of some note prepared by a court officer; (3) under the hearsay exception based on official writings, official court reports or notes may be admitted; (4) a witness may rely on his own written notes made at the time of the former testimony. These notes come in under the past recollection recorded rule.

NOTES:

PEOPLE v. ENSKAT
State (P) v. Motion picture exhibitor (D)
20 Cal. App.3d Supp.1 (1971).

NATURE OF CASE: Appeal from conviction of exhibiting obscene motion pictures.

FACT SUMMARY: The prosecution did not present the allegedly obscene motion picture in a prosecution of Enskat for exhibiting lewd material.

CONCISE RULE OF LAW: The best evidence rule (unless otherwise explained, secondary evidence of the contents of a writing is inadmissible in the absence of the original writing) applies to motion pictures.

FACTS: Enskat (D) was charged with exhibiting obscene motion pictures. At Enskat's (D) trial, the prosecution failed, without offering any explanation, to produce the allegedly obscene films.

ISSUE: Does the best evidence rule apply to motion pictures?

HOLDING AND DECISION: (Zack, J.) Yes. The best evidence rule (unless otherwise explained, secondary evidence of the contents of a writing is inadmissible in the absence of the original writing) applies to motion pictures. A photographic transparency—or "slide"—has been held to be a "writing." A motion picture film is a series of such slides. While a motion picture gives the optical illusion that the sequences are continuous, this does not alter the fact that the motion picture is composed of a series of single "writings." Arguably, the moving image portrayed is not recorded. However, the moving image can only be realized through the use of a projector and screen. The moving image is totally dependent on the recorded frames of the filmstrip. It is better for the trier of fact to see a filmstrip than to have it described. Hence, the prosecution must produce the films themselves for viewing by the court.

EDITOR'S ANALYSIS: Recognizing the best evidence rule problems posed by the use of the microfilm, many States' statutes, and at least the federal courts, will admit microfilm without requiring any proof on the original records. All that need be proved is that the films were made in good faith as part of a regular business practice, and that each roll of microfilm contain some acknowledgment of authentication.

UNITED STATES v. DOCKINS
Federal government (P) v. Firearm possessors (D)
986 F.2d 888 (5th Cir. 1993).

NATURE OF CASE: Appeal from a conviction for illegal possession of a firearm by a convicted felon.

FACT SUMMARY: Dockins (D) argued that the documents introduced as evidence of his status as a convicted felon were not properly authenticated.

CONCISE RULE OF LAW: As a condition precedent to admissibility, documents that are not self-authenticating require authentication or identification by evidence sufficient to show they are what their proponent claims.

FACTS: At Dockins's (D) trial for illegal possession of a firearm by a convicted felon, the United States (P) introduced evidence, purportedly from the Denver Police Department, to show that Dockins (D) had been convicted of a felony using the name of Carl Smith. Different individual testified that Smith's fingerprints matched those of Dockins (D) and that the signature on the fingerprint card matched Dockins's (D) handwriting. The court admitted the evidence over Dockins's (D) objection on grounds of authentication. After the trial, Dockins (D) moved for a judgment of acquittal n.o.v. or for a new trial. At a hearing on the authenticity of the two exhibits, Jantz, an officer with the Denver Police Department, testified that the documents were exact copies of the records in his file. Without relying on Jantz's testimony, the court found the documents to be admissible. Dockins (D) appealed.

ISSUE: As a condition precedent to admissibility, do documents that are not self-authenticating require authentication or identification by evidence sufficient to show they are what their proponent claims?

HOLDING AND DECISION: (Higginbotham, J.) Yes. As a condition precedent to admissibility, documents that are not self-authenticating require authentication or identification by evidence sufficient to show they are what their proponent claims. The parties agree that the documents at issue here are not self-authenticating. The testimony at trial as to the documents had nothing to do with their source. Jantz was the custodian of those documents, but he did not testify at trial, nor was circumstantial evidence introduced to show that the documents came from the Denver Police Department. Thus, a reasonable jury could not conclude that they were what they purported to be. However, admission of the documents constituted harmless error since other evidence proved beyond a reasonable doubt that Dockins (D) was a convicted felon. Affirmed.

EDITOR'S ANAYSIS: The court here was applying Fed. R. Evid. 901. In *United States v. Jimenez Lopez*, 873 F.2d 769 (5th Cir. 1989), the government successfully offered a copy of a document as proof of a prior conviction. However, in that case, a border patrol agent testified that he personally requested and received the document, establishing a chain of custody. The testimony of the agent, while he was not the custodian of the document, provided circumstantial evidence to support the conclusion that the document was an official record.

NOTES:

FIRST STATE BANK OF DENTON v.
MARYLAND CASUALTY CO.

Executor of estate (P) v. Insurance company (D)

918 F.2d 38 (5th Cir. 1990).

NATURE OF CASE: Appeal from denial of award of insurance proceeds.

FACT SUMMARY: Mills' second home was destroyed by fire, but when Denton (P), the executor of Mills' estate sought to recover the proceeds from a fire insurance policy on the home issued by Maryland Casualty (D), Maryland Casualty (D) asserted that Mills had intentionally started the fire, relying on a police dispatcher's telephone call to Mills' first home during which the answerer stated that Mills was not there.

CONCISE RULE OF LAW: Under Federal Rule of Evidence 901(b)(6), when a person places a telephone call to a listed number and the answering party identifies himself as the expected party, the call is properly authenticated.

FACTS: Mills' second home was insured by a $133,000 fire insurance policy issued by Maryland Casualty (D). When a fire completely destroyed the home, Maryland Casualty (D) asserted that Mills had intentionally started the fire. Mills died before he could file a suit against Maryland Casualty (D), so the executor of his estate, First State Bank of Denton (P), filed the suit to recover the proceeds. In its defense at trial, Maryland Casualty (D) introduced evidence that Mills's second home had been unoccupied for many weeks before the fire, but that three hours before the blaze, a neighbor saw a light in the home. Further, Mills was the only one with a key to the house; he owned a pick-up truck; and a neighbor saw a pick-up truck drive away from the home after the fire had started. Further, when a police dispatcher tried to contact Mills by telephone at his primary residence after the fire had begun, someone answered the telephone and stated that he was not there. It was also proven that Mills was in financial trouble because he had bought his primary residence before selling the home that eventually burned down. Denton (P) moved to exclude admission of the evidence of the dispatcher's call as hearsay and unauthenticated, but the trial court admitted it. Denton (P) lost the lawsuit and appealed.

ISSUE: Under Fed. R. Evid. 901(b)(6), when a person places a telephone call to a listed number, and the answering party identifies himself as the expected party, is the call properly authenticated?

HOLDING AND DECISION: (Smith, Cir. J.) Yes. Under Federal Rule of Evidence 901(b)(6), when a person places a telephone call to a listed number and the answering party identifies himself as the expected party, the call is properly authenticated. Fed. R. Evid. 901 provides that all evidence must be authenticated before being admitted, and that this requirement is satisfied by evidence reliable enough to show that it is what its proponent claims it to be. Rule 901(b)(6), by way of illustration but not by exclusion, provides that authentication can occur for a telephone call when a person places a call to a listed number and the answering party identifies himself as the expected party. The calling of the number assigned by the telephone company reasonably supports the assumption that the listing is correct and that the number is the one reached. The telephone system is assumed accurate, and there is no motive to falsify transmission of the call. Here, however, Denton (P) demands that authentication requires that Mills himself have answered the telephone in order for the police dispatcher call to be admissible. This ignores the true reason for requiring self-identification, which is that the phone company usually is accurate. Therefore, all that needs to be established by the answerer is a prima facie case on the issue of identity, which may be resolved by the jury. Affirmed.

EDITOR'S ANALYSIS: In one notorious case, a husband was allowed to authenticate the voice he heard on the phone making an obscene call to his wife as the voice of a prominent judge where the husband had later heard the judge give a law-and-order speech to the husband's service club. Note also that jurors may infer the identity of a disputed voice on a recording of a telephone call in comparison with a recorded exemplar of the defendant's voice, if available, or with the actual sound of the defendant's voice as he testifies.

NOTES:

CHAPTER NINE
COMPETENCY OF WITNESSES

QUICK REFERENCE RULES OF LAW

1. **Competence of Minors as Witnesses.** The competency of a minor to testify lies in the discretion of the trial judge. (Hill v. Skinner)

2. **Witness Competency.** Hypnotically induced recall testimony is per se inadmissible. (State ex rel. Collins v. Superior Court)

3. **Witness Competency.** A state may not categorically prohibit the introduction of a defendant's hypnotically refreshed testimony. (Rock v. Arkansas)

4. **Juror Impeachment of Verdict.** Juror testimony may not be admitted to impeach a jury verdict unless there is proof of tampering or external influence or proof that a juror was insane or mentally incompetent immediately before or after the trial. (Tanner v. United States)

HILL v. SKINNER
Injured child (P) v. Dog owner (D)
Ohio Ct. App., 81 Ohio App. 375, 79 N.E.2d 787 (1947).

NATURE OF CASE: Appeal from award of damages in dog bite case.

FACT SUMMARY: Cary Hill, a four-year old, was bit by Chang, Skinner's (D) dog, in the head and mouth while he was attempting to "love" Chang.

CONCISE RULE OF LAW: The competency of a minor to testify lies in the discretion of the trial judge.

FACTS: Cary Hill (P), a four-year-old child, approached and petted Chang, Skinner's (D) dog, when Chang wandered onto Hill's (P) property. Chang responded by biting Hill (P) on the head and mouth. Hill (P) sued Skinner (D) for personal injuries, and the trial judge allowed Hill (P) to testify about the dog's response to Hill's (P) "loving," despite his age and an Ohio statute providing that children under ten were incompetent to testify unless they were capable of "receiving just impressions of the facts and transactions respecting which they are examined." The jury awarded the child $500 in damages, and Skinner (D) appealed on the grounds that Hill's (P) testimony was incompetent and improperly admitted.

ISSUE: Does the competency of a minor to testify lie in the discretion of the trial judge?

HOLDING AND DECISION: (Doyle, J.) Yes. The determination of whether a minor child is competent to testify lies in the sound discretion of the trial judge. The essential test of an infant witness is his comprehension of the obligation to tell the truth and his intellectual capacity of observation, recollection and communication. Here, the trial court examined the child at length in chambers before allowing him to testify, and little Hill (P) admitted that "God won't love me" if he didn't tell the truth. The judge properly exercised his discretion in admitting Hill's (P) testimony. Affirmed, but modified to provide for destruction of Chang.

EDITOR'S ANALYSIS: Competence is frequently determined by asking the witness a series of silly questions such as, "Do you know what happens to people who tell lies?"; a person who thinks that liars go to the White House instead of Hell is likely to be thought unfit to be a witness. A better method of determining witness competence is expert testimony on the ability of the witness to perceive and communicate. Note that for purposes of determining competence, children have often been judged according to the same rules applied to adults with mental infirmities; the primary consideration is whether the person to testify is capable of understanding his duty to tell the truth.

NOTES:

STATE EX REL. COLLINS v. SUPERIOR COURT
State (P) v. Rape suspect (D)
Ariz. Sup. Ct., 132 Ariz. 180, 644 P.2d 1266 (1982).

NATURE OF CASE: Motion for a new hearing on the admissibility of testimony based on hypnotically induced recall.

FACT SUMMARY: Arizona (P) petitioned the Arizona Supreme Court for a rehearing on the admissibility of testimony based on hypnotically induced recall.

CONCISE RULE OF LAW: Hypnotically induced recall testimony is per se inadmissible.

FACTS: Between August 1977 and May 1980, 18 rapes were reported in unpopulated areas in Phoenix, Arizona. The assaults followed a similar pattern. A masked male, carrying a pistol and ropes, blindfolds, and a ground cloth, would approach couples in cars from behind. He would tie the couple up, blindfold them, and rape the woman. The local sheriffs and police departments investigated the rapes, including hypnotizing seven victims to obtain additional information. Subsequently, Silva (D) was arrested as he approached a decoy vehicle containing a male and a female police officer. He was masked and carrying a pistol, ropes, blindfolds, and a ground cloth. Silva (D) moved to suppress the use of the testimony of the seven witnesses who had been hypnotized. The testimony was held inadmissible by the Arizona Supreme Court and Arizona (P) petitioned for a rehearing, contending that recent decisions of that court had suggested that hypnotically induced recall testimony might be admissible if proper safeguards were used to diminish suggestibility. The Arizona Supreme Court granted a hearing.

ISSUE: Is hypnotically induced recall testimony per se inadmissible?

HOLDING AND DECISION: (Feldman, J.) Yes. Hypnotically induced recall testimony is inadmissible per se. A hypnotized subject is afforded the ability to experience a heightened recall of events he previously experienced. However, along with this ability, he may have pseudomemories of facts he did not experience but were consciously or unconsciously suggested to him by the hypnotist. These then become part of his recall. The most dangerous aspect of this is that during the hypnotic session, neither the hypnotist nor the subject can distinguish between true memories and pseudomemories. Further, when the subject repeats his recall upon awakening, neither an expert witness nor a lay observer can make the distinction. Therefore, these dangers, plus the hypersuggestibility and hypercompliance characteristic of the effect of the hypnotic trance, require a rule which renders hypnotically induced recall testimony per se inadmissible. Original judgment and holding of the Arizona Supreme Court upheld.

EDITOR'S ANALYSIS: In this case, the court also held that hypnosis was a valuable investigatory tool, and that its holding in this case should not be interpreted as rendering witnesses who have been hypnotized incompetent to testify to facts demonstrably recalled prior to hypnosis. Therefore, witnesses may be allowed to testify to establish the elements of a crime even if they are subsequently hypnotized to relate identifying facts.

NOTES:

ROCK v. ARKANSAS
Hypnotized defendant (D) v. State (P)
483 U.S. 44 (1987).

NATURE OF CASE: Appeal of conviction for voluntary manslaughter.

FACT SUMMARY: Arkansas's per se rule of inadmissibility of hypnotically refreshed testimony prevented Rock (D) from testifying regarding key details of the shooting incident that led to her manslaughter prosecution.

CONCISE RULE OF LAW: A state may not categorically prohibit the introduction of a defendant's hypnotically refreshed testimony.

FACTS: Rock (D) became involved in a heated argument with her husband, which culminated in his being fatally shot. Rock's recollection of the event was, according to her, fuzzy. Under hypnosis, she purportedly recalled that she pointed the gun at him, but her finger was not on the trigger. Nonetheless, the gun discharged. An expert's examination of the gun revealed that it was defective and did indeed have a tendency to fire when handled without the trigger being pulled. Nonetheless, the trial court, per Arkansas law prohibiting hypnotically refreshed testimony from being introduced, excluded Rock's (D) post-hypnosis recollections. Rock (D) was convicted, and this was affirmed on appeal. The Supreme Court accepted review.

ISSUE: May a state categorically prohibit the introduction of a defendant's hypnotically refreshed testimony?

HOLDING AND DECISION: (Blackmun, J.) No. A state may not categorically prohibit the introduction of a defendant's hypnotically refreshed testimony. It is beyond question that a defendant has the right to testify in his or her own behalf. This right has several sources in the Constitution. These include the fourteenth amendment's due process clause, the compulsory process clause of the sixth amendment, and the fifth amendment's guarantee against compelled testimony, which has as a logical corollary the right to testify if the defendant so desires. The right to testify in one's own behalf is meaningless, however, if the state can arbitrarily limit the scope of the defendant's testimony. While the state has a legitimate interest in the prevention of unreliable or unnecessary testimony, its rules in this regard may not go farther than necessary to effectuate this goal. Here, Arkansas' rule is a per se prohibition against hypnotically refreshed testimony, regardless of its reliability. While a state could conceivably limit such testimony to that obtained by an expert psychologist or psychiatrist, and require corroborating evidence, a per se rule sweeps too broadly. Reversed and remanded.

DISSENT: (Rehnquist, C.J.) Hypnotically induced testimony is inherently unreliable, due to the uncertain state of the art with respect to eliciting it. No set of procedures can make it reliable. A state is free to exclude such inherently untrustworthy categories of testimony.

EDITOR'S ANALYSIS: At early common law, there were many categorical rules of witness incompetency. In fact, at one time parties to a litigation were incompetent to testify due to their interest in the outcome of the litigation. The trend ever since has been to jettison rules of incompetency and hold that the factors once giving rise to incompetency should instead go to weight given the testimony in question.

NOTES:

TANNER v. UNITED STATES
Conspiracy convict (D) v. Federal government (P)
483 U.S. 107 (1987).

NATURE OF CASE: Appeal from denial of motions for new trial and for leave to interview jurors after verdict in fraud action.

FACT SUMMARY: Tanner (P) was convicted of conspiracy to defraud and mail fraud by a jury he later learned was intoxicated during much of the trial.

CONCISE RULE OF LAW: Juror testimony may not be admitted to impeach a jury verdict unless there is proof of tampering or external influence or proof that a juror was insane or mentally incompetent immediately before or after the trial.

FACTS: Tanner (P) was convicted in a federal trial of conspiracy to defraud and of mail fraud. After the trial, however, Tanner's (P) attorney received an unsolicited telephone call from one of the jurors at Tanner's (P) trial. The juror stated that many of the jurors drank alcohol during recesses and lunch breaks and were asleep during the afternoon. The district court continued Tanner's (P) sentencing date, and heard argument on motions to interview jurors, but ultimately denied the motions on the ground that evidence of juror intoxication was inadmissible under Fed. R. Evid. 606(b) to impeach the jury's verdict. While the denial of Tanner's (P) motion was on appeal to the Eleventh Circuit, another juror approached Tanner's (P) attorney with many details of drug abuse and intoxication. This juror told of chugging pitchers of beer, martinis at lunch, smoking marijuana and ingesting cocaine, and he concluded that the jurors had been "on one big party." The district court, taking note of the supplemental allegations, again denied the motion to interview the jurors, and the Eleventh Circuit affirmed. The Supreme Court granted certiorari to consider whether the district court was required to hold an evidentiary hearing, including juror testimony, on juror alcohol and drug use during the trial.

ISSUE: May juror testimony be admitted to impeach a jury verdict in the absence of proof of tampering or external influence or proof that a juror was insane or mentally incompetent immediately before or after the trial?

HOLDING AND DECISION: (O'Connor, J.) No. Juror testimony may not be admitted to impeach a jury verdict unless there is proof of tampering or external influence or proof that a juror was insane or mentally incompetent immediately before or after the trial. In deciding whether to allow juror testimony after a verdict has been handed down, courts have long adhered to the external/internal distinction. If the allegation for which testimony is sought involves a juror's inability to hear or comprehend at trial, it is treated as internal and testimony is disallowed. Internal abnormalities in a jury will not be inquired into except in the gravest and most important cases. This rule is based on the rationale that allegations of juror misconduct, incompetency, or inattentiveness raised for the first time days, weeks, or months after the verdict, seriously disrupt the finality of the process. Moreover, frank and full discussion in the jury room, jurors' willingness to return an unpopular verdict, and the community's trust in a system that relies on the decisions of lay people would be undermined by a barrage of postverdict scrutiny of juror conduct. Here, substance abuse cannot be considered an improper "outside" or "external" influence any more than a virus, lack of sleep, or poorly prepared food. Further, the legislative history underlying Fed. R. Evid. 606(b), which allows jury impeachment of the verdict under appropriate circumstances, demonstrates that Congress expressly considered, and rejected, consideration of juror intoxication as grounds for impeachment. Affirmed.

EDITOR'S ANALYSIS: Courts will be more willing to consider juror testimony to impeach a verdict when the allegations concern juror consideration of prejudicial or extraneous information not admitted into evidence. See *Mattox v. United States*, 146 U.S. 140, 149 (1982). Prior testimony of influence by outsiders was also admitted in *Parker v. Gladden*, 385 U.S. 363, 365 (1966) (bailiff's comments on defendant) and *Remmer v. United States*, 347 U.S. 227, 228-230 (1954) (bribe offered to juror). See also *Smith v. Phillips*, 455 U.S. 209 (1982) (juror in criminal trial had submitted an application for employment at the district attorney's office).

NOTES:

CHAPTER TEN
ADJUDICATIVE FACTS

QUICK REFERENCE RULES OF LAW

1. **Judicial Notice.** Courts should take notice of whatever is or ought to be generally known, within the limits of their jurisdiction. (Varcoe v. Lee)

2. **Effect of Judicial Notice.** The taking of judicial notice of commonly known evidentiary facts does not establish them so conclusively as to prevent the presentation of contrary evidence or the making of a finding to the contrary. (State v. Lawrence)

3. **Evidentiary Procedure.** An exhibit which has been introduced into evidence may be retained by the jury for its inspection and use in the course of deliberations only if the jury has been instructed against conducting independent experiments without the knowledge of the parties and the court. (Higgins v. Los Angeles Gas & Electric Co.)

VARCOE v. LEE
Parents of decedent (P) v. Chauffered car driver (D)
Cal. Sup. Ct., 180 Cal. 338, 181 P. 223 (1919).

NATURE OF CASE: Appeal from award of damages for wrongful death.

FACT SUMMARY: In Varcoe's (P) action against Lee (D) to recover damages for the wrongful death of Varcoe's (P) child, Varcoe (P) contended that Lee's (D) chauffeur, Nicholas, was driving Lee's (D) auto along Mission Street at the time the accident in which the child was killed at a speed greater than 15 miles per hour in violation of city and state law, and that such speed was negligence in itself.

CONCISE RULE OF LAW: Courts should take notice of whatever is or ought to be generally known, within the limits of their jurisdiction.

FACTS: Varcoe's (P) child was run over by Lee's (D) auto, being driven at the time by Lee's (D) chauffeur, Nichols. Varcoe's (P) right to recover was based on Nichol's negligence in operating the auto above the speed limit. Varcoe (P) contended that Nichols was driving the car along Mission Street at the time of the accident at a speed greater than 15 miles per hour, in violation of city and state laws. Varcoe (P) claimed that such speed was negligence in itself. The jury returned a verdict for Varcoe (P), and Nichols (D) appealed, arguing that it was error for the trial judge to charge the jury that the accident had occurred in a "business district" and that this question should not have been taken from the jury because Nichols would automatically be considered negligent under state law if he was driving faster than 15 miles per hour in a business district.

ISSUE: Should courts take notice of whatever is or ought to be generally known, within the limits of their jurisdiction?

HOLDING AND DECISION: (Olney, J.) Yes. Courts should take notice of whatever is or ought to be known, within the limits of their jurisdiction. So far as the record itself goes, there is little to show what the character of Mission Street between Twentieth and Twenty-Second Streets is. Nichols (D), himself, referred to it in his testimony as part of the "downtown district," undoubtedly meaning thereby part of the business district of the City of San Francisco. The probabilities are that every person in the courtroom at the trial knew perfectly well what the character of the location was. This court is now asked to reverse the judgment because the trial court assumed, without submitting to the jury, what could not be disputed, and what he and practically every resident in the county for which the court was sitting knew to be a fact. The conclusion follows that the charge of the trial court that Mission Street, between Twentieth and Twenty-Second Streets, was a business district, was not error. Affirmed.

EDITOR'S ANALYSIS: In the above case, it should be noted that the facts of which judicial notice was taken were "adjudicative facts." They were facts about the particular event which gave rise to the lawsuit and, like all adjudicative facts, helped to explain who did what, when, where, how, and with what intent. Also, either because they were facts so commonly known in the jurisdiction or so easily verified, they were facts reasonably informed people in the community would regard as propositions not reasonably subject to dispute.

NOTES:

STATE v. LAWRENCE
State (P) v. Larceny suspect (D)
Utah Sup. Ct., 120 Utah 323, 234 P.2d 600 (1951).

NATURE OF CASE: Appeal from a conviction of grand larceny.

FACT SUMMARY: At Lawrence's (D) larceny trial there was no evidence of value, except a description of the stolen car as a 1947 Ford sedan in good condition. The court instructed the jury that the car's value was greater than $50, so if Lawrence (D) was guilty at all, he was guilty of grand larceny.

CONCISE RULE OF LAW: The taking of judicial notice of commonly known evidentiary facts does not establish them so conclusively as to prevent the presentation of contrary evidence or the making of a finding to the contrary.

FACTS: At the conclusion of the evidence at Lawrence's (D) larceny trial, Lawrence's (D) counsel moved for a directed verdict on the ground that there had been no evidence of the value of the stolen car. The court denied the motion and took judicial notice of the fact that the car's value was more than $50. It had been shown that the car was a 1947 Ford sedan which was in good condition. The court instructed the jury, "In this case you will take the value of the property as being in excess of $50 and, therefore, the defendant, if he is guilty at all, is guilty of grand larceny."

ISSUE: Does the taking of judicial notice of commonly known evidentiary facts establish them so conclusively as to prevent the presentation of contrary evidence or the making of a finding to the contrary?

HOLDING AND DECISION: (Crockett, J.) No. The taking of judicial notice of commonly known evidentiary facts does not establish them so conclusively as to prevent the presentation of contrary evidence or the making of a finding to the contrary. Judicial notice is not binding on the jury. The process of notice is intended chiefly for expedition of proof and it remains possible for the jury to negate it. Hence, in this case, if it is assumed that the value of the car is of that class of fact which is so well known that judicial notice should be taken of it, that would not necessarily be conclusive upon the jury. Had witnesses testified that the car was worth more than $50, and had there been no evidence to the contrary, the court could not tell the jury that they had to believe such testimony. The accused person's right to a trial by jury extends to each and all the facts which must be found to be present in order to constitute the crime charged. Such right may not be invaded by the judge's telling the jury that any of the facts are established by the evidence. A new trial is ordered.

DISSENT: (Wolfe, C.J.) If a fact is so well known that judicial notice should be taken of it, it then is the court's duty to inform the jury that the matter should be taken to be established.

EDITOR'S ANALYSIS: There is disagreement as to whether judicial notice may be taken only of facts which are indisputably true or also of facts which are more than likely true. It is argued, that if it is the function of the jury to resolve disputed questions of fact, judges should not make decisions about facts unless they are indisputable facts. If this argument is accepted, it follows that once a fact has been judicially noticed, evidence contradicting the truth of the fact is inadmissible, since the only facts capable of being judicially noticed are those which are indisputable and which the jury must be instructed to accept as true. If, on the other hand, the function of judicial notice is to expedite the trial of cases, it can be argued that judges should dispense with the need for time-consuming formal evidence when the fact in question is more than likely true. Hence, evidence contradicting the judicially noticed fact is admissible, and the jury may accept or reject the truth of such fact. The court in *Lawrence* followed the latter line of reasoning.

NOTES:

HIGGINS v. LOS ANGELES GAS & ELECTRIC CO.
Building owner (P) v. Utility company (D)
Cal. Sup. Ct., 159 Cal. 651, 115 P.313 (1911).

NATURE OF CASE: Action to recover for damages to a building.

FACT SUMMARY: Higgins (P) sued the Los Angeles Gas & Electric Company (D) for damages to his building as the result of an explosion which, he alleged, occurred when a spark from a flashlight carried by an employee of the Gas Company (D) ignited leaking gas. The court permitted a flashlight similar to the one which allegedly caused the explosion to be examined by the jury in the course of its deliberations, which action, the Gas Company (D) claimed, constituted reversible error.

CONCISE RULE OF LAW: An exhibit which has been introduced into evidence may be retained by the jury for its inspection and use in the course of deliberations only if the jury has been instructed against conducting independent experiments without the knowledge of the parties and the court.

FACTS: Higgins (P) sued the Los Angeles Gas & Electric Company (D) for damages to his building resulting from an explosion which occurred in a restaurant operated by one of his tenants. Upon discovery of a gas leak in a dark location, employees of the Gas Company (D) approached the source of the leak, carrying an electric flashlight. Higgins (P) claimed that a spark from this flashlight ignited the seeping gas, but the Gas Company (D) attributed the explosion to the flame of a stove which burned nearby, and introduced into evidence a flashlight similar to that used by its employees, arguing that it was impossible for such a device to produce a spark of the type required to cause the explosion. Higgins (P) called an expert witness to show how the flashlight could have produced such a spark, but the court halted his presentation, and refused to permit any experiment which did not involve conditions similar to those existing at the time of the explosion. The jury, however, was permitted to inspect the flashlight and retain it for their use during the course of deliberations. Special interrogatories were submitted in which the jury concluded that the explosion had been caused by a spark from the flashlight, and not by the gas stove. From a verdict in favor of Higgins (P) and an order denying its motion for a new trial, the Gas Company (D) appealed, alleging that the court had erred in permitting the jurors to have the flashlight with them during their deliberations.

ISSUE: May exhibits which have been introduced into evidence be retained by the jury for inspection and use in the course of its deliberations if the jury has been instructed against conducting independent experiments without the knowledge of the parties and the court?

HOLDING AND DECISION: (Henshaw, J.) Yes. An exhibit which has been introduced into evidence may be retained by the jury for its inspection and use in the course of deliberations only if the jury has been instructed against conducting independent experiments without the knowledge of the parties and the court. Although juries, in the course of their deliberations, are permitted by statute to examine papers which have been introduced as exhibits, no statutory provision is made for the use of exhibits of other types. However, the rule which has evolved from the common law is that jurors may retain any exhibit for examination in the course of their deliberations if circumstances dictate its retention, and if it consists of evidence introduced in open court with the knowledge of both parties. However, although the jury may examine an exhibit, and may even scrutinize it more critically than did the parties or the court, the jurors must be instructed that they may not conduct any experiments in addition to those performed in open court. This is because in performing independent experiments the jury would, in effect, be accepting evidence which neither party would have an opportunity to challenge. In the present case, it was error to permit the jury to retain the flashlight without instructing against the conducting of experiments, but since the Gas Company (D) would have been liable whether the explosion was caused by a spark from the flashlight or by the gas stove, the error did not affect the outcome of the trial, and was therefore not prejudicial.

EDITOR'S ANALYSIS: It has been suggested that cases attempting to apply the rule of *Higgins v. Los Angeles Gas & Electric Company* are not reconcilable with one another. The *Higgins* courts attempt to distill a single rule from its examination of the *Wilson* and *Taylor* cases seems to confirm this assertion. The *Higgins* trial court, by submitting to the jury the question of how the explosion occurred, effectively refused to take judicial notice of the impossibility of creating a spark from a flashlight. It is, however, the weight of authority that a jury may not, in such a case, perform independent experimentation in order to discover or disprove that which the court was unwilling to note.

NOTES:

CHAPTER ELEVEN
THE BURDEN OF PROOF AND PRESUMPTIONS

QUICK REFERENCE RULES OF LAW

1. **Preponderance of Evidence Standard.** A proposition is proved by the preponderance of the evidence if it is made to appear more likely or probable in the sense that actual belief in its truth, derived from the evidence, exists in the mind or minds of the tribunal notwithstanding any doubts that may still linger there. Mathematical evidence may not be introduced without some supporting direct evidence. (Smith v. Rapid Transit, Inc.)

2. **Evidentiary Procedure.** Where a plaintiff will be unable to present any witnesses at trial who will testify to his allegations, summary judgment must be directed against him. (Dyer v. MacDougall)

3. **Conflicting Presumptions.** A case involving contrary presumptions should not be summarily disposed of by assessing their relative strength and deciding which one should prevail. (Legille v. Dann)

4. **Conflicting Presumptions.** If two presumptions arise which are conflicting with each other, the court shall apply the presumption which is founded on the weightier considerations of policy and logic, and if there is no such preponderance both presumptions shall be disregarded. (Atkinson v. Hall)

5. **Criminal Presumption.** A statute creating a mandatory presumption which works to shift to the defendant the burden of disproving an element of the crime is unconstitutional. (People v. Roder)

SMITH v. RAPID TRANSIT, INC.
Driver of damaged car (P) v. Bus company (D)
Mass. Sup. Jud. Ct., 317 Mass. 469, 58 N.E.2d 754 (1945).

NATURE OF CASE: Action for personal injuries as the result of negligent operation of a bus.

FACT SUMMARY: Although unable to find out which bus company owned the vehicle which forced her off the road, Smith (P) sued Rapid Transit, Inc. (D) on the theory that the bus was most probably owned by them.

CONCISE RULE OF LAW: A proposition is proved by the preponderance of the evidence if it is made to appear more likely or probable in the sense that actual belief in its truth, derived from the evidence, exists in the mind or minds of the tribunal notwithstanding any doubts that may still linger there. Mathematical evidence may not be introduced without some supporting direct evidence.

FACTS: Betty Smith (P) was driving her automobile at 1:00 A.M. on Main Street, Winthrop. A bus coming toward her forced her to swerve to the right to avoid being hit. Her automobile collided with a parked car. Smith (P) could not see who owned the bus. Smith (P) brought suit against Rapid Transit (D) on the theory that they were the only local bus company licensed to use Main Street as a route; and that they had buses running at the time of the accident which could have, based on the company's timetable, been where Smith (P) was injured at about 1:00 A.M. This made it mathematically more certain than not that Smith (P) was injured by Rapid Transit's (D) bus. The judge directed the verdict for Rapid Transit (D), and Smith (P) appealed.

ISSUE: Should a case be allowed to go to the jury where the only proof of guilt is that it is mathematically more likely than not that the defendant is guilty?

HOLDING AND DECISION: (Spalding, J.) No. A proposition is proved by the preponderance of the evidence if it is made to appear more likely or probable in the sense that actual belief in its truth, derived from the evidence, exists in the mind or minds of the tribunal notwithstanding any doubts that may still linger there. Mathematical evidence may not be introduced without some supporting direct evidence. The ownership of the bus was a matter of conjecture. Other buslines could have been using Main Street (private, chartered, etc.). It is not enough that mathematically the chances somewhat favor the proposition to be proven. Proof by preponderance of the evidence means that the trier of fact believes in the truth of the fact asserted, based on the evidence presented, notwithstanding any lingering doubts. It is necessary to present some non-statistical and individualized proof of identity before compelling a party to pay damages, and even before compelling him to come forward with defensive evidence, absent an adequate explanation of the failure to present such individualized proof.

EDITOR'S ANALYSIS: This case stands for the proposition that mere mathematical inference of guilt, regardless of its high probability, will be insufficient to allow the case to go to the jury without non-statistical evidence to support it. Mere probability lacks an evidential foundation from which a valid inference can be drawn. Without adequate proof of the underlying proposition, the inference would merely be an unproven supposition. Mathematics alone cannot supply this evidential base.

NOTES:

DYER v. MacDOUGALL
Libel claimant (P) v. Alleged slanderer (D)
201 F.2d 265 (2d Cir. 1952).

NATURE OF CASE: Appeal from summary judgment denying damages for libel and slander.

FACT SUMMARY: MacDougall (D) moved for summary judgment when, through depositions, he learned that none of Dyer's (P) witnesses would testify that he had heard any slander.

CONCISE RULE OF LAW: Where a plaintiff will be unable to present any witnesses at trial who will testify to his allegations, summary judgment must be directed against him.

FACTS: In his complaint for libel and slander, Dyer (P) alleged that MacDougall (D) had written a libelous letter about him to a Mrs. Hope, and had made slanderous statements to Almirall. Depositions of these prospective witnesses disclosed, however, that they denied having heard or read the slanders uttered. The trial court, in considering MacDougall's (D) motion for summary judgment, offered to hold off its decision until Dyer (P) himself could take depositions of Hope and Almirall, but Dyer (P) failed to do so. Finding that Dyer (P) would be unable to present at trial any witnesses who would testify to having heard the alleged slanders, the trial court, ruling that there was no "genuine issue" under Fed. R. Civ. P. 56(c), granted MacDougall's (D) motion for summary judgment.

ISSUE: Where a plaintiff will be unable to present any witnesses at trial who will testify to his allegations, must summary judgment be directed against him?

HOLDING AND DECISION: (Hand, J.) Yes. Where a plaintiff will be unable to present any witnesses at trial who will testify to his allegations, summary judgment must be directed against him. Only when it appears that there will be a "genuine issue" at trial will a motion for summary judgment pursuant to Fed. R. Civ. P. 56(c) be denied. Here, Dyer's (P) prospective witnesses will deny having heard the utterances. Arguably, Dyer (P) might still be able, by placing Hope and Almirall on the stand, to convince the jury of the truth of his allegations. The jury, in studying the witnesses' demeanors, might believe that they were lying in their denials and assume the opposite. Notwithstanding this possibility, the motion for summary judgment must still be granted. Otherwise, in cases like this, there could not be an effective appeal from the judge's disposition of a motion for a directed verdict; demeanor cannot be reflected in a record on appeal. Affirmed.

CONCURRENCE: (Frank, J.) The holding of this case should be limited to the peculiarity of its facts. The majority's worry about

preserving the record for appeal is unfounded, since the trial judge's attitude towards demeanor is not a factor on appeal.

EDITOR'S ANALYSIS: Upon its introduction, Rule 56 was interpreted as providing that an action which is well pleaded is not subject to dismissal through the summary judgment device. This, however, undermined the device's purpose to eliminate frivolous or meritless actions prior to trial. Rule 56, as a result, was amended by a new subsection (e), which obligates the adverse party to respond with counteraffidavits, or other evidence, in opposing a well-made and supported motion.

NOTES:

LEGILLE v. DANN
Public official (D) v. Patent applicant (P)
544 F.2d 1 (D.C. Cir. 1976).

NATURE OF CASE: Action to compel certain action by the Commissioner of Patents.

FACT SUMMARY: Commissioner of Patents Legille (D) claimed the practice of stamping patent applications as received rebutted the presumption that Dann's (P) patent application, once mailed, was delivered in due course and without delay, and not on the late date stamped on it by the Patent Office.

CONCISE RULE OF LAW: A case involving contrary presumptions should not be summarily disposed of by assessing their relative strength and deciding which one should prevail.

FACTS: Dann (P) sought an order directing the Commissioner of Patents, Legille (D), to reassign an earlier filing date to his patent application. He wanted a date no later than March 6, 1973, arguing that the law presumes something mailed will be delivered in due course and without unreasonable delay. Legille (D) offered evidence as to the routine practice of stamping patent applications as received, claiming a presumption of procedural regularity attached to rebut the presumption that the mailed patent application arrived without delay. The district court held the rebuttable presumption of delivery in due course could not be overcome by invoking another conflicting presumption but had to be rebutted by positive evidence that the presumption was inapplicable in a particular case. It thus granted Dann (P) a summary judgment.

ISSUE: Should a summary disposition of a case be made by deciding the relative strength of two contrary presumptions involved in the case and deciding which one should prevail?

HOLDING AND DECISION: (Robinson, J.) No. Where contrary presumptions are involved in a case, it should not be summarily disposed of by assessing the relative strength of each and deciding which one should prevail and govern the outcome. Presumptions are mere procedural devices incapable of waging war among themselves. An issue of material fact, the date of receipt, was presented and should not have been summarily disposed of without considering the conflicting evidence. Reversed and remanded.

EDITOR'S ANALYSIS: The Federal Rules of Evidence, the Model Code of Evidence, and the Supreme Court adhere to the "bursting bubble" theory of presumptions. It says that once some evidence contrary to a presumption is offered, the presumption disappears as a rule of law and leaves the case in the fact-finder's hands free of any rule.

NOTES:

ATKINSON v. HALL
Paternity claimant (P) v. Ex-lover (D)
Me. Sup. Ct., 556 A.2d 651 (1989).

NATURE OF CASE: Appeal from determination of paternity suit.

FACT SUMMARY: The trial judge in Atkinson's (P) paternity suit against her ex-lover Hall (D) disregarded two conflicting presumptions, the first that Atkinson's (P) son was legitimate because she bore him while married, and the second that Atkinson's (P) son was conceived with Hall (D) because Hall's (D) blood tests showed the probability of his paternity as 98.3%.

CONCISE RULE OF LAW: If two presumptions arise which are conflicting with each other, the court shall apply the presumption which is founded on the weightier considerations of policy and logic, and if there is no such preponderance both presumptions shall be disregarded.

FACTS: Atkinson (P) and Hall (D) slept together a few months before she married Marshall and Hall (D) returned to prison. Atkinson (P) visited Hall (D) in prison and told him she had married Marshall, and that she was about to have a son. Atkinson (P) believed she told Hall (D) that the son was his, but Hall (D) believed that Atkinson (P) told him the son was Marshall's. Atkinson (P) named her son after Marshall on his birth certificate, but soon divorced Marshall. Atkinson (P), many years later, brought a paternity suit against Hall (D). At the time of trial, the son was 15, and was over six feet tall, whereas both Hall (D) and Atkinson (P) were short. Nevertheless, Hall's (D) blood test revealed a 98.3% probability that he was the father. This fact, under Maine law, raised a presumption of paternity that could only be rebutted by clear and convincing evidence. However, the fact that the son was born of a legal marriage raised a counter-presumption that Atkinson (P) bore the burden of producing evidence and proving beyond a reasonable doubt that Hall (D) was the boy's father. The trial judge disregarded both presumptions and instructed the jury that Atkinson (P) had the burden of proving her case under the ordinary civil standard of preponderance of the evidence. The jury found for Hall (D) and Atkinson (P) appealed.

ISSUE: If two presumptions arise which are conflicting, shall the court apply the presumption which is founded on the weightier considerations of policy and logic, and if there is no such preponderance is the court entitled to disregard both presumptions?

HOLDING AND DECISION: (Hornby, J.) Yes. If two conflicting presumptions arise, the court shall apply the presumption which is founded on the weightier considerations of policy and logic, and if there is no such preponderance both presumptions shall be disregarded. In terms of logic, presuming paternity from a 98.3% blood test seems weightier than presuming legitimacy from the mere fact of marriage. In terms of policy, however, there is no particular weight to the blood test presumption since a jury is able to hear and evaluate testimony concerning the blood test without the presumption and make a rational decision as to who is the biological father in any event. The presumption of legitimacy, however, is clearly designed to minimize official intrusion into marital and family relations; it is one of the strongest known to law. At the very least, then, the paternity presumption is not founded on weightier considerations than the legitimacy presumption. Therefore, Atkinson (P) was not prejudiced when the superior court instructed the jury to decide this case under the ordinary civil standard of a preponderance of the evidence. Affirmed.

EDITOR'S ANALYSIS: Wisconsin takes the position that when presumptions conflict, they always cancel each other out so that the burden of proof remains where it was initially placed. However, much depends on whether the presumptions are of the "Thayer-Wigmore" (affecting the burden of producing evidence) or "Morgan-McCormick" (affecting the burden of proof) variety. Two "Thayer-Wigmore" presumptions cannot conflict because the inference from the basic facts of one presumption would be sufficient evidence of the nonexistence of the presumed fact to cause the other presumption to "burst." Further, since "Morgan-McCormick" presumptions do not disappear when contrary evidence is introduced, it is possible that two presumptions could simultaneously place the burden of proof on two different parties, giving rise to the problem that Wisconsin and Maine have decided somewhat differently.

NOTES:

PEOPLE v. RODER
State (P) v. Second-hand shop owner (D)
Cal. Sup. Ct., 33 Cal. 3d 491, 658 P.2d 1302 (1983).

NATURE OF CASE: Appeal from conviction for receiving stolen property.

FACT SUMMARY: Roder (D) contended that the trial court committed constitutional error in instructing the jury to the effect that the burden of proof shifted to him to disprove an element of the crime of which he was charged.

CONCISE RULE OF LAW: A statute creating a mandatory presumption which works to shift to the defendant the burden of disproving an element of the crime is unconstitutional.

FACTS: Roder (D) was the proprietor of a second-hand shop. The police, pursuant to a warrant, searched the shop and found a distinctive clarinet which had been reported stolen. Roder (D) was charged with receiving stolen property. The owner of the clarinet testified that after it was stolen he inquired about it at several second-hand stores, including Roder's (D), yet he never heard back from Roder (D). Roder (D) testified he did not recall meeting the owner, but did not deny doing so. He said most of the store's inventory was purchased at flea markets, that he did not buy it, and the first time he saw it it was already part of the store's inventory. At the conclusion of the evidence, the court instructed the jury on the elements of receiving stolen property, and that, under California Penal Code § 496, if the jury found that (1) Roder (D) was a dealer in second-hand merchandise; (2) he bought stolen property; (3) he bought such property under circumstances which should have induced him to inquire whether the person from whom it bought the property had the legal right to sell it; and (4) that he failed to make such inquiry, then it was to presume Roder (D) bought the property with knowledge of it being stolen, unless it had a reasonable doubt concerning the conclusion. Roder (D) was convicted and appealed, contending that because knowledge that the property was stolen is an essential element of the crime, the prosecution had the burden of proving it beyond a reasonable doubt. He argued that the presumption articulated by the court effectively shifted the burden to him to disprove the presumption of his knowledge, and therefore the statutory presumption was unconstitutional.

ISSUE: Is a statutory mandatory presumption which works to shift to the defendant the burden of disproving an element of the crime charged unconstitutional?

HOLDING AND DECISION: (Kaus, J.) Yes. A statutory mandatory presumption which works to shift to the defendant the burden of disproving an element of the crime charged is unconstitutional. The presumption in this case impermissibly lightens the prosecution's burden of proof. First, if the prosecution proves the first three elements, the jury is compelled to find the fourth unless the defendant disproves its existence. The jury was led to believe that it was the defendant's failure to present sufficient evidence to raise a reasonable doubt concerning his knowledge the property was stolen that established this element, rather than the prosecution's proving it beyond a reasonable doubt. As a result, the presumption shifted the burden of proof to the defendant and was unconstitutional. Reversed.

EDITOR'S ANALYSIS: A presumption is not considered evidence. Rather, it is a procedural device implemented through jury instructions, which mandates the drawing of certain inferences leading to the finding of ultimate facts. A conclusive or mandatory presumption requires the trier to find certain ultimate facts upon finding the existence of the basic facts. In this case, if the jury found Roder (D) was a second-hand dealer, that he purchased stolen property, and that he did so without inquiring as to the true owner where circumstances required it, then the jury, from finding these basic facts, was required to find he knew the property was stolen, the ultimate fact.

NOTES:

CHAPTER TWELVE
OPINION, EXPERTISE AND EXPERTS;
SCIENTIFIC AND DEMONSTRATIVE EVIDENCE

QUICK REFERENCE RULES OF LAW

1. **Personal Knowledge of Witness.** Testimony of a witness as to his opinion of the intentions manifested by the accused in a certain semaphoric signal (e.g., wink) should be inadmissible as outside the witness's personal knowledge. (Commonwealth v. Holden)

2. **Lay Witness Opinions.** Under Federal Rule of Evidence 701, if a witness is not testifying as an expert, his testimony in the form of opinions or inferences is limited to those that are rationally based on the perception of the witness and helpful to a clear understanding of his testimony. (Government of the Virgin Islands v. Knight)

3. **Ultimate Issue Rule.** A duly qualified expert may characterize a defendant's conduct based on his experience in terms which parallel the language of the statutory offense when that language also constitutes the ordinary parlance or expression of persons in everyday life. (State v. Odom)

4. **Basis of Expert Opinion Testimony.** Experts may not give opinions embodying legal conclusions expressed in statutory or regulatory language, or offer an opinion as to relevant facts based on their assessment of the trustworthiness or accuracy of another witness's testimony. (United States v. Scop)

5. **Hypothetical Questions Asked of Experts.** (1) To be competent, a hypothetical question may include only facts which are already in evidence or those which the jury might logically infer therefrom. (2) The opinion of an expert witness may not be predicated in whole or in part upon the opinions, inferences, or conclusions of other witnesses, whether they be expert or lay, unless their testimony is put hypothetically as an assumed fact. (Ingram v. McCuiston)

6. **Evidence Relied on by Experts.** (1) Hearsay evidence relied on by an expert in forming his opinion, provided it is of a type regularly relied on by experts in the field, is a "firmly rooted" exception to the hearsay rule, and therefore not violative of a criminal defendant's constitutional confrontation rights. (2) A court does not abuse its discretion in a criminal case by excluding evidence referred to but not relied on by an expert where the opposing party seeks to cross-examine on that evidence. (United States v. Brown)

7. **Reliance on Inadmissible Data.** Expert opinion evidence is inadmissible where the expert has relied on underlying data that is itself inadmissible and is not the type of data reasonably relied on by experts in the field. (United States v. Tran Trong Cuong)

8. **Hypothetical Assumptions.** An expert may render opinion testimony on the basis of facts given in a hypothetical question that asks the expert to assume their truth. (People v. Gardeley)

9. **Proper Forum of Questions Directed to Experts.** Federal Rule of Evidence 704(b) does not bar mental health experts from offering opinions as to whether a defendant possessed a certain mental state at the time of a crime in response to questions tracking the exact language of the applicable legal test for determination of guilt. (United States v. Kristiansen)

10. **Expert Opinions.** If scientific knowledge will assist the trier of fact to understand the evidence or to determine a fact in issue, a witness qualified as an expert by knowledge, skill, experience, training, or education may testify thereto in the form of an opinion or otherwise. (Daubert v. Merrell Dow Pharmaceuticals Inc.)

11. Reliability of Scientific Testimony. A trial judge has a special obligation to ensure that any and all scientific testimony is not only relevant, but reliable. (Kuhmo Tire Company, Ltd. v. Carmichael)

12. Handwriting Analysis Testimony. The testimony of a forensic document analyst to show the similarities and differences between handwriting samples is inadmissible under the Federal Rules of Evidence. (United States v. Saelee)

13. Polygraph Evidence. (1) The federal standard for the admissibility of scientific evidence is applicable in state cases in Connecticut. (2) Polygraph evidence is per se inadmissible because its prejudicial effect far outweighs its probative value. (State v. Porter)

14. Exception to Polygraph Inadmissibility. The results of polygraph tests are admissible when: (1) the parties stipulate in advance as to the circumstances of the test and the scope of admissibility; (2) the test is used to impeach or corroborate the testimony of a witness at trial after notice to and opportunity for the opposing side to conduct its own lie detector test; and (3) the trial court has determined its probative value outweighs prejudice to the jury. (United States v. Piccinonna)

15. Constitutionality of Polygraph Inadmissibility. Military Rule of Evidence 707, which makes polygraph evidence inadmissible in court-martial proceedings, does not unconstitutionally abridge the right of the accused members of the military to present a defense. (United States v. Scheffer)

16. Admissibility of Field Sobriety Tests. The results of properly administered standard field sobriety tests (SFSTs) may not be admitted under Fed. R. Evid. 702 as direct evidence of a specific Blood Alcohol Content (BAC). (United States v. Horn)

17. Expert Testimony. Expert testimony on the defects of eyewitness identifications is admissible if there is: (1) a qualified expert; (2) a proper subject; (3) conformity with generally accepted explanatory theory; and (4) probative value compared to prejudicial effect. (State v. Chapple)

18. Circumstantial Evidence. Wholly circumstantial evidence can establish a prima facie case of criminal wrongdoing. (Ellis v. State)

COMMONWEALTH v. HOLDEN
State (P) v. Convicted murderer (D)
Pa. Sup. Ct., 390 Pa. 221, 134 A.2d 868 (1957).

NATURE OF CASE: Dissent in murder appeal.

FACT SUMMARY: Holden (D) was convicted of murdering Cora Smith based, in part, upon testimony by Jones that Holden (D) had indicated to him with a wink that he wanted Jones to supply an alibi for him.

CONCISE RULE OF LAW: Testimony of a witness as to his opinion of the intentions manifested by the accused in a certain semaphoric signal (e.g., wink) should be inadmissible as outside the witness's personal knowledge.

FACTS: Holden (D) was tried and convicted of murdering Cora Smith by striking her over the head some time between 5:15 and 6:40 A.M. on December 31, 1965. At the trial, the prosecution presented the testimony of Jones, who had been with Holden (D) the night prior to the murder. Jones testified that, while being questioned by police in Holden's (D) presence, Holden (D) had winked at him. After stating that he did not know whether this had been intentional or merely the result of Holden's (D) having something in his eye, Jones was confronted by the prosecutor with a prior statement which he had made to the police, namely, "I think he was trying to get me to make an alibi for him to cover up some of his actions and I don't know nothing about any of his actions." Holden (D) was convicted. His appeal was denied without the majority ever reaching the issue presented herein by the dissent of Justice Musmanno. Only this dissent appears in the casebook.

ISSUE: May a witness properly testify as to the meaning manifested by the accused in a signal apparently communicated to the witness?

DISSENT: (Musmanno, J.) No. Testimony of a witness as to his opinion of the intentions manifested by the accused in a certain semaphoric signal (e.g., wink) should be inadmissible as outside the witness's personal knowledge. The question asked of Jones required that he indulge in pure speculation as to the goings on of Holden's (D) mind. Permitting it is no different than permitting him to speculate as to the answer to the question: "What was he thinking at the time?" The refusal of the court to reverse this conviction "would suggest that here the law has not only winked, but closed both eyes."

EDITOR'S ANALYSIS: By the modern view, a lay witness may offer his opinion as to "normal observations" (e.g., time, speed, etc.) where such is based on his personal knowledge and is helpful or necessary to the jury's deliberations. The dissent herein presents a clear, albeit nitpicking example of the fine line between that which is based upon personal observation and that which is based upon mere speculation. Note that the question of what Jones contemporaneously interpreted Holden's (D) wink to mean would not involve opinion and would be admissible if somehow relevant (it is not probative on whether Holden (D) did in fact attempt to induce an alibi). However, when Jones went further to speculate as to the intentions of Holden (D), he entered the realm of inadmissible opinion.

NOTES:

GOVERNMENT OF THE VIRGIN ISLANDS v. KNIGHT

Federal government (P) v. Convicted murderer (D)

989 F.2d 619 (3d Cir. 1993).

NATURE OF CASE: Appeal from a conviction of voluntary manslaughter and two weapons charges.

FACT SUMMARY: After the gun Knight (D) used to beat Miller discharged, killing Miller, Knight (D) objected to the trial court's refusal to allow an eyewitness and the investigating police officer to give opinion testimony as to Knight's (D) contention that the gun discharged accidentally.

CONCISE RULE OF LAW: Under Federal Rule of Evidence 701, if a witness is not testifying as an expert, his testimony in the form of opinions or inferences is limited to those that are rationally based on the perception of the witness and helpful to a clear understanding of his testimony.

FACTS: While Knight (D) repeatedly struck Miller in the head with a pistol, the pistol went off, killing Miller. Knight (D) was charged and tried for second degree murder and two firearm violations. During the trial, Knight (D) contended that the gun had gone off accidentally. However, the court refused to allow a lay eyewitness or the investigating police officer to offer their opinions on this issue. Knight (D) argued that the trial court erred in refusing to allow this opinion testimony. The jury found Knight (D) guilty as charged. Knight (D) appealed.

ISSUE: If a witness is not testifying as an expert, is his testimony in the form of opinions or inferences limited to those which are rationally based on the perception of the witness and helpful to a clear understanding of his testimony?

HOLDING AND DECISION: (Cowen, J.) Yes. Under Fed. R. Evid. 701, if a witness is not testifying as an expert, his testimony in the form of opinions or inferences is limited to those that are rationally based on the perception of the witness and helpful to a clear understanding of his testimony. In this case, the district court properly excluded the investigating police officer's opinion because he did not observe the assault. In contrast, the eyewitness obviously had firsthand knowledge of the facts from which his opinion was formed. The witness's opinion that the gunshot was accidental would have permitted him to relate the facts with greater clarity and hence would have aided the jury. Based on an assessment of the witness's credibility, the jury could then attach an appropriate weight to this lay opinion. However, the exclusion of this opinion testimony was harmless error. The government (P) all but conceded that the shooting was an accident. Thus, the trial court's ruling could not have significantly prejudiced Knight (D), and a reversal is not warranted. Affirmed.

EDITOR'S ANALYSIS: While the general rule excludes opinion or conclusion testimony by a layperson, the modern trend favors admissibility of lay opinion testimony. The relaxation of the standards governing the admissibility of such testimony relies on cross-examination to reveal any weaknesses in the witness's conclusions.

NOTES:

STATE v. ODOM
State (P) v. Convicted drug dealer (D)
N.J. Sup. Ct., 116 N.J. 65, 560 A.2d 1198 (1989).

NATURE OF CASE: Appeal from reversal of conviction of possession of controlled substances with intent to distribute.

FACT SUMMARY: In Odom's (D) trial for possession of crack cocaine with intent to distribute, the prosecutor called as an expert witness a narcotics squad officer who based his opinion that Odom (D) had intended to distribute the crack found in his possession on his experience and the facts surrounding Odom's (D) arrest.

CONCISE RULE OF LAW: A duly-qualified expert may characterize a defendant's conduct based on his experience in terms which parallel the language of the statutory offense when that language also constitutes the ordinary parlance or expression of persons in everyday life.

FACTS: Odom (D) was arrested in his attic by a narcotics officer with a search warrant. Odom (D), who was found with a juvenile, had 18 vials of crack cocaine in a pillowcase on the bed as well as $24 in cash. No other drugs or drug paraphernalia were found. Odom (D) was arrested for possession of controlled substances with intent to distribute. At trial, Odom (D) testified that he was a crack addict and that the 18 vials were for his personal use. The prosecutor put a narcotics officer on the stand as an expert witness. The officer had over nine years' experience in narcotics, had been involved in over 400 crack investigations, had arrested over 100 people who were distributing crack, had interviewed 50 crack dealers, and had testified as an expert in over 1,000 trials. After being presented with the facts surrounding Odom's (D) arrest, the officer was asked to give an expert opinion as to whether Odom (D) possessed crack with the intent to distribute, and he replied that Odom (D) had. Odom (D) was convicted, but the appellate division reversed on the ground that the expert's use of the phrase "intent to distribute" amounted to a determination of the truth of the charge. The State (P) appealed.

ISSUE: May a duly-qualified expert characterize a defendant's conduct based on his experience in terms which parallel the language of the statutory offense when that language also constitutes the ordinary parlance or expression of persons in everyday life?

HOLDING AND DECISION: (Handler, J.) Yes. A duly-qualified expert may characterize a defendant's conduct based on his experience in terms which parallel the language of the statutory offense when that language also constitutes the ordinary parlance or expression of persons in everyday life. However, an expert may not express an ultimate opinion on the guilt of the particular defendant—the determination of guilt or innocence is the exclusive province of the jury. Further, the hypothetical question to the expert should be carefully phrased to refer only to the testimony and evidence adduced, and the expert's opinion should not be based on facts not in evidence. No reference to the defendant's particular name should be included in the hypothetical or the expert's response. With these precautions, however, the opinion of an expert, such as the narcotics officer here, which relates to a relevant subject that is beyond the understanding of the average person of ordinary experience, education, and knowledge can be highly useful to the jury. Here, the officer's opinion was based exclusively on the surrounding facts relating to the quantity and packaging of the drugs found at Odom's (D) flat, the addictive quality of those drugs, and the absence of drug-use paraphernalia. The conclusion he drew was derived from his experience and was permissibly stated in layman's language. Reversed.

EDITOR'S ANALYSIS: See also *State v. Landeros*, 20 N.J. 69, 74, 118 A.2d 521 (1955) (improper for expert, when asked if the defendant was guilty, to reply, "He is as guilty as Mrs. Murphy's pet pig") and *Shutka v. Pennsylvania R.R. Co.*, 74 N.J. Super. 381, 401-402, 181 A.2d 400 (App. Div. 1962) (court allowed expert opinion regarding the ultimate issue, noting, however, that expert testimony that expressed "his belief as to how the case should be decided" would be improper). Note also that in cases in which the expert used language characterizing defendant's conduct which paralleled statutory language, the expert's opinions were only allowed when the language was in common usage. See, e.g., *State v. Morton*, 74 N.J.Super. 531, 181 A.2d 785 (police officer in drunk-driving case allowed to testify that the defendant was under the influence of alcohol); see also *State v. Rucker*, 46 N.J.Super. 162, 166, 134 A.2d 409 (App.Div.) (police experts in gambling prosecution allowed to testify as experts that certain papers were for use in a lottery).

NOTES:

UNITED STATES v. SCOP
Federal government (P) v. Auto dealer (D)
846 F.2d 135 (2d Cir. 1988).

NATURE OF CASE: Appeal from conviction for mail and securities fraud.

FACT SUMMARY: Scop (D) and others were involved in a scheme to artificially inflate the price of automobile dealership stock they owned, but at their trial for mail and securities fraud, the government (P) introduced an expert witness who characterized their conduct in conclusory terms based on the exact language of the federal fraud statutes.

CONCISE RULE OF LAW: Experts may not give opinions embodying legal conclusions expressed in statutory or regulatory language, or offer an opinion as to relevant facts based on their assessment of the trustworthiness or accuracy of another witness's testimony.

FACTS: Scop (D) and others were investors and traders in the stock of an automobile dealership which became involved in a scheme with one Sarcinelli to inflate the value of their holdings. Sarcinelli brought in customers for the stock and "matched" orders or trades such that both sides—buying and selling—of the transaction were covered by the same person. However, when the stock price did not rise as expected, Sarcinelli began to suspect that one of his partners was "back dooring" him by selling the stock on the open market, and he abandoned the scheme. When Sarcinelli withdrew, the stock value plummeted. At the trial of Scop (D) and the other investors for mail and securities fraud, the government (P) introduced as an expert witness the chief investigator for the Securities and Exchange Commission in Chicago. The expert had also been a stockbroker for eight years, had spent over 1,000 hours over four years on the case involving Scop (D), and had interviewed over 70 witnesses. As an expert in securities trading, he was asked to express his opinion solely on the testimony and documentary evidence at trial. When asked whether there was a scheme to defraud, the expert opined that Scop (D) and the others "had engaged in a manipulative and fraudulent scheme," and were "material" and "active" participants in the manipulation of the dealership stock prices. He repeated this conclusion many times during the course of his testimony. The expert's characterizations drew directly on the language of the mail and securities fraud statutes under which Scop (D) was being prosecuted. Scop (D) and the other investors were convicted and on appeal contended that the expert's opinions should have been excluded as legal conclusions.

ISSUE: May experts give opinions embodying legal conclusions expressed In statutory or regulatory language or offer opinions as to relevant facts based on their assessment of the trustworthiness or accuracy of another witness's testimony?

HOLDING AND DECISION: (Winter, Cir. J.) No. Experts may not give opinions embodying legal conclusions expressed in statutory or regulatory language, or offer an opinion as to relevant facts based on their assessment of the trustworthiness or accuracy of another witness's testimony. Testimony in the form of an opinion or inference otherwise admissible is not objectionable because it embraces an ultimate issue to be decided by the trier of fact. Fed. R. Evid. 704. However, Rule 704 does not allow experts to give opinions embodying legal conclusions. Repeated use of opinions expressed in language drawn from the statute or regulation under which a defendant is charged constitutes the worst form of testifying as to legal conclusions. Nor may experts evaluate the credibility of witnesses in offering an opinion on relevant facts; the trier of fact is the best evaluator of credibility. Here, the government's (P) expert repeatedly concluded that Scop (D) and the other investors had engaged in "fraudulent manipulative practices" and were "material" and "active" participants in that scheme, language drawn from the mail and securities fraud statutes. These were not self-defining terms, but impermissible ultimate conclusions of law. Further, the government's (P) expert made it clear he believed Sarcinelli told the truth while on the stand; this independent assessment of Sarcinelli's trustworthiness and the accuracy of his opinions invaded the province of the jury. Thus, the admission of the expert's opinion was reversible error. Reversed.

CONCURRENCE: (Pierce, J.) It is up to the cross-examiner to question an expert's reliance on the testimony of a witness whose credibility is in question; an appellate court should not set up a per se rule precluding expert opinions based on personal assessment of witness credibility.

EDITOR'S ANALYSIS: The court also based its rule forbidding experts from couching their opinions in the language of applicable statutes and regulations on the rationale that the absence of such a restriction would have the effect of allowing the expert, not the court, to "instruct" the jury on the applicable law of the case. See *FAA v. Landy*, 705 F.2d 624, 632 (2nd Cir.), cert. denied, 464 U.S. 895 (1983) ("It is not for witnesses to instruct the jury as to applicable principles of law, but for the judge."). Further, the court concluded that the Advisory Committee Note to Rule 703, while allowing experts to base their conclusions on technically inadmissible evidence (such as unauthenticated X-rays and oral reports), did not purport to allow experts to assess the credibility of testimony given in the same case.

INGRAM v. McCUISTON
Injured driver (P) v. Driver (D)
N.C. Sup. Ct., 261 N.C. 392, 134 S.E.2d 705 (1964).

NATURE OF CASE: Action to recover damages for personal injuries.

FACT SUMMARY: Ingram's (P) lawyer propounded to an expert witness a hypothetical question which contained facts which were not supported by evidence in the record and which was based in part upon the opinion of a second expert witness.

CONCISE RULE OF LAW: (1) To be competent, a hypothetical question may include only facts which are already in evidence or those which the jury might logically infer therefrom. (2) The opinion of an expert witness may not be predicated in whole or in part upon the opinions, inferences, or conclusions of other witnesses, whether they be expert or lay, unless their testimony is put hypothetically as an assumed fact.

FACTS: Ingram (P) was in an automobile accident when McCuiston (D) rear-ended her Volkswagen at a stop light and pushed Ingram (P) into the car in front. Ingram (P) is a nervous individual and was 3-months pregnant at the time of the accident. At trial, Ingram's (P) counsel posed a long hypothetical question to Dr. Miller, an orthopedic specialist, to which defendant objected, but the objection was overruled and the question was permitted. The jury found in favor of Ingram (P) and awarded substantial damages. Defendant appealed.

ISSUE: (1) Must a hypothetical question include only facts which are already in evidence or those which the jury might logically infer therefrom? (2) Can a hypothetical question be based upon the opinion of another witness?

HOLDING AND DECISION: (Sharp, J.) (1) Yes. To be competent, a hypothetical question may include only facts which are already in evidence or those which the jury might logically infer therefrom. Hence, the question propounded here was improper, since it was based upon facts which were not supported by evidence in the record. (2) No. The opinion of an expert witness may not be predicated in whole or in part upon the opinions, inferences, or conclusions of other witnesses, whether they be expert or lay, unless their testimony is put hypothetically as an assumed fact. Stated another way, although an expert may base his opinion on facts testified to by another expert, the witness may not have submitted to him, as part of facts to be considered in the formation of his inference and conclusion, the opinion of such other expert. Since the opinion contained in the hypothetical question was not put hypothetically here, the question was improper. Nor are six pages required to state a proper hypothetical question based on the evidence in this case. Judgment for Ingram (P) is reversed.

EDITOR'S ANALYSIS: Commentators agree that the hypothetical question is an ingenious and logical device for enabling the jury to apply the expert's knowledge to the facts of the case. They also agree that it is a failure in practice and an obstruction to the administration of justice. If it is required that the question recite all the relevant facts, it becomes intolerably wordy. If counsel is allowed to choose the facts to include, there is the risk of a partisan slanting of the question.

NOTES:

UNITED STATES v. BROWN

Federal government (P) v. Convicted drug carrier (D)

299 F.3d 1252 (11th Cir. 1999).

NATURE OF CASE: Appeal from convictions for drug crimes.

FACT SUMMARY: Brown (D) was convicted of transporting cocaine base from Jamaica to Bermuda via Miami. She challenged the exclusion of a Drug Enforcement Administration (DEA) price list referred to, but not relied on, by the prosecution's (P) expert in forming an opinion as to the value of the cocaine base in Bermuda.

CONCISE RULE OF LAW: (1) Hearsay evidence relied on by an expert in forming his opinion, provided it is of a type regularly relied on by experts in the field, is a "firmly rooted" exception to the hearsay rule, and therefore not violative of a criminal defendant's constitutional confrontation rights. (2) A court does not abuse its discretion in a criminal case by excluding evidence referred to but not relied on by an expert where the opposing party seeks to cross-examine on that evidence.

FACTS: Brown (D) was traveling from Jamaica to Bermuda via Miami, when customs officers found cocaine base in her luggage. She claimed to have no knowledge of the cocaine. At trial, to prove Brown's (D) knowledge of the presence of the cocaine, the prosecution (P) relied on the opinion of a DEA expert on drug valuation, who testified that the value of the discovered cocaine base in Bermuda was $217,000. He based this value on information he received from another DEA officer, who in turn had conferred with Bermuda authorities to arrive at an estimated value. Brown (D) did not object at trial to the admission of this testimony. The government (P) argued that an unknowing innocent would not have been entrusted with such valuable contraband. Brown (D) attempted to contradict this testimony with a written DEA price list referred to by the DEA expert, but upon which he did not rely in forming his opinion. The district court excluded the price list and disallowed cross-examination on the information contained therein. Over Brown's (D) objection to this evidentiary ruling, Brown (D) was convicted, and then appealed to the court of appeals.

ISSUE: (1) Is hearsay evidence relied on by an expert in forming his opinion, provided it is of a type regularly relied on by experts in the field, a "firmly rooted" exception to the hearsay rule, and therefore not violative of a criminal defendant's constitutional confrontation rights? (2) Does a court abuse its discretion in a criminal case by excluding evidence referred to but not relied on by an expert where the opposing party seeks to cross-examine on that evidence?

HOLDING AND DECISION: (Kravitch, J.) (1) Yes. Hearsay evidence relied on by an expert in forming his opinion, provided it is of a type regularly relied on by experts in the field, is a "firmly rooted" exception to the hearsay rule, and therefore not violative of a criminal defendant's constitutional confrontation rights. Because Brown (D) did not object to the admission of the DEA expert's testimony, the trial court's ruling is reviewed for plain error. Here, the DEA expert had substantial experience investigating narcotics smuggling and drug valuation. The expert conceded that he relied on information and expertise from non-testifying parties, and, therefore, that part of his testimony was hearsay. Fed. R. Evid. 703 permits experts to rely on data that itself is inadmissible hearsay, if this data is "of a type reasonably relied upon by experts in the particular field in forming opinions." That rule applies in cases such as this one, where the expert bases his opinion on his experience and expertise in conjunction with hearsay data that is regularly relied on in the field. Given that the expert was a long-time agent in this area, the trial court would have been justified in concluding that he possessed the professional knowledge and ability to determine if the hearsay on which he based his opinion was reliable. Therefore, the district court did not commit plain error in admitting his testimony. Criminal cases, however, present heightened concern for the defendant's constitutional confrontation right. The Sixth Amendment prohibits hearsay unless it falls into a "firmly rooted hearsay exception," or is particularly trustworthy. Rule 703 and the long-established practice of admitting expert opinion based on hearsay when it is of a type regularly relied on by experts in the field establish that this evidentiary principle is a "firmly rooted" exception to the hearsay rule. Brown (D) could and did cross-examine the expert on the reliability of the hearsay sources and his resulting opinion; therefore, Brown's (D) confrontation rights were not violated. (2) No. A court does not abuse its discretion in a criminal case by excluding evidence referred to but not relied on by an expert where the opposing party seeks to cross-examine on that evidence. Here, the price list made no reference to cocaine base at all, and did not make reference to drug prices in either Jamaica or Bermuda. Thus, admitting the price list for other types of cocaine in other countries could well have misled the jury. Moreover, Brown's (D) substantial rights were not affected by the exclusion of the price list because the DEA expert himself testified to great discrepancies between the price of cocaine in different countries. Brown (D) could have cross-examined on these

Continued on next page.

significant price differences, and the reasons for such differences, but failed to. Therefore, the district court did not commit abuse of discretion in excluding the price list. Affirmed.

EDITOR'S ANALYSIS: In criminal cases, where an expert for the prosecution bases an important opinion on otherwise inadmissible hearsay that is of the type regularly relied on by experts in the field, generally challenges to the opinion on Confrontation Clause grounds fail. However, where the expert is merely being used as a conduit to report the substance of otherwise inadmissible out-of-court statements by third persons, a challenge to the expert's opinions would most likely be upheld on constitutional grounds.

NOTES:

UNITED STATES v. TRAN TRONG CUONG
Federal government (P) v. Physician (D)
18 F.3d. 1132 (4th Cir. 1994).

NATURE OF CASE: Appeal from a conviction for unlawfully prescribing controlled substances.

FACT SUMMARY: Tran (D), a physician who was convicted of unlawfully prescribing controlled substances, claimed that Federal Rule of Evidence 703 was violated when MacIntosh, a medical expert, was allowed to testify that based on his review of another physician's (Stevenson's) report on Tran's (D) patients, it was his opinion that his findings and Stevenson's were "essentially the same." Tran (D) claimed that since Stevenson's report was not introduced into evidence and that Stevenson was unavailable to testify, MacIntosh's statement was prejudicial hearsay not based on the type of data reasonably relied on by experts in the field.

CONCISE RULE OF LAW: Expert opinion evidence is inadmissible where the expert has relied on underlying data that is itself inadmissible and is not of the type of data reasonably relied on by experts in the field.

FACTS: Tran (D), a physician practicing medicine in Virginia, was convicted of prescribing controlled substances to patients who were known drug abusers. At trial, the government (P) presented the testimony of MacIntosh, a medical expert in the area of family medicine (the area in which Tran (D) practiced) who had reviewed charts belonging to the patients listed in the indictment, and who had prepared a written report summarizing his findings. MacIntosh also testified as to the qualifications of Stevenson, another doctor who had also prepared a report on some of Tran's (D) patients. MacIntosh indicated that Stevenson was his friend, a highly regarded general surgeon, a lawyer, and president of the Medical Society. MacIntosh also testified that he had reviewed Stevenson's report, and, based on this review, he opined that his findings were "essentially the same" as Stevenson's. Stevenson's report was not introduced into evidence and Stevenson was unavailable to testify. Tran (D) objected to MacIntosh's opinion, claiming that Fed. R. Evid. 703 had been violated because Stevenson's report was prejudicial hearsay that was not of the type relied on by experts in the field.

ISSUE: Is expert opinion evidence admissible where the expert has relied on underlying data that is itself inadmissible and is not of the type of data reasonably relied on by experts in the field?

HOLDING AND DECISION: (Chapman, J.) No. Expert opinion evidence is inadmissible where the expert has relied on underlying data that is itself inadmissible and is not of the type of data reasonably relied on by experts in the field. Stevenson's report was clearly hearsay and prejudicial to Tran (D). Although MacIntosh could permissibly testify that he had reviewed Stevenson's report and that he had relied on it in reaching his opinion, he could not go further and bolster his testimony by saying that his and Stevenson's opinions or reports were essentially the same, unless Stevenson were called as a witness and his report put into evidence. Under Fed. R. Evid. 703, expert opinion evidence is not objectionable where the expert has relied on underlying data that is itself inadmissible, provided that it is the type of data reasonably relied on by experts in the field. Here, there was no indication that Stevenson's report was of such a type. The report was prepared for the prosecution, and was thus a forensic opinion or report. It is doubtful that MacIntosh relies on forensic medical opinions in forming his opinions in his field of expertise—family medicine. Moreover, reports specifically prepared for litigation are not, by definition "of a type reasonably relied on by experts in the particular field." Furthermore, Stevenson was not properly qualified as an expert in family medicine. Thus, MacIntosh's attempt to put before the jury Stevenson's opinion without subjecting Stevenson to cross-examination denied Tran (D) his fundamental cross-examination right. Reversed.

EDITOR'S ANALYSIS: Fed. R. Evid. 703 codifies what had been a widely recognized exception to the rule against hearsay evidence. Even before the enactment of Fed. R. Evid. 703, it had long been the rule that an expert witness could express an opinion even though her opinion was based in part, or even solely, on hearsay sources. The rationale for this "exception" is that the expert, because of her professional knowledge and ability, is competent to judge for herself the reliability of the records and statements on which she bases her expert opinion.

QUICKNOTES

CROSS-EXAMINATION - The interrogation of a witness by an adverse party either to further inquire as to the subject matter of the direct examination or to call into question the witness' credibility.

EXPERT WITNESS - A witness providing testimony at trial who is specially qualified regarding the particular subject matter involved.

HEARSAY - An out-of-court statement made by a person other than the witness testifying at trial that is offered in order to prove the truth of the matter asserted.

PEOPLE v. GARDELEY
State (P) v. Gang members (D)
Cal. Sup. Ct., 927 P.2d 713 (1996).

NATURE OF CASE: Review of reversal of an enhanced criminal sentence.

FACT SUMMARY: Sentence enhancements based on gang affiliation were struck down on appeal because the expert witness allegedly did not have personal knowledge of the facts.

CONCISE RULE OF LAW: An expert may render opinion testimony on the basis of facts given in a hypothetical question that asks the expert to assume their truth.

FACTS: Following a street attack on Bruno, a white boy who stopped in an area controlled by the Family Crip gang in San Jose, California, Gardeley (D) was charged with attempted murder, assault with a deadly weapon with a great bodily harm enhancement, and robbery. A police detective with many years of experience investigating criminal street gang activity had interviewed Gardeley (D) and the other assailants and testified at the trial about other criminal activities of the Family Crip gang in the area. The prosecution gave the witness a scenario using the facts from the events in this case, and the witness testified that it was a classic example of how a gang used violence to secure its drug-dealing stronghold. The jury convicted Gardeley (D) and the other defendants of assault committed for the benefit of, at the direction of, or in association with, a criminal street gang. Under the provisions of the Street Terrorism Enforcement and Prevention (STEP) Act, the trial court imposed increased sentences. The court of appeals struck down the sentence enhancements on the ground that the prosecution (P) had failed to prove the requisite pattern of criminal gang activity. The court of appeals held that evidence of two or more predicate offenses by gang members can establish a pattern of criminal gang activity only if each such offense is shown to be gang-related. The Attorney General (P) petitioned the state supreme court for review.

ISSUE: May an expert render opinion testimony on the basis of facts given in a hypothetical question that asks the expert to assume their truth?

HOLDING AND DECISION: (Kennard, J.) Yes. An expert may render opinion testimony on the basis of facts given in a hypothetical question that asks the expert to assume their truth. The testimony by the police detective provided a basis from which the jury could reasonably find that the Family Crip gang met the requirements of the STEP Act. Since the predicate offenses need not themselves be gang-related, the prosecution (P) adequately proved a pattern of criminal gang activity. Reversed.

EDITOR'S ANALYSIS: The STEP Act was enacted in 1988. A criminal street gang is defined by the Act as any ongoing association of three or more persons that shares a common name or common identifying sign or symbol; has as one of its primary activities the commission of specified criminal offenses; and engages through its members in a pattern of criminal gang activity. Pattern of criminal gang activity means that gang members have committed or attempted to commit two or more specified criminal offenses (so-called predicate offenses.)

QUICKNOTES

EXPERT WITNESS - A person with specialized knowledge or experience called to trial to testify as to facts which require such specialized experience to be helpful to the triers-of-fact.

HEARSAY - An out-of-court statement made by a person other than the witness testifying at trial that is offered in order to prove the truth of the matter asserted.

NOTES:

UNITED STATES v. KRISTIANSEN
Federal government (P) v. Prisoner (D)
901 F.2d 1463 (8th Cir. 1990).

NATURE OF CASE: Appeal from conviction for escaping from custody.

FACT SUMMARY: Kristiansen (D), who was residing in a halfway house facility, failed to return after calling in "sick." He was convicted of escaping from custody after a psychiatrist gave an expert opinion that Kristiansen (D)—though antisocial—was able to appreciate the nature and quality of the wrongfulness of his acts.

CONCISE RULE OF LAW: Federal Rule of Evidence 704(b) does not bar mental health experts from offering opinions as to whether a defendant possessed a certain mental state at the time of a crime in response to questions tracking the exact language of the applicable legal test for determination of guilt.

FACTS: Kristiansen (D) was residing in a halfway house facility. On three consecutive nights he telephoned the facility and informed it that he was unable to return because he was "sick." Although advised to keep the facility informed of his intentions and whereabouts, Kristiansen (D) failed to do so and was apprehended by the federal marshal and indicted for escaping from custody. At trial Kristiansen's (D) attorney argued that Kristiansen (D) lacked, by reason of mental disease or defect, the willful intent to escape because he was a cocaine addict and was under the influence of cocaine at the time he failed to return. Kristiansen's (D) counsel put a psychiatrist on the stand as its expert and asked the question: "Would an individual . . . with this severe mental disease or defect . . . [be able] to appreciate the nature and quality of the wrongfulness of his acts?" The trial court refused to allow the expert to answer this question because use of the word "would" asked for an answer that reached the ultimate issue in the case. However, the court did allow a question that substituted the word "could" for "would," and Kristiansen's (D) expert merely noted that Kristiansen (D) had demonstrated antisocial behavior. On cross-examination, however, the expert testified that Kristiansen (D) was not insane or psychotic to the degree that he would not be legally accountable for his actions. Kristiansen's (D) counsel did not object to this testimony, and Kristiansen (D) was convicted of escaping from custody. He appealed (D) on the ground that the trial court abused its discretion in allowing the expert's testimony on cross-examination, which permitted the expert to testify as to an ultimate issue in the case, i.e., Kristiansen's (D) culpability.

ISSUE: Does Fed. R. Evid. 704(b) bar mental health experts from offering opinions as to whether a defendant possessed a certain mental state at the time of a crime in response to questions tracking the exact language of the applicable legal test for determination of guilt?

HOLDING AND DECISION: (Heaney, J.) No. Federal Rule of Evidence 704(b) does not bar mental health experts from offering opinions as to whether a defendant possessed a certain mental state at the time of a crime in response to questions tracking the exact language of the applicable legal test for determination of guilt. Although Fed. R. Evid. 704(b) prohibits mental health experts from offering opinions as to whether the defendant possessed the required mental state at the time of the crime, it was not meant to prohibit testimony that describes the qualities of a mental disease. The fact that part of the wording of a question may track the legal test by asking if the disease prevents one suffering from it from understanding the nature and quality of an act does not violate the rule. Here, the trial court should have allowed the defense to ask the question about Kristiansen's (D) comprehension of the nature and the quality of his acts using the word "would," but the allowance of the same question with the word "could" means that the trial court's error was harmless. However, the government's (P) questioning of the expert was not harmless because it elicited the expert's opinion on the ultimate issue in the case, i.e., whether Kristiansen (D) had the mental state requisite for escaping from custody. However, this was not reversible error because the defense waived its right to object by failing to object at the time the testimony was introduced. Affirmed.

EDITOR'S ANALYSIS: The ultimate issue rule was based on the notion that jurors might be unduly swayed by the opinion of some witness about how the case ought to be decided. This rule has some basis in reason because jurors justifiably will not want to be appear ignorant by disregarding the opinions of those who are certifiably learned. But there is seldom a consensus of experts, and in reality jurors will not be prejudicially influenced merely because one expert has responded to a question which is framed in language parroting the ultimate legal standard in the case.

NOTES:

DAUBERT v. MERRELL DOW PHARMACEUTICALS, INC.
Birth defect claimant (P) v. Drug manufacturer (D)
509 U.S. 579 (1993).

NATURE OF CASE: Appeal from a grant of defendant's motion for summary judgment in an action to recover damages for personal injuries.

FACT SUMMARY: In Daubert's (P) suit to recover damages for serious birth defects allegedly caused by a drug marketed by Merrell Dow (D), the court granted Merrell Dow's (D) motion for summary judgment after applying the general acceptance, or "Frye," rule to the scientific evidence of Daubert's (P) expert witnesses.

CONCISE RULE OF LAW: If scientific knowledge will assist the trier of fact to understand the evidence or to determine a fact in issue, a witness qualified as an expert by knowledge, skill, experience, training, or education may testify thereto in the form of an opinion or otherwise.

FACTS: Jason Daubert (P) and Eric Schuller (P) brought this suit for damages, alleging that their serious birth defects had been caused by their mothers' ingestion of Benedectin, a drug marketed by Merrell Dow (D). Merrell Dow (D) moved for summary judgment, submitting an affidavit by its expert witness, who concluded, after reviewing more than thirty published studies, that maternal use of Benedectin during the first trimester of pregnancy was not a risk factor for human birth defects. Daubert's (P) and Schuller's (P) eight experts conducted their own studies and reanalyzed previously published studies, concluding that Benedectin can cause birth defects. The court granted Merrell Dow's (D) motion for summary judgment, holding that scientific evidence must be generally accepted to be admissible. The court of appeals affirmed. Daubert (P) and Schuller (P) appealed.

ISSUE: If scientific knowledge will assist the trier of fact to understand the evidence or to determine a fact in issue, may a witness qualified as an expert by knowledge, skill, experience, training, or education testify thereto in the form of an opinion or otherwise?

HOLDING AND DECISION: (Blackmun, J.) Yes. If scientific knowledge will assist the trier of fact to understand the evidence or to determine a fact in issue, a witness qualified as an expert by knowledge, skill, experience, training, or education may testify thereto in the form of an opinion or otherwise. The general acceptance test established by *Frye v. United States*, 293 F. 1013 (1923), has been displaced by the Federal Rules of Evidence. The current inquiry to be made under Fed. R. Evid. 702 is the scientific validity, and thus the evidentiary relevance and reliability, of the principles underlying a proposed submission.

Unlike an ordinary witness, an expert is permitted wide latitude to offer opinions. Accordingly, the judgment of the court of appeals is vacated, and the case is remanded for further proceedings.

EDITOR'S ANALYSIS: The Rules of Evidence assign to the trial judge the task of ensuring that an expert's testimony both rests on a reliable foundation and is relevant to the task at hand. Pertinent evidence based on scientifically valid principles will satisfy those demands. While publication, peer review, and general acceptance can have a bearing on the court's inquiry, they are not dispositive.

NOTES:

KUHMO TIRE COMPANY, LTD. v. CARMICHAEL
Tire manufacturer (D) v. Customer (P)
526 U.S. 137 (1999).

NATURE OF CASE: Review of order declaring evidence inadmissible and judgment for defendant.

FACT SUMMARY: Carmichael (P) claimed that his expert witness testimony was improperly excluded at trial and successfully appealed the trial court's application of the Daubert factors to determine the admissibility of technical evidence.

CONCISE RULE OF LAW: A trial judge has a special obligation to ensure that any and all scientific testimony is not only relevant, but reliable.

FACTS: The right rear tire on Carmichael's (P) minivan blew out and caused an accident in which one passenger died and others were severely injured. Carmichael (P) alleged that the tire was defective and sued the manufacturer, Kumho (D). Carmichael (P) rested his case in significant part upon deposition testimony provided by an expert in tire failure analysis, who intended to testify in support of his conclusion. Kumho's (D) motion to exclude that testimony was granted, on the ground that the tire expert's methodology failed Rule 702's reliability requirement. The court agreed with Kumho (D) that it should act as a *Daubert*-type gatekeeper, even though one might consider the testimony technical, rather than scientific. Carmichael's (P) motion for reconsideration was then granted, but the court later affirmed its earlier order and granted Kuhmo's (D) motion for summary judgment. The Eleventh Circuit reversed, concluding that the testimony fell outside the scope of *Daubert*, which applied only to scientific principles, and not to skill or experience-based observation. Kuhmo (D) appealed, and the Supreme Court granted certiorari.

ISSUE: Does a trial judge have a special obligation to ensure that any and all scientific testimony is not only relevant, but reliable?

HOLDING AND DECISION: (Breyer, J.) Yes. A trial judge has a special obligation to ensure that any and all scientific testimony is not only relevant, but reliable. Some of *Daubert*'s questions may help to evaluate the reliability of even experience-based testimony. Whether *Daubert*'s specific factors are, or are not, reasonable measures of reliability in a particular case are a matter that the law grants the trial judge broad latitude to determine. The trial judge in this court determined that the testimony fell outside the area where experts might reasonably differ, and where the jury must decide among the conflicting views of different experts, even though the evidence is shaky. The doubts that triggered the trial court's initial inquiry here were reasonable, as was the court's ultimate conclusion. Reversed.

CONCURRENCE: (Scalia, J.) The trial court discretion, endorsed here, in choosing the manner of testing expert reliability is not the discretion to abandon the gatekeeping function.

CONCURRENCE AND DISSENT: (Stevens, J.) The only question we granted certiorari to decide was whether a trial judge may consider the four factors set out in *Daubert v. Merrill Dow Pharmaceuticals, Inc.*, 509 U.S. 579 (1993), in a rule 702 analysis of admissibility of an engineering expert's testimony. I join the majority in its answer to that question. The different question of whether the trial judge abused his discretion when he excluded testimony should not be reached here because it was not raised by the certiorari petition.

EDITOR'S ANALYSIS: Justice Stevens concurred with the first two parts of the court's decision here, but dissented from the disposition of the case. He wrote that the question of the exclusion of the expert testimony should be decided by the court of appeals since it involved a study of the record. *Daubert* itself made clear that its list of factors was meant to be helpful, not definitive.

QUICKNOTES

***DAUBERT* RULE -** Provides that scientific evidence offered as expert testimony need not be based solely on procedures that have been generally accepted in the particular field to which it belongs.

EXPERT WITNESS - A person with specialized knowledge or experience called to trial to testify as to facts which require such specialized experience to be helpful to the triers-of-fact.

NOTES:

UNITED STATES v. SAELEE
Federal government (P) v. Alleged drug importer (D)
162 F. Supp.2d 1097 (D. Alaska, 2001).

NATURE OF CASE: Appeal from motion in limine excluding testimony by a forensic document analyst.

FACT SUMMARY: The government (P) claimed that Saelee (D) imported opium by using the mails and sought to introduce the testimony of a forensic document analyst, Cawley, about the similarities and differences between Saelee's (D) handwriting and the handwriting on the mailings.

CONCISE RULE OF LAW: The testimony of a forensic document analyst to show the similarities and differences between handwriting samples is inadmissible under the Federal Rules of Evidence.

FACTS: Saelee (D) was indicted for importing opium from Thailand. The opium was concealed in Butterfinger candy bars that appeared to have been express mailed from the United States but then returned to the sender after delivery was unsuccessful. The government (P) had Cawley, a forensic document analyst, compare hand printing exemplars provided by defendant with the hand printing on the address labels on the packages in question. Cawley concluded that Saelee (D) was the writer of one of the questioned writings and was probably the writer of another. The government (P) originally proposed to have Cawley testify as to his conclusions at trial, but then changed its position to have Cawley testify only as to the differences and similarities between the handwriting samples. The government (P) sought to have the testimony admitted under Fed. R. Evid. 701, which governs the admissibility of lay opinion testimony. Saelee (D) argued that the testimony was admissible, if at all, only under Fed. R. Evid. 702, which governs expert testimony, and asserted that a *Daubert* hearing was necessary. At the *Daubert* hearing, the government (P) changed course again, arguing that Cawley's testimony was admissible under Fed. R. Evid. 901, which deals with the authentication and identification of evidence. The court granted Saelee's (D) motion in limine to exclude the handwriting comparison evidence. The government (P) appealed to the district court.

ISSUE: Is the testimony of a forensic document analyst to show the similarities and differences between handwriting samples admissible under the Federal Rules of Evidence?

HOLDING AND DECISION: (Holland, J.) No. The testimony of a forensic document analyst to show the similarities and differences between handwriting samples is inadmissible under the Federal Rules of Evidence. Cawley's testimony is not admissible under Federal Rules of Evidence 701, 702, or 901.

Fed. R. Evid. 701, as amended, expressly limits lay opinion testimony to that which is not based on scientific, technical, or other specialized knowledge within the scope of Fed. R. Evid. 702. It is clear that Cawley is not a lay person who proposes to offer testimony based on sensory perception. Rather, he is a trained analyst who relies on handwriting identification principles, scientific examinations, and specialized knowledge, as well as 24 years of experience in this area. Therefore, such testimony must be examined under Fed. R. Evid. 702, which requires judges to exclude unreliable expert testimony. Various factors are used to test the reliability of expert testimony. Factors that "fit" the instant case are whether the theories and techniques of handwriting comparison have been tested, whether they have been subjected to peer review, the known or potential error rate of forensic document examiners, the existence of standards in making comparisons between known writings and questioned documents, and the general acceptance by the forensic evidence community. The government (P) bears the burden of proving that its expert's proffered testimony is sufficiently reliable to be admissible; here, the government (P) has failed to meet its burden. First, there has been a dearth of empirical testing of the theories and techniques used by forensic document analysts, and the few tests that have been conducted have not conclusively established that the experts in this area are better than lay persons in identifying genuine signatures or analyzing handwriting. This field also suffers from a lack of peer review, and little is known about the error rates of forensic document examiners. The little testing that has been done raises serious questions about the reliability of the methods currently in use. The field also suffers from a lack of controlling standards. Thus, the technique of comparing known writings with questioned documents appears to be entirely subjective. Finally, although there is general acceptance of the theories and techniques involved in this field among the closed universe of forensic document examiners, this proves nothing; just because this type of evidence was generally accepted by courts in the past does not mean that it should be accepted now. Other courts that recently have examined this issue have also found numerous problems with handwriting comparison testimony and severely limited it at trial. However, Cawley's testimony should be excluded in its entirety because in the absence of tested principles for making comparisons, his testimony as to similarities would itself be nothing more than a set of subjective observations, and could, therefore, mislead a jury. Finally, nothing in the Federal Rules of

Continued on next page.

171

Evidence requires a different result. Fed. R. Evid. 901 must be read in conjunction with Fed. R. Evid. 702. Fed. R. Evid. 901(b)(3) contemplates testimony by an expert—but before an expert's testimony can be admitted, it must pass through the gates of Fed. R. Evid. 702. As Cawley's testimony did not make it past Fed. R. Evid. 702, Fed. R. Evid. 901 is irrelevant to the question of whether his testimony is admissible. Motion to exclude is granted.

EDITOR'S ANALYSIS: *Saelee* is a leading case for exclusion of expert testimony of forensic document analysts under the Federal Rules of Evidence. As the case itself indicates, other courts have permitted the analyst to testify as to the similarities and differences between the writing at issue and the defendant's writing, and some courts continue the tradition of allowing the analyst to testify without limit.

NOTES:

STATE v. PORTER

State (P) v. Convicted arsonist (D)
Conn. Sup. Ct., 698 A.2d 739 (1997).

NATURE OF CASE: Appeal.

FACT SUMMARY: [Facts not stated in casebook excerpt.]

CONCISE RULE OF LAW: (1) The federal standard for the admissibility of scientific evidence is applicable in state cases in Connecticut. (2) Polygraph evidence is per se inadmissible because its prejudicial effect far outweighs its probative value.

FACTS: [Facts not stated in casebook excerpt.]

ISSUE: (1) Is the federal standard for the admissibility of scientific evidence applicable in state cases in Connecticut? (2) Is polygraph evidence per se inadmissible because its prejudicial effect far outweighs its probative value?

HOLDING AND DECISION: (Borden, J.) (1) Yes. The federal standard for the admissibility of scientific evidence is applicable in state cases in Connecticut. That standard, set forth by the United States Supreme Court in *Daubert v. Merrell Dow Pharmaceuticals, Inc.*, 509 U.S. 579 (1993), is adopted by this court. (2) Polygraph evidence is per se inadmissible because its prejudicial effect far outweighs its probative value. The *Daubert*, 509 U.S. 579 (1993), approach should govern the admissibility of scientific evidence. Assuming that polygraph evidence meets the admissibility threshold established by *Daubert*, such evidence nevertheless should be excluded per se because its prejudicial impact greatly exceeds its probative value. This conclusion is supported by case law and extensive scientific literature. The polygraph test rests on the assumptions that there is a regular relationship between deception and certain emotional states, and that there is a regular relationship between those emotional states and physiological changes in the body that can be measured and recorded. However, it is acknowledged that there is no known physiological response or pattern of responses that is unique to deception. Thus, while polygraphs can accurately gauge a subject's physiological profile, they cannot determine the underlying psychological profile. It is, therefore, up to the polygrapher to translate the physiological data into an assessment of truth or lying. The "control question test" is the polygraph method most commonly used in criminal cases, and is based on the theory that fear of detection causes psychological stress. The test, therefore, is really measuring fear of detection, not deception per se. As part of the procedure of this type of test, the examiner asks three kinds of questions: (1) neutral, which is entirely nonconfrontational and is used to measure the subject's baseline physiological state; (2) relevant, directed specifically at the subject under investigation; and (3) control, concerning an act of wrongdoing similar to the main incident under investigation and designed to be a question to which the subject, in all probability, will lie. The theory is that a truthful person will respond more to the control questions than to the relevant questions, because they are more of a threat, and that the liar will respond more to the relevant questions for the same reason. Thus, the examiner looks to the relative strength of the responses to a series of questions that includes all three types of questions, and that is repeated several times. The examiner then assigns numerical values to the responses. The validity of such tests depends on their "accuracy" and "predictive value." As to accuracy, there is agreement that false positives (specificity) outnumber false negatives (sensitivity), i.e., that a truthful subject is incorrectly labeled as a liar more often than a liar is incorrectly labeled as truthful. However, there is disagreement as to the actual sensitivity and specificity values for a well-run test. A review of the literature reveals that even if one accepts studies that favor polygraph exams, polygraph evidence is of questionable validity because according to even the most favorable studies, such exams can cause almost half of those who are in fact truthful to be labeled as deceptive, and can cause about 13 percent of those who are in fact deceptive to be labeled as truthful. The actual probative value of polygraph evidence as a signifier of guilt or innocence is even more questionable. This relates to the predictive value of the exam. The questions related to predictive value are: how likely is it that a person really is lying given that the polygraph labels the subject as deceptive (this is called "predictive value positive"); and how likely is it that a subject really is truthful given that the polygraph labels the subject as not deceptive (this is called "predictive value negative"). The predictive values, in turn, depend on "base rate" of deceptiveness among the people tested by the polygraph. Unfortunately, there is no reliable measure of this base rate. Given the complete absence of reliable data on base rates, legally, there is no way of assessing the probative value of the polygraph test. Furthermore, with training, subjects are able to take countermeasures to induce false negatives so as to pass the test. For all these reasons, the probative value polygraph evidence is very low, even if it satisfies *Daubert*, and any limited evidentiary value it might have is substantially outweighed by its prejudicial effects. A basic problem with polygraph evidence is that it usurps the fact-finding province of the jury because it allows one person, the polygrapher, to label a witness as honest or as dishonest based solely on the same type of indirect evidence that it takes an entire jury to evaluate. Affirmed.

EDITOR'S ANALYSIS: Under the *Daubert* approach, the court must determine the admissibility of scientific evidence by evaluating the underlying validity of two separate aspects of the evidence: (1) its scientific method; and (2) the application of that method to the factual inquiry under consideration. The court in this case, by evaluating the scientific validity of polygraph evidence, as well as evaluating the test's probative value, has taken such an approach.

UNITED STATES v. PICCINONNA
Federal government (P) v. Convicted perjurer (D)
885 F.2d 1529 (11th Cir. 1989).

NATURE OF CASE: Appeal from conviction for perjury.

FACT SUMMARY: Piccinonna (D) testified before a grand jury that he had not heard of an agreement between garbage companies in Florida not to compete with each other, but Piccinonna (D) was implicated in the anticompetitive scheme by other witnesses and convicted of perjury despite his passing a polygraph test.

CONCISE RULE OF LAW: The results of polygraph tests are admissible when: (1) the parties stipulate in advance as to the circumstances of the test and the scope of admissibility; (2) the test is used to impeach or corroborate the testimony of a witness at trial after notice to and opportunity for the opposing side to conduct its own lie detector test; and (3) the trial court has determined its probative value outweighs prejudice to the jury.

FACTS: Piccinonna (D) was in the waste disposal business in South Florida. He agreed to testify about antitrust violations in the garbage business before the grand jury in return for a grant of immunity. However, when Piccinonna (D) testified, he stated that he had not heard of an alleged agreement between garbage companies not to compete for each other's accounts and to compensate each other for accounts stolen from one firm by another. Other witnesses before the grand jury, however, implicated Piccinonna (D) in the anti-competitive scheme, and Piccinonna (D) was indicted for perjury. Prior to his perjury trial, Piccinonna (D) asked the government (P) to stipulate to admission of the results of a subsequent polygraph examination, but the government (P) refused to do so. Piccinonna (D) had a lie detector test performed anyway, and the results indicated that he was telling the truth. After his conviction for perjury, Piccinonna (D) appealed the trial court's denial of admission of the results of the test.

ISSUE: Are the results of a polygraph test admissible at trial when: (1) the parties stipulate in advance as to the circumstances of the test and the scope of its admissibility; (2) the test is used to impeach or corroborate the testimony of a witness at trial after notice to the opposing side and an opportunity for the opposing party to conduct its own lie detector test; and (3) the trial court determines that the probative value of the test outweighs its possible prejudicial impact on the jury?

HOLDING AND DECISION: (Fay, J.) Yes. The results of a polygraph test are admissible when both parties stipulate in advance as to the circumstances of the test and as to the scope of its admissibility. They are also admissible when used to impeach or corroborate the testimony of a witness at trial; but first, the party planning to use the evidence must provide adequate notice to the opposing party, and second, the opposing party must be given a reasonable opportunity to have its own polygraph expert administer a test covering substantially the same questions. Further, these two modifications of the per se exclusionary rule should not be construed to preempt or limit in any way the trial court's discretion to exclude lie detector test results or polygraph expert testimony on the grounds that the prejudicial impact of such evidence outweighs its probative value. Further, the trial court may exclude lie detector test evidence because the polygraph examiner's qualifications are unacceptable, the test procedure was unfairly prejudicial or the test was poorly administered, or the questions asked during the test were irrelevant or improper. Vacated and remanded.

CONCURRENCE AND DISSENT: (Johnson, J.) Polygraph evidence should be admissible when both parties stipulate in advance to the circumstances of the test and the scope of its admissibility. However, the majority is incorrect in asserting that the polygraph has gained widespread acceptance in the scientific community, and that therefore the per se rule of exclusion should be modified.

EDITOR'S ANALYSIS: Controversy continues over the admissibility of polygraph test results. The dissent in this opinion challenges the assumptions underlying the reliability of the lie detector test. It asserts: (1) that some individuals may be able to control their physiological responses to the stress of lying; (2) that it is not necessarily true that stress produces the same types of responses in all people such that all stress will be monitored by the test; (3) that dishonesty may not necessarily affect blood pressure, heart rate, respiration, and perspiration; and (4) that emotions are not automatically triggered by exposure to stimuli, but that they are processed or assessed before producing an emotion.

NOTES:

UNITED STATES v. SCHEFFER
Federal government (P) v. Airman (D)
523 U.S. 303 (1998).

NATURE OF CASE: Review of reversal of conviction for drug use.

FACT SUMMARY: The results from Scheffer's (D) drug test indicated the presence of methamphetamine, while a polygraph examination "indicated no deception" when Scheffer (D) denied using drugs since joining the Air Force.

CONCISE RULE OF LAW: Military Rule of Evidence 707, which makes polygraph evidence inadmissible in court-martial proceedings, does not unconstitutionally abridge the right of the accused members of the military to present a defense.

FACTS: Scheffer (D) was an airman stationed at March Air Force Base when he volunteered to work as an informant on drug investigations. As part of his duty, he was required to submit to drug tests and polygraph examinations. On one occasion, Scheffer (D) was asked to submit to a urine test and a polygraph examination. The results from the urinalysis indicated the presence of methamphetamine. However, the results from the polygraph examination revealed that Scheffer (D) "indicated no deception" when he denied using drugs since joining the Air Force. At trial, Scheffer (D) claimed "innocent ingestion" of the drug and sought to introduce the polygraph evidence to support his claim. The judge determined that Rule 707 was constitutional, and Scheffer (D) was convicted. Upon appeal, the court reversed, holding that a per se exclusion of Scheffer's (D) polygraph evidence violated his Sixth Amendment rights and was therefore unconstitutional. The government (P) petitioned for certiorari.

ISSUE: Does Military Rule of Evidence 707, which makes polygraph evidence inadmissible in court-martial proceedings, unconstitutionally abridge the right of the accused members of the military to present a defense?

HOLDING AND DECISION: (Thomas, J.) No. Military Rule of Evidence 707, which makes polygraph evidence inadmissible in court-martial proceedings, does not unconstitutionally abridge the right of the accused members of the military to present a defense. A defendant's right to present relevant evidence is limited and subject to reasonable restrictions that serve the legitimate interests of the criminal trial process. Rules that make evidence inadmissible are unconstitutional when they are arbitrary or disproportionate to the purposes they are designed to serve. Rule 707 was formulated to ensure that only reliable evidence is introduced at trial, preserving the jury's role in determining the credibility of its witnesses and evidence, and avoiding litigation on collateral issues. Viewed in this context, excluding polygraph evidence is neither arbitrary nor disproportionate in promoting these ends. Reversed.

EDITOR'S ANALYSIS: Most states maintain per se rules excluding polygraph evidence. Only New Mexico makes polygraph evidence generally admissible without the prior stipulation of the parties. However, both state and federal courts continue to express doubt about whether such evidence is reliable.

NOTES:

UNITED STATES v. HORN
Federal government (P) v. Allegedly intoxicated driver (D)
185 F. Supp.2d 530 (D. Md. 2002).

NATURE OF CASE: Motion in limine to exclude evidence of performance on field sobriety tests.

FACT SUMMARY: Horn (D), who was charged with driving under the influence, moved in limine to exclude evidence of his performance on standard field sobriety tests (SFSTs) on the grounds that they were not scientifically reliable or valid under Federal Rule of Evidence 702.

CONCISE RULE OF LAW: The results of properly administered standard field sobriety tests (SFSTs) may not be admitted under Federal Rule of Evidence 702 as direct evidence of a specific Blood Alcohol Content (BAC).

FACTS: Officer Jarrell suspected Horn (P) was driving under the influence of alcohol, and detained and questioned Horn (D). Jarrell also administered three standard field sobriety tests (SFTSs): the Walk and Turn (WAT) test; the One Leg Stand (OLS) test; and the Horizontal Gaze Nystagmus (HGN) test. As a result of his performance on these tests, Horn (D) was charged with driving while intoxicated. He moved in limine to exclude the evidence of his performance on the SFSTs on the grounds that they were not scientifically reliable under Fed. R. Evid. 702. The most "scientific" or "technical" of the three tests is HGN. Nystagmus is the involuntary jerking of the eyes, occurring as the eyes gaze toward the side. Also, nystagmus is a natural, normal phenomenon. Alcohol and certain other drugs do not cause this phenomenon, they merely exaggerate it or magnify it. The HGN SFST requires the investigating officer to look for three "clues": (1) the inability of the suspect to follow a slowly moving stimulus smoothly with his or her eyes, (2) the presence of "distinct" nystagmus when the suspect has moved his or her eyes as far to the left or right as possible and held them in this position for approximately four seconds, and (3) the presence of nystagmus before the eyes have moved 45 degrees to the left or right, which according to proponents of this test usually means that the subject has a Blood Alcohol Content (BAC) above 0.10 The officer is trained to look for each of the above three "clues" for each of the suspect's eyes, meaning there are six possible "clues." If the officer observes four or more clues this means that it is likely that the suspect's BAC is above 0.10. The test is valid only if the test procedures are performed properly and the investigating officer has been thoroughly trained in administering the test and interpreting its results. Much depends on the officer's subjective evaluation of the presence of the "standardized clues." The WAT test requires the suspect to place his feet in the heel-to-toe stance on a straight line. The subject then is instructed to place his right foot on the line ahead of the left foot, with the heel of the right foot against the toe of the left. The suspect also is told to keep his arms down at his side and to maintain this position until the officer instructs him to begin the test. Once told to start, the suspect is to take nine heel-to-toe steps down the line, then to turn around in a prescribed manner, and take nine heel-to-toe steps back up the line. While walking, the suspect is to keep his hands at his side, watch his feet, and count his steps out loud. Also, the suspect is told not to stop the test until completed, once told to start. As with the HGN test, the National Highway Traffic Safety Administration (NHTSA) Manual used to train investigating officers, asserts that there are eight standardized clues that "[r]esearch . . . has demonstrated . . . are the most likely to be observed in someone with a BAC above 0.10." Further, the Manual states "[i]f the suspect exhibits two or more distinct clues on this test or fails to complete it, classify the suspect's BAC as above 0.10." Once again, it is the officer's subjective evaluation of the suspect that results in the determination of whether a "clue" is present or not. In the OLS test, the suspect is told to stand with her feet together, arms at her sides. She then is told not to start the test until told to do so. To perform the OLS test, the suspect must raise whichever leg she chooses, approximately six inches from the ground, toes pointed out. While holding this position, the suspect then must count out loud for thirty seconds, by saying "one-one thousand, two-one thousand," etc. The Manual identifies four "standardized clues" for the OLS test and instructs law enforcement officers that "[i]f an individual shows two or more clues or fails to complete the [test] . . . there is a good chance the BAC is above 0.10." It is claimed that when the WAT and HGN tests are combined, using a decision matrix, an officer can achieve 80% accuracy in identifying suspects with BACs in excess of 0.10. Horn (D) challenged the reliability, validity and relevance of the SFSTs to prove driver intoxication. Horn's (D) experts were sharply critical of the claims of accuracy made for the test, and framed these objections in terms of the factors discussed in the *Daubert/Kumho Tire* decisions. Horn's experts (Caplan, Cole, Brull, and Wiesen) challenged the reliability and validity of the SFSTs under Fed. R. Evid. 702. In the context of scientific or technical testing, such as may be the case with SFSTs, reliability means the ability of a test to be duplicated, producing the same or substantially same results when successively performed under the same conditions. A test is valid if it has a logical nexus with the issue to be determined in a case. Cole was highly critical of the reliability of the SFSTs if used to prove the precise level of a suspect's alcohol intoxication or impairment. He theorized that the SFSTs, particularly the WAT and OLS tests, required subjects to perform unfamiliar, unpracticed motions and noted that a very few miscues result in a conclusion that the subject failed and had a BAC in excess of 0.10. His hypothesis was that individuals could be classified as intoxicated/impaired as a result of unfamiliarity with the test, rather than actual BAC. He supported his theory with research

Continued on next page.

that showed that officers' perceptions of impairment were faulty. Cole also criticized NHTSA reports, showing that their claims of 80% accuracy were misleading and below rates of reliability accepted by the scientific community (.77 versus .8 or higher). He also pointed out that use of the SFSTs resulted in an a high erroneous arrest rate. Moreover, he criticized claims that the SFSTs were validated in a field setting, when, in fact, validating tests were conducted in a laboratory setting and were, by the NHTSA's own admission, not adequately tested in the field. Finally, he pointed out that studies regarding the SFSTs were not peer-reviewed and did not appear in scientific peer-review journals. Wiesen was likewise critical of the SFST studies, saying they were inadequate, and concluded that the SFSTs did not meet reasonable professional and scientific standards. Brull testified that the accuracy of the SFSTs was less than desired and well below the level expected for tests of human performance, and that the "field" studies were not well documented, and produced unknown error rates.

The government (P) introduced the SFST studies (of which Horn's (D) experts had been highly critical), the Manual, an article on HGN, and the expert testimony of Rabin, an optometrist who testified that alcohol ingestion can enhance the presence of nystagmus in the human eye at BAC levels as low as .04. He expressed the opinion that "there is a very good correlation between the results of the . . . [HGN] test and breath analysis for intoxication." He also stated that the three "clues" that officers are taught to look for in connection with the HGN SFST "are indicative of alcohol consumption with possible intoxication." Rabin further expressed his belief that police officers could be trained adequately to administer the HGN test and interpret its results. He did acknowledge, however, that he acquired his knowledge of, and formed his opinions about, the SFSTs in connection with performing duties as an expert witness for Army prosecutors in two courts martial, not as a result of any independent research that he had done. Further, the references to the HGN SFST that he read in peer review literature published by the *American Journal of Optometry* was based primarily on the NHTSA studies, rather than any independent research by that organization. He also acknowledged that there are many causes of exaggerated nystagmus in the human eye that are unrelated to the ingestion of alcohol.

ISSUE: May the results of properly administered standard field sobriety tests (SFSTs) be admitted under Fed. R. Evid. 702 as direct evidence of a specific Blood Alcohol Content (BAC)?

HOLDING AND DECISION: (Grimm, J.) No. The results of properly administered standard field sobriety tests (SFSTs) may not be admitted under Fed. R. Evid. 702 as direct evidence of a specific Blood Alcohol Content (BAC). Regarding the Horizontal Gaze Nystagmus (HGN) test, it cannot be disputed that there is a sufficient factual basis to support the causal connection between observable exaggerated HGN in a suspect's eye and the ingestion of alcohol by that person. This connection is so well

established that it is appropriate to be judicially noted under Rule 201. That being said, however, it must quickly be added that there also are many other causes of nystagmus that are unrelated to alcohol consumption. Thus, the detectable presence of exaggerated HGN in a driver clearly is circumstantial, not direct, evidence of alcohol consumption. With regard to the SFSTs' accuracy, Horn's (D) experts and the literature they cite, establish that presently there is insufficient data to support claims of accuracy. Thus, BAC levels may not be proved by SFSTs alone. This conclusion regarding the reliability of the methods and principles underlying the SFSTs takes into account the evidence introduced by Horn (D) about the methods used to develop these tests, and the error rates associated therewith—the first two *Daubert/Kumho Tire* factors. This alone precludes their admissibility to prove specific BAC. Also, as Horn's (D) experts showed, most of the publications regarding the SFST test were not peer reviewed. Merely because many state courts have concluded that the SFSTs have received general acceptance among criminologists, law enforcement personnel, highway safety experts and prosecutors, this is sufficient for purposes of *Daubert* and *Kumho Tire*. Acceptance by a relevant scientific or technical community implies that that community has the expertise critically to evaluate the methods and principles that underlie the test or opinion in question. However skilled law enforcement officials, highway safety specialists, prosecutors and criminologists may be in their fields, this does not at all mean that these communities have the expertise needed to evaluate the methods and procedures underlying human performance tests such as the SFSTs. For these reasons, SFST evidence in this case does not, at this time, meet the requirements of *Daubert/ Kumho Tire* and Fed. R. Evid. 702 as to be admissible as direct evidence of intoxication or impairment.

A more difficult question, however, is whether the SFSTs may be used as circumstantial evidence of alcohol consumption and, if so, just how. On the record presented in this case, there are not sufficient facts or data about the One Leg Stand (OLS) and Walk and Turn (WAT) SFSTs to support the conclusion that, if a suspect exhibits two out of eight possible clues on the WAT test or two out of four clues on the OLS, he has "failed" the tests. To permit a police officer to testify about each of the SFSTs in detail, their claimed accuracy rates, the number of standardized clues applicable to each, the number of clues exhibited by the suspect, and then offer an opinion about whether he or she passed or failed, stopping just short of expressing an opinion as to specific BAC, invites the risk of allowing through the back door of circumstantial proof evidence that is not reliable enough to enter through the front door of direct proof of intoxication or impairment. Such testimony clearly is technical, if not scientific, and may not be admitted unless shown to be reliable under the standards

Continued on next page.

imposed by Fed. R. Evid. 702 and *Daubert/Kumho Tire*, which has not been done in this case. Accordingly, if offered as circumstantial evidence of alcohol intoxication or impairment, the probative value of the SFSTs derives from their basic nature as observations of human behavior, which is not scientific, technical or specialized knowledge. Therefore, when testifying about the SFSTs, a police officer must be limited to describing the procedure administered and the observations of how the defendant performed it, without resort to terms such as "test," "standardized clues," "pass" or "fail," unless the government first has established a foundation that satisfies Fed. R. Evid. 702 and the *Daubert/Kumho Tire* factors regarding the reliability and validity of the scientific or technical underpinnings of the National Highway Traffic Safety Administration (NHTSA) assertions that there are a stated number of clues that support an opinion that the suspect has "failed" the test. This is not to say that a police officer may not express an opinion as a lay witness that the defendant was intoxicated or impaired, if otherwise admissible under Fed. R. Evid. 701, which permits lay opinion testimony if: (a) rationally based upon the perception of the witness, (b) helpful to the fact finder and (c) if the opinion does not involve scientific, technical or specialized information. There is near universal agreement that lay opinion testimony about whether someone was intoxicated is admissible if it meets the above criteria. A police officer certainly may testify about his or her observations of a defendant's appearance, coordination, mood, ability to follow instructions, balance, the presence of the smell of an alcoholic beverage, as well as the presence of exaggerated HGN, and the observations of the defendant's performance of the SFSTs. The officer should not, however, be permitted to interject technical or specialized comments to embellish the opinion based on any special training or experience he or she has in investigating Driving While Intoxicated/Driving Under the Influence (DWI/DUI) cases.

What these rules mean for this case is that Jarrell may testify as to his administration of the SFSTs, but only as to the instruction he has received in administering the tests, but he may not offer opinions about the tests' accuracy. If he testifies about the results of the HGN test, he may testify as to his qualifications to detect exaggerated HGN, and his observations of exaggerated HGN in Horn (D), but may not, absent being qualified under Fed. R. Evid. 702 to do so, testify as to the causal nexus between alcohol consumption and exaggerated HGN. When testifying about Horn's (D) performance of the SFSTs, Jarrell may describe the SFSTs he required Horn (D) to perform and describe Horn's (D) performance, but he may not use language such as "test," "standardized clues" or express the opinion that Horn (D) "passed" or "failed." Under Fed. R. Evid. 701, Jarrell may give lay opinon testimony that Horn (D) was intoxicated, based on his

observations of Horn (D). Also, the government (P) may prove the causal connection between exaggerated HGN in Horn's (D) eyes and alcohol consumption through several routes: judicial notice (Fed. R. Evid. 201); expert testimony (Fed. R. Evid. 702); or learned treatises (Fed. R. Evid. 803(18)). Horn (D) then can prove there are other causes of HGN other than alcohol through similar means.

EDITOR'S ANALYSIS: This case shows how the recently amended Fed. R. Evid. 702, which incorporates the *Daubert/Kumho Tire* standards, can be used to force courts to reckon with the factors that really do determine whether certain "scientific" evidence is reliable, relevant, and fits the case at issue. Such evaluation, even of theories and methods that have been long accepted, compels courts to abandon long existing per se rules of admissibility or inadmissibility that were grounded on *Frye*, which focused on general acceptance. Most courts, before the enactment of amended Fed. R. Evid. 702 in 2000, did not conduct a detailed analysis of the factual sufficiency, reliability, and validity of SFSTs. However, under Fed. R. Evid. 702, as demonstrated by this case, evidence that long has been routinely admitted may now be excluded.

NOTES:

STATE v. CHAPPLE
State (P) v. Convicted murderer (D)
Ariz. Sup. Ct., 135 Ariz. 281, 660 P.2d 1208 (1983).

NATURE OF CASE: Appeal from a murder conviction.

FACT SUMMARY: The State (P) contended that the expert testimony on the defects of the eyewitness testimony would not aid the jury and was therefore inadmissible.

CONCISE RULE OF LAW: Expert testimony on the defects of eyewitness identifications is admissible if there is: (1) a qualified expert; (2) a proper subject; (3) conformity with generally accepted explanatory theory; and (4) probative value compared to prejudicial effect.

FACTS: Chapple (D) was charged with murder after his picture was selected by witnesses as one of the people involved. The witnesses were exposed to Chapple's (D) picture in two separate photographic line-ups. In the first he was not identified. In the second, conducted over a month later, his picture was identified. At trial, Chapple (D) asserted an alibi defense and contended the eyewitness identification was erroneous. Chapple (D) attempted to extract testimony from Dr. Loftus, an expert in accuracy and defects of eyewitness identification, to rebut the prosecution witness' testimony. The trial court granted the State's (P) motion to suppress, holding the shortcomings of eyewitness identification was common knowledge, and therefore such expert testimony would not aid the jury. Chapple (D) was convicted and appealed, contending suppression of the testimony was reversible error.

ISSUE: Is expert testimony concerning the defects in eyewitness identifications admissible if there is: (1) a qualified expert; (2) a proper subject; (3) conformity with generally accepted explanatory theory; and (4) probative value compared to prejudicial effect?

HOLDING AND DECISION: (Feldman, J.) Yes. Expert testimony on the defects of eyewitness identifications is admissible if there is: (1) a qualified expert; (2) a proper subject; (3) conformity with generally accepted explanatory theory; and (4) probative value compared to prejudicial impact. In this case, the State (P) conceded Dr. Loftus was qualified as an expert on the subject and that her testimony would follow generally accepted explanatory theory. The testimony was clearly probative in that it would have related to the value of the eyewitness identifications and affected the jury findings. Finally, the testimony was a proper subject for expert testimony because it could offer information not commonly known and thereby aid the jury. For example, the jury might know that memory fades over time. However, it might not know that forgetting occurs very rapidly and then tends to level out. Therefore, the more immediate the identification, the more reliable it is. In this case, the line-up in which Chapple's (D) picture was identified occurred over a month after the first line-up where it was not identified. Based on Dr. Loftus' testimony, the jury could have found the earlier line-up more reliable, and discounted the later one. As a result, the testimony should have been admitted. Reversed.

DISSENT: (Hays, J.) The average juror knows that an immediate identification is more trustworthy than a later one. Therefore, the expert testimony would not aid in the findings of fact.

EDITOR'S ANALYSIS: There is a split between the common law and the Federal Rules of Evidence in the requirements for admissibility of expert testimony. Fed. R. Evid. 703 allows expert testimony if it will aid the trier of fact. The common law follows a rule of strict necessity under which expert testimony must relate to matters beyond common knowledge and experience. In this case, the testimony would have met either test.

NOTES:

ELLIS v. STATE
Convicted larcenist (D) v. State (P)
Okla. Ct. Crim. App., 643 P.2d 330 (1982).

NATURE OF CASE: Appeal from conviction for larceny of a domestic animal.

FACT SUMMARY: Ellis (D) claimed that the evidence that he had stolen a calf was insufficient to sustain his conviction of larceny of a domestic animal.

CONCISE RULE OF LAW: Wholly circumstantial evidence can establish a prima facie case of criminal wrongdoing.

FACTS: Owens noticed that one of his newborn calves was missing. Three days later, his son spotted a calf fitting the description of the missing calf in a shed with other calves on an adjoining neighbor's property. The neighbor testified that the calves belonged to Ellis (D). The calf was taken to Owens's pasture, where the mother cow came running across the open field bawling, immediately licked the calf, and allowed it to nurse. According to the uncontroverted expert testimony of lifelong cattlemen, these actions of claiming a calf by a cow in an open field constitute the accepted test for determining maternal lineage. Ellis (D) claimed he had purchased the calf, and had a receipt to prove it, but had never mentioned this to anyone before trial. A friend of Ellis's (D) testified that he had sold a calf fitting the description of Owens's calf to Ellis. Ellis (D) argued that the evidence was insufficient to sustain the verdict, and that the court erred in failing to instruct the jury to acquit him.

ISSUE: Can wholly circumstantial evidence establish a prima facie case of criminal wrongdoing?

HOLDING AND DECISION: [Judge not stated in casebook excerpt.] Yes. Wholly circumstantial evidence can establish a prima facie case of criminal wrongdoing. Although the evidence here is wholly circumstantial, it has established a prima facie case. Therefore, the trial court properly denied Ellis's (D) motion for a directed verdict. Affirmed.

EDITOR'S ANALYSIS: The court did not expressly state, but instead implied, that the test for determining maternal lineage exercised in this case was sufficiently probative that the calf originally belonged to Owens.

NOTES:

GLOSSARY
COMMON LATIN WORDS AND PHRASES ENCOUNTERED IN THE LAW

A FORTIORI: Because one fact exists or has been proven, therefore a second fact that is related to the first fact must also exist.

A PRIORI: From the cause to the effect. A term of logic used to denote that when one generally accepted truth is shown to be a cause, another particular effect must necessarily follow.

AB INITIO: From the beginning; a condition which has existed throughout, as in a marriage which was void ab initio.

ACTUS REUS: The wrongful act; in criminal law, such action sufficient to trigger criminal liability.

AD VALOREM: According to value; an ad valorem tax is imposed upon an item located within the taxing jurisdiction calculated by the value of such item.

AMICUS CURIAE: Friend of the court. Its most common usage takes the form of an amicus curiae brief, filed by a person who is not a party to an action but is nonetheless allowed to offer an argument supporting his legal interests.

ARGUENDO: In arguing. A statement, possibly hypothetical, made for the purpose of argument, is one made arguendo.

BILL QUIA TIMET: A bill to quiet title (establish ownership) to real property.

BONA FIDE: True, honest, or genuine. May refer to a person's legal position based on good faith or lacking notice of fraud (such as a bona fide purchaser for value) or to the authenticity of a particular document (such as a bona fide last will and testament).

CAUSA MORTIS: With approaching death in mind. A gift causa mortis is a gift given by a party who feels certain that death is imminent.

CAVEAT EMPTOR: Let the buyer beware. This maxim is reflected in the rule of law that a buyer purchases at his own risk because it is his responsibility to examine, judge, test, and otherwise inspect what he is buying.

CERTIORARI: A writ of review. Petitions for review of a case by the United States Supreme Court are most often done by means of a writ of certiorari.

CONTRA: On the other hand. Opposite. Contrary to.

CORAM NOBIS: Before us; writs of error directed to the court that originally rendered the judgment.

CORAM VOBIS: Before you; writs of error directed by an appellate court to a lower court to correct a factual error.

CORPUS DELICTI: The body of the crime; the requisite elements of a crime amounting to objective proof that a crime has been committed.

CUM TESTAMENTO ANNEXO, ADMINISTRATOR (ADMINISTRATOR C.T.A.): With will annexed; an administrator c.t.a. settles an estate pursuant to a will in which he is not appointed.

DE BONIS NON, ADMINISTRATOR (ADMINISTRATOR D.B.N.): Of goods not administered; an administrator d.b.n. settles a partially settled estate.

DE FACTO: In fact; in reality; actually. Existing in fact but not officially approved or engendered.

DE JURE: By right; lawful. Describes a condition that is legitimate "as a matter of law," in contrast to the term "de facto," which connotes something existing in fact but not legally sanctioned or authorized. For example, de facto segregation refers to segregation brought about by housing patterns, etc., whereas de jure segregation refers to segregation created by law.

DE MINIMUS: Of minimal importance; insignificant; a trifle; not worth bothering about.

DE NOVO: Anew; a second time; afresh. A trial de novo is a new trial held at the appellate level as if the case originated there and the trial at a lower level had not taken place.

DICTA: Generally used as an abbreviated form of obiter dicta, a term describing those portions of a judicial opinion incidental or not necessary to resolution of the specific question before the court. Such nonessential statements and remarks are not considered to be binding precedent.

DUCES TECUM: Refers to a particular type of writ or subpoena requesting a party or organization to produce certain documents in their possession.

EN BANC: Full bench. Where a court sits with all justices present rather than the usual quorum.

EX PARTE: For one side or one party only. An ex parte proceeding is one undertaken for the benefit of only one party, without notice to, or an appearance by, an adverse party.

EX POST FACTO: After the fact. An ex post facto law is a law that retroactively changes the consequences of a prior act.

EX REL.: Abbreviated form of the term ex relatione, meaning, upon relation or information. When the state brings an action in which it has no interest against an individual at the instigation of one who has a private interest in the matter.

FORUM NON CONVENIENS: Inconvenient forum. Although a court may have jurisdiction over the case, the action should be tried in a more conveniently located court, one to which parties and witnesses may more easily travel, for example.

GUARDIAN AD LITEM: A guardian of an infant as to litigation, appointed to represent the infant and pursue his/her rights.

HABEAS CORPUS: You have the body. The modern writ of habeas corpus is a writ directing that a person (body) being detained (such as a prisoner) be brought before the court so that the legality of his detention can be judicially ascertained.

IN CAMERA: In private, in chambers. When a hearing is held before a judge in his chambers or when all spectators are excluded from the courtroom.

IN FORMA PAUPERIS: In the manner of a pauper. A party who proceeds in forma pauperis because of his poverty is one who is allowed to bring suit without liability for costs.

INFRA: Below, under. A word referring the reader to a later part of a book. (The opposite of supra.)

IN LOCO PARENTIS: In the place of a parent.

IN PARI DELICTO: Equally wrong; a court of equity will not grant requested relief to an applicant who is in pari delicto, or as much at fault in the transactions giving rise to the controversy as is the opponent of the applicant.

IN PARI MATERIA: On like subject matter or upon the same matter. Statutes relating to the same person or things are said to be in pari materia. It is a general rule of statutory construction that such statutes should be construed together, i.e., looked at as if they together constituted one law.

IN PERSONAM: Against the person. Jurisdiction over the person of an individual.

IN RE: In the matter of. Used to designate a proceeding involving an estate or other property.

IN REM: A term that signifies an action against the res, or thing. An action in rem is basically one that is taken directly against property, as distinguished from an action in personam, i.e., against the person.

INTER ALIA: Among other things. Used to show that the whole of a statement, pleading, list, statute, etc., has not been set forth in its entirety.

INTER PARTES: Between the parties. May refer to contracts, conveyances or other transactions having legal significance.

INTER VIVOS: Between the living. An inter vivos gift is a gift made by a living grantor, as distinguished from bequests contained in a will, which pass upon the death of the testator.

IPSO FACTO: By the mere fact itself.

JUS: Law or the entire body of law.

LEX LOCI: The law of the place; the notion that the rights of parties to a legal proceeding are governed by the law of the place where those rights arose.

MALUM IN SE: Evil or wrong in and of itself; inherently wrong. This term describes an act that is wrong by its very nature, as opposed to one which would not be wrong but for the fact that there is a specific legal prohibition against it (malum prohibitum).

MALUM PROHIBITUM: Wrong because prohibited, but not inherently evil. Used to describe something that is wrong because it is expressly forbidden by law but that is not in and of itself evil, e.g., speeding.

MANDAMUS: We command. A writ directing an official to take a certain action.

MENS REA: A guilty mind; a criminal intent. A term used to signify the mental state that accompanies a crime or other prohibited act. Some crimes require only a general mens rea (general intent to do the prohibited act), but others, like assault with intent to murder, require the existence of a specific mens rea.

MODUS OPERANDI: Method of operating; generally refers to the manner or style of a criminal in committing crimes, admissible in appropriate cases as evidence of the identity of a defendant.

NEXUS: A connection to.

NISI PRIUS: A court of first impression. A nisi prius court is one where issues of fact are tried before a judge or jury.

N.O.V. (NON OBSTANTE VEREDICTO): Notwithstanding the verdict. A judgment n.o.v. is a judgment given in favor of one party despite the fact that a verdict was returned in favor of the other party, the justification being that the verdict either had no reasonable support in fact or was contrary to law.

NUNC PRO TUNC: Now for then. This phrase refers to actions that may be taken and will then have full retroactive effect.

PENDENTE LITE: Pending the suit; pending litigation underway.

PER CAPITA: By head; beneficiaries of an estate, if they take in equal shares, take per capita.

PER CURIAM: By the court; signifies an opinion ostensibly written "by the whole court" and with no identified author.

PER SE: By itself, in itself; inherently.

PER STIRPES: By representation. Used primarily in the law of wills to describe the method of distribution where a person, generally because of death, is unable to take that which is left to him by the will of another, and therefore his heirs divide such property between them rather than take under the will individually.

PRIMA FACIE: On its face, at first sight. A prima facie case is one that is sufficient on its face, meaning that the evidence supporting it is adequate to establish the case until contradicted or overcome by other evidence.

PRO TANTO: For so much; as far as it goes. Often used in eminent domain cases when a property owner receives partial payment for his land without prejudice to his right to bring suit for the full amount he claims his land to be worth.

QUANTUM MERUIT: As much as he deserves. Refers to recovery based on the doctrine of unjust enrichment in those cases in which a party has rendered valuable services or furnished materials that were accepted and enjoyed by another under circumstances that would reasonably notify the recipient that the rendering party expected to be paid. In essence, the law implies a contract to pay the reasonable value of the services or materials furnished.

QUASI: Almost like; as if; nearly. This term is essentially used to signify that one subject or thing is almost analogous to another but that material differences between them do exist. For example, a quasi-criminal proceeding is one that is not strictly criminal but shares enough of the same characteristics to require some of the same safeguards (e.g., procedural due process must be followed in a parole hearing).

QUID PRO QUO: Something for something. In contract law, the consideration, something of value, passed between the parties to render the contract binding.

RES GESTAE: Things done; in evidence law, this principle justifies the admission of a statement that would otherwise be hearsay when it is made so closely to the event in question as to be said to be a part of it, or with such spontaneity as not to have the possibility of falsehood.

RES IPSA LOQUITUR: The thing speaks for itself. This doctrine gives rise to a rebuttable presumption of negligence when the instrumentality causing the injury was within the exclusive control of the defendant, and the injury was one that does not normally occur unless a person has been negligent.

RES JUDICATA: A matter adjudged. Doctrine which provides that once a court of competent jurisdiction has rendered a final judgment or decree on the merits, that judgment or decree is conclusive upon the parties to the case and prevents them from engaging in any other litigation on the points and issues determined therein.

RESPONDEAT SUPERIOR: Let the master reply. This doctrine holds the master liable for the wrongful acts of his servant (or the principal for his agent) in those cases in which the servant (or agent) was acting within the scope of his authority at the time of the injury.

STARE DECISIS: To stand by or adhere to that which has been decided. The common law doctrine of stare decisis attempts to give security and certainty to the law by following the policy that once a principle of law as applicable to a certain set of facts has been set forth in a decision, it forms a precedent which will subsequently be followed, even though a different decision might be made were it the first time the question had arisen. Of course, stare decisis is not an inviolable principle and is departed from in instances where there is good cause (e.g., considerations of public policy led the Supreme Court to disregard prior decisions sanctioning segregation).

SUPRA: Above. A word referring a reader to an earlier part of a book.

ULTRA VIRES: Beyond the power. This phrase is most commonly used to refer to actions taken by a corporation that are beyond the power or legal authority of the corporation.

ADDENDUM OF FRENCH DERIVATIVES

IN PAIS: Not pursuant to legal proceedings.

CHATTEL: Tangible personal property.

CY PRES: Doctrine permitting courts to apply trust funds to purposes not expressed in the trust but necessary to carry out the settlor's intent.

PER AUTRE VIE: For another's life; in property law, an estate may be granted that will terminate upon the death of someone other than the grantee.

PROFIT A PRENDRE: A license to remove minerals or other produce from land.

VOIR DIRE: Process of questioning jurors as to their predispositions about the case or parties to a proceeding in order to identify those jurors displaying bias or prejudice.

REV 1-95

CASENOTE LEGAL BRIEFS

Administrative Law .... Asimow, Bonfield & Levin
Administrative Law .... Breyer, Stewart, Sunstein & Spitzer
Administrative Law .... Cass, Diver & Beermann
Administrative Law .... Funk, Shapiro & Weaver
Administrative Law .... Reese
Administrative Law .... Mashaw, Merrill & Shane
Administrative Law .... Strauss, Rakoff & Farina (Gellhorn & Byse)
Agency & Partnership .... Hynes & Loewenstein
Antitrust .... Pitofsky, Goldschmid & Wood
Antitrust .... Sullivan & Hovenkamp
Banking Law .... Macey, Miller & Carnell
Bankruptcy .... Warren & Bussel
Bankruptcy .... Warren & Westbrook
Business Organizations .... Eisenberg (Abridged & Unabridged)
Business Organizations .... Choper, Coffee & Gilson
Business Organizations .... Hamilton
Business Organizations .... Klein, Ramseyer & Bainbridge
Business Organizations .... O'Kelley & Thompson
Business Organizations .... Soderquist, Sommer, Chew & Smiddy
Business Organizations .... Bauman, Weiss & Palmiter
Civil Procedure .... Cound, Friedenthal, Miller & Sexton
Civil Procedure .... Field, Kaplan & Clermont
Civil Procedure .... Freer & Perdue
Civil Procedure .... Hazard, Tait & Fletcher
Civil Procedure .... Marcus, Redish & Sherman
Civil Procedure .... Subrin, Minow, Brodin & Main
Civil Procedure .... Yeazell
Commercial Law .... Lopucki, Warren, Keating & Mann
Commercial Law (Sales/Sec.Tr/Pay.Law) .... Speidel, Summers & White
Commercial Law .... Warren & Walt
Commercial Law .... Whaley
Community Property .... Bird
Community Property .... Blumberg
Complex Litigation .... Marcus & Sherman
Conflicts .... Brilmayer & Goldsmith
Conflicts .... Currie, Kay & Kramer
Conflicts .... Hay, Weintraub & Borchers
Conflicts .... Symeonides, Perdue & Von Mehren
Constitutional Law .... Brest, Levinson, Balkin & Amar
Constitutional Law .... Chemerinsky
Constitutional Law .... Choper, Fallon, Kamisar & Shiffrin (Lockhart)
Constitutional Law .... Cohen & Varat
Constitutional Law .... Farber, Eskridge & Frickey
Constitutional Law .... Rotunda
Constitutional Law .... Sullivan & Gunther
Constitutional Law .... Stone, Seidman, Sunstein & Tushnet
Contracts .... Barnett
Contracts .... Burton
Contracts .... Calamari, Perillo & Bender
Contracts .... Crandall & Whaley
Contracts .... Dawson, Harvey & Henderson
Contracts .... Farnsworth, Young & Sanger
Contracts .... Fuller & Eisenberg
Contracts .... Knapp, Crystal & Prince
Contracts .... Murphy, Speidel & Ayres
Contracts .... Rosett & Bussel
Copyright .... Goldstein
Copyright .... Joyce, Leaffer, Jaszi & Ochoa
Criminal Law .... Bonnie, Coughlin, Jeffries & Low
Criminal Law .... Boyce & Perkins
Criminal Law .... Dressler
Criminal Law .... Johnson & Cloud
Criminal Law .... Kadish & Schulhofer
Criminal Law .... Kaplan, Weisberg & Binder
Criminal Procedure .... Allen, Stuntz, Hoffmann & Livingston
Criminal Procedure .... Dressler & Thomas
Criminal Procedure .... Haddad, Marsh, Zagel, Meyer, Starkman & Bauer
Criminal Procedure .... Kamisar, La Fave, Israel & King
Criminal Procedure .... Saltzburg & Capra
Criminal Procedure .... Weaver, Abramson, Bacigal, Burkhoff, Hancock & Lively
Criminal Procedure .... Weinreb
Employment Discrimination .... Friedman & Strickler
Employment Discrimination .... Zimmer, Sullivan, Richards & Calloway
Employment Law .... Rothstein & Liebman
Environmental Law .... Menell & Stewart
Environmental Law .... Percival, Miller, Schroder & Leape
Environmental Law .... Plater, Abrams, Goldfarb, Graham, Heinzerling & Wirth
Evidence .... Broun, Mosteller & Giannelli

Evidence .... Mueller & Kirkpatrick
Evidence .... Sklansky
Evidence .... Waltz & Park
Evidence .... Weinstein, Mansfield, Abrams & Berger
Evidence .... Wellborn
Family Law .... Areen
Family Law .... Ellman, Kurtz & Scott
Family Law .... Harris & Teitelbaum
Family Law .... Krause, Elrod, Garrison & Oldham
Family Law .... Wadlington & O'Brien
Family Law .... Weisberg & Appleton
Federal Courts .... Fallon, Meltzer & Shapiro (Hart & Wechsler)
Federal Courts .... Low & Jeffries
Federal Courts .... Redish & Sherry
First Amendment .... Shiffrin & Choper
Gender and Law .... Bartlett & Harris
Health Care Law .... Hall, Bobinski & Orentlicher
Health Law .... Furrow, Greaney, Johnson, Jost & Schwartz
Immigration Law .... Aleinikoff, Martin & Motomura
Immigration Law .... Legomsky
Indian Law .... Getches, Wilkinson & Williams
Insurance Law .... Abraham
Intellectual Property .... Merges, Menell & Lemley
International Business Transactions .... Folsom, Gordon & Spanogle
International Law .... Carter & Trimble
International Law .... Damrosch, Henkin, Pugh, Schachter & Smit
International Law .... Dunoff, Ratner & Wippman
International Law .... Firmage, Blakesley, Scott & Williams (Sweeny & Oliver)
Labor Law .... Cox, Bok, Gorman & Finkin
Land Use .... Callies, Freilich & Roberts
Legislation .... Eskridge, Frickey & Garrett
Mass Media .... Franklin, Anderson & Cate
Oil & Gas .... Kuntz, Lowe, Anderson, Smith & Pierce
Patent Law .... Adelman, Radner, Thomas & Wegner
Patent Law .... Francis & Collins
Products Liability .... Owen, Montgomery & Keeton
Professional Responsibility .... Gillers
Professional Responsibility .... Hazard, Koniak & Cramton
Professional Responsibility .... Morgan & Rotunda
Professional Responsibility .... Schwartz, Wydick & Perschbacher
Property .... Casner, Leach, French, Korngold & VanderVelde
Property .... Cribbet, Johnson, Findley & Smith
Property .... Donahue, Kauper & Martin
Property .... Dukeminier & Krier
Property .... Haar & Liebman
Property .... Kurtz & Hovenkamp
Property .... Nelson, Stoebuck & Whitman
Property .... Rabin, Kwall & Kwall
Property .... Singer
Real Estate .... Berger & Johnstone
Real Estate .... Korngold & Goldstein
Real Estate Transactions .... Nelson & Whitman
Remedies .... Rendleman (Bauman & York)
Remedies .... Laycock
Remedies .... Leavell, Love, Nelson & Kovacic-Fleisher
Remedies .... Re & Re
Remedies .... Shoben, Tabb & Janutis
Securities Regulation .... Cox, Hillman & Langevoort
Securities Regulation .... Coffee & Seligman
Software and Internet Law .... Lemley, Menell, Merges & Samuelson
Sports Law .... Weiler & Roberts
Sports Law .... Yasser, McCurdy, Goplerud & Weston
Taxation (Corporate) .... Lind, Schwartz, Lathrope & Rosenberg
Taxation (Estate & Gift) .... Bittker, Clark & McCouch
Taxation (Individual) .... Burke & Friel
Taxation (Individual) .... Freeland, Lathrope, Lind & Stephens
Taxation (Individual) .... Graetz & Schenk
Taxation (Individual) .... Klein, Bankman & Shaviro
Torts .... Dobbs & Hayden
Torts .... Epstein
Torts .... Franklin & Rabin
Torts .... Henderson, Pearson & Siliciano
Torts .... Wade, Schwartz, Kelly & Partlett (Prosser)
Wills, Trusts, & Estates .... Dukeminier & Johanson
Wills, Trusts, & Estates .... Dobris, Sterk & Leslie
Wills, Trusts, & Estates .... Scoles, Halbach, Link & Roberts
Wills, Trusts, & Estates .... Waggoner, Alexander, Fellows & Gallanis